The Sound of Finnish Angels

Musical Signification
in Five Instrumental Compositions by
Einojuhani Rautavaara

The Sound of Finnish Angels

Musical Signification in Five Instrumental Compositions by Einojuhani Rautavaara

by
Wojciech Stępień

MUSIC IN INTERDISCIPLINARY DIALOGUE No. 9
Siglind Bruhn, General Editor

PENDRAGON PRESS
Hillsdale, NY

Other Titles in the INTERPLAY Series

No. 1 *Masqued Mysteries Unmasked:*
Pythagoreanism and Early Modern North European Music Theater
by Kristin Rygg (2000)

No. 2 *Musical Ekphrasis: Composers Responding to Poetry and Painting*
by Siglind Bruhn (2000)

No. 3 *Voicing the Ineffable: Musical Representation of Religious Experience*
Eleven essays edited by Siglind Bruhn (2001)

No. 4 *The Musical Order of the World: Kepler, Hesse, Hindemith*
by Siglind Bruhn (2004)

No. 5 *Neo-Mythologism in Music:*
From Scriabin and Schoenberg to Schnittke and Crumb
by Victoria Adamenko (2007)

No. 6 *Sonic Transformations of Literary Texts:*
From Program Music to Musical Ekphrasis
Nine essays edited by Siglind Bruhn (2008)

No. 7 *The Orpheus Myth and the Powers of Music*
by Vladimir L. Marchenkov (2009)

No. 8 *Musical Functionalism:*
The Musical Thoughts of Arnold Schoenberg and Paul Hindemith
by Magnar Breivik (2011)

Cover design by Stuart Ross, based on *Angel of Light* by Susan Blasius (b. 1963), a painting inspired by Einojuhani Rautavaara's Symphony No. VII of the same title (acrylic on canvas, 40 x 55 inches; www.susan-blasius.de). The photo on the back cover, showing the author and the composer, was taken by Sini Rautavaara.

Library of Congress Cataloging-in-Publication Data

Stępień, Wojciech.
 The sound of Finnish angels : musical signification in five instrumental compositions by Einojuhani Rautavaara / by Wojciech Stępień.
 p. cm. -- (Interplay : music in interdisciplinary dialogue ; no. 9)
 Includes bibliographical references and index.
 ISBN 978-1-57647-171-5 (alk. paper)
 1. Rautavaara, Einojuhani, 1928- Instrumental music. 2. Angels--Songs and music--History and criticism. I. Title. II. Series.
  ML410.R229S74 2011
  784.092--dc22

2011009527

Copyright 2011 by Wojciech Stępień

For my parents

PLATE 1: Einojuhani Rautavaara on the balcony of his home in Helsinki. Photographed by Wojciech Stępień, summer 2008.

Table of Contents

Preface	xi
Acknowledgments	xiii
Introduction	xv

PART I: THEORETICAL BACKGROUNDS

Chapter 1: Musical Syntax or Semantics?	3
Theories of Musical Representation as Methodological Tools	7
The Art of Musical Rhetoric	10
Actor, Actant, and Musical Persona	11
Mythical Narration	12
The Uncanny	14
Topics	16
Ekphrasis	17
Chapter 2: Angels in Religions and Beliefs	21
Pre-Christian Angels	22
Jewish Angelology and the Kabbalah	24
Christian Angels	25
Islamic Angels	29
New Age Angels	30
Chapter 3: Musical Approaches to Angels	33
Musica coelestis: the Theory of Angelic Choirs	35
Angelic Modes and Scales	38
The *Diabolus in Musica*: Angelic and Demonic Intervals	41
The Angel as a Number	43
The Angel as an Actor	46
The Angel as an Instrument	47
The *Dies irae* and Apocalyptic Angels	49
The Angel as a Rhetorical Figure	51
Angels and National Spirits	53
Angelic Dreams	55

Representations of Angels in 20th-century Instrumental Music 56
  Berg's Violin Concerto "Dem Andenken eines Engels" 56
  Hindemith's Symphony "Mathis der Maler" *and* Marienleben 57
  Crumb's String Quartet Black Angels 59
  Messiaen's Theology of Angels 60
  Pop-angels: the Destruction of the Angelic Symbol in Popular Music 66

Chapter 4: Rautavaara's Mystical Aesthetics 69
  Rautavaara's Output as Macrotext 71
  The Artist as a Medium 74
  Between Past and Present: Childhood Memories, Dreams, and Psychology 75
  The Aesthetic of the Double 80
    Literary and Philosophical Associations 83
    Titles as Mantras 84
    Pictorial Aspects of Music 86
  Personal Myth as Universal Myth 88

PART II: ANALYSIS

Chapter 5: Analysis of Rautavaara's Instrumental Works about Angels 93
  Archangel Michael Fighting the Antichrist 94
  Angels and Visitations (Angel Trilogy, Part I) 103
  The Double Bass Concerto *Angel of Dusk* (Angel Trilogy, Part II) 118
    "*His first appearance*" 120
    "*His monologue*" 124
    "*His last appearance*" 128
    Conclusion 134
  Monologue with Angels 135
  The Seventh Symphony "*Angel of Light*" (Angel Trilogy, Part III) 137
    Movement I 142
    Movement II 147
    Movement III 151
    Movement IV 154
  Playgrounds for Angels 158
    Three Timbral Groups in Asynchronous Sections 159
    Instrumental Interactions and Relations 165
    Conclusion 167

Table of Contents ix

PART III: INTERPRETATIONS AND ASSOCIATIONS

Chapter 6: "Angelic" Features in Rautavaara's Instrumental Works	173
The "Disturbance" Technique	173
Musica Automata / Senza Espressivo	178
Mechanical Elements	180
The Signification of Musica Automata	191
Signification of Instruments	195
Woodwinds	197
Metallophones	199
Strings	200
Brass	202
The Rest of the Percussion Group	203
Solo Instruments	203
Dark versus Light	205
Mandala Form	212
Chapter 7: Musical Ekphrasis	219
The Angel in Rilke's *Duino Elegies*	220
Rilke's *Duino Elegies* in Rautavaara's Music	223
Rilke's Angel as a Jungian Archetype	228
Rilke's Terrifying Angels in Rautavaara's Instrumental Music	231
Aspects of the Uncanny in Rilke's and Rautavaara's Angels	234
Beyond Rilke: Rautavaara's Musical (Self-)Ekphrasis	236
Conclusion	243
Appendix: Text of Rilke's *Die erste Elegie / The First Elegy*	245
Bibliography	247
List of Illustrations	257
Index of Names	261
About the Author	265

Preface

Many musicologists and music theorists investigating the music of Einojuhani Rautavaara (b. 1928) explore it through detailed analysis only on the syntactic level, leaving the semantic content aside. Such an approach, which risks creating an incomplete image of Rautavaara's music, needs to be complemented by an understanding of its wider cultural context. The present study attempts to fill this gap by focusing on five instrumental compositions whose titles refer to angels: the orchestral overture *Angels and Visitations* (1978), the Double Bass Concerto *Angel of Dusk* (1980), *Playgrounds for Angels* for brass ensemble (1981), the Seventh Symphony *Angel of Light* (1994), and "Archangel Michael Fighting the Antichrist" from the piano suite *Icons* (1955) and the later orchestral adaptation in *Before the Icons* (2006). The aim is to explore the link between musical phenomena and their extramusical references both in the case of the individual works and in the composer's general aesthetics. Rautavaara is an erudite composer whose interests extend beyond music to philosophy, psychology, literature, the visual arts, and spirituality. He is a talented writer of books, poems, and opera librettos, as well as an amateur painter. Such extramusical interests also characterize his music. They leave their traces in his program notes, commentaries, titles, and writings, which together provide a rich source of knowledge about his aesthetics and philosophy. As a result, much of his music can be read semantically, in some cases in the sense of the mildly programmatic tendency of contemporary music, in others as an example of musical ekphrasis.

Not all of Rautavaara's compositions have obvious extramusical connections; notable exceptions are his dodecaphonic works from his first serial period (1957-1965). The group of instrumental compositions referring to angels, however, provides an excellent case for an investigation of how the semantic content of the work titles plays itself out in the compositional technique, from smallest details such as the use of motifs and scales through the structure of particular movements to the layout and characteristics of whole compositions. Moreover, as Rautavaara in his instrumental works tends to incorporate aspects that relate to the vocal style of his operas and songs, many non-vocal parameters must be examined for their potential to represent, or correspond to, narration in stage drama.

In order to prepare the ground for the examination of Rautavaara's musical reflection on angels, the study begins with an overview of angelic representations in the history of Western music. Rautavaara uses some of the same methods of representation in his compositions depicting angelic beings, thereby making his music a continuation of traditional approaches. Other musical techniques, unique to Rautavaara's angelic series, create something like his private musical signature. This is particularly evident in cases where similar or identical musical ideas seem to inform related titles. On examining the composer's aesthetic, many of these ideas can be shown to belong to a philosophical outlook that he also discusses in his writings. Although Rautavaara's thoughts about his works are not central to this study, they are taken into consideration insofar as they provide an important context for the music. The focus, however, is on the way in which the titles invite listeners to consider the spirituality of the music. The angel is an important symbol for the composer, which he interprets in religious, poetic, and aesthetic dimensions. An investigation of Rautavaara's instrumental music referring to angels thus opens a window toward the essence of his extramusical attitude. In a wider context, it is thus hoped that this book may provide a helpful tool for the semantic analysis also of the composer's other instrumental works.

Acknowledgments

"No man is an Island."
John Donne

Paraphrasing Donne, one might say that no scholar is an island. My research is not solely the product of my own scientific and artistic discoveries: I feel humble and thankful for the input of others. Considerably portions of this study represent my reactions to the reflections and observations of other scholars, whose books I read, with whom I had discussions, and whom I sought to emulate. It is therefore impossible to express my gratitude fully to all the people without whom my dissertation and the revised version of it in this book would never have come into existence.

First of all I would like to express my gratitude to the Department of Musicology at the University of Helsinki and its Head, Professor Eero Tarasti. Thanks to his invitation to the Doctoral and Postdoctoral Seminar in Music Semiotics in 2005, I was able to travel to Finland for the first time and had the chance to present my early ideas on Rautavaara's music; thanks to his open-mindedness, I felt encouraged to embark on my own intellectual journey into the work of Rautavaara. Without Professor Tarasti's help with many practical aspects during my stay in Helsinki I could never completed this study. Also, I do not know how my book could have gotten anywhere without the support of Susanna Välimäki. Her kind advice and detailed comments were the first significant opinions I received about my work. Furthermore, I had great pleasure in discussing my ideas with Professor Anne Sivuoja-Gunaratnam from the Sibelius Academy in Helsinki, who turned my attention toward many unfamiliar aspects of Rautavaara's music as well as to bibliographic sources I might not have discovered without her. I owe the idea to undertake studies in Helsinki to the encouragement of Dr. Danuta Mirka from the University of Southampton. She was the first person with whom I discussed my project, and it was she who advised me to study with Professor Tarasti. During the writing of the book she often appeared to me like a "guardian angel" since she helped in many places with the sometimes difficult methodological problems and analyses.

Finally, I was very fortunate to meet Dr. Siglind Bruhn from the University of Michigan, first in her capacity as my external doctoral examiner and opponent during my defense in Helsinki, and subsequently as my wonderfully helpful editor for the *Interplay* series published at Pendragon

Press. She encouraged me to publish a revised version of my dissertation as a book and advised me throughout the editorial process. Without her positive attitude toward my work I would never have undertaken the thorough revision of my original study. I would also like to thank Mr. Robert J. Kessler, Managing Director of Pendragon Press, who agreed to publish a text by a young scholar from a foreign country, and Dr. h.c. Claire Brook for polishing my language.

My research would have been impossible without the financial aid of several Finnish and Polish foundations and institutions. I am grateful to the Niilo Helander Foundation, the Pro Musica Foundation, CIMO (the Centre for International Mobility), The Cultural Department of Katowice, The University of Helsinki, and the Academy of Music in Katowice. Two Finnish institutions in particular, Fennica Gehrman and the Finnish Music Information Centre, kindly allowed me access to Rautavaara's scores, books, and recordings. Excerpts from Rautavaara's works are reprinted by kind permission of Fennica Gehrman Oy, Helsinki ©Warner/Chappel Music Finland Oy.

Among the many people who further helped me in matters both big and small I wish to mention Professor Eugeniusz Knapik, Dr. Marcin Trzęsiok, Agata Knapik-Mikołajczak, Stanisław Bromboszcz from the Academy of Music in Katowice; Irma Vierimaa and Paul Forsell from the University of Helsinki; Dr. Edward Venn from Lancaster University; Professor Richard Littlefield from Central Michigan University, as well as Pekka Hako, Kalevi Aho, Samuli Tiikkaja, Laura Gutman-Hanhivaara, Ari Nieminen, Kristiina Vuorela, Agnieszka Terho, Filip Sikorski, and Otto Lehto.

My greatest debt is to the composer himself. I am immensely grateful to have been allowed to meet with Einojuhani Rautavaara in his home in Helsinki and to have the opportunity to interview him on several occasions. Each time, it was a wonderful experience to sit on the sofa in his living room and listen to a composer whose music I love. Although his health is frail and he is still very active as a composer, he always found time for me. He gave me wonderful insights into his compositions both during our personal encounter and in e-mail correspondence. His wife Sini also supported me with books, scores, and addresses. Without the help of this extraordinary couple my work would be a dry collection of thoughts.

My special thanks go to my parents Weronika and Jan Stępień who brought me up, allowed me to study music and make many mistakes, who were my support, and who gave me strength. Finally my warmest gratitude goes to my wife Dorota and our daughter Weronisia for their faith in me and my work, and their "angelic" patience for their husband and father who was not always an "angel" during the long process of writing this book.

Helsinki – Katowice, Christmas 2010

Introduction

The music of Einojuhani Rautavaara has recently received much attention, most particularly in the wake of the composer's international breakthrough in the middle of the 1990s. The interest of music scholars at home and broad prompted Rautavaara to reconsider his so-called "withdrawal decision" of 1978, in which he had pledged not to give any interviews about his music.[1] However, his growing fame resulted in a change of attitude toward public attention. Since then, Rautavaara has regularly agreed interviews as well as radio and TV talks. With the assistance of his wife, he has even published his private recollections, which appeared in 2001 under the title *Säveltäjä ja Muusa*.[2] Rautavaara was not the only relatively unknown composer to attract the attention of the international musical audience: John Tavener from England, Arvo Pärt from Estonia and Henryk Mikołaj Górecki from Poland all came to prominence at this time. It is interesting how similar the aesthetics of these composers are, with their music rapidly coming to be called spiritual, although the claims for spirituality to be found in popular music journals and magazines have not received any systematic research.

This study of Rautavaara's instrumental compositions concerning angels is based on various existing approaches to his music. The most important of these theories are those of Anne Sivuoja-Gunaratnam, Kalevi Aho, and Samuli Tiikkaja. Probably the most revealing studies, which provide the basic assumptions underpinning my work, have been those of Sivuoja-Gunaratnam in her doctoral dissertation[3] and in various articles. Although her focus was primarily on the composer's earliest period and his dodecaphonic technique, her study draws attention to the most important problems raised by the composer's techniques, and in particularly the omnipresent

---

[1] Kalevi Aho, "Einojuhani Rautavaara – Avant-Gardist, Mystic and Upholder of Values," *Highlights* 5 (1998): 3.

[2] Einojuhani Rautavaara, Sini Rautavaara, *Säveltäjä ja Muusa* [Composer and Muse] (Juva: Werner Söderström Osakeyhtiö, 2001).

[3] Anne Sivuoja-Gunaratnam, *Narrating with Twelve Tones: Einojuhani Rautavaara's First Serial Period (ca. 1957-1965)* (Helsinki: The Finnish Academy of Science and Letters, 1997).

xvi   Introduction

intertextuality.[4] In her articles on Rautavaara's operas, Sivuoja-Gunaratnam turns her attention to those elements of the plot that are based on the same symbols, and notes the connections between female characters, birdsong, and angels. She draws on the psychocritical theory of Charles Mauron in order to analyze Rautavaara's output, and positions his intertextual references, interpreted as variations on the same theme, in the context of Claude Lévi-Strauss's notion of *bricolage*. She also examines the temporal dimensions of Rautavaara's operas, noting how time is presented in a nonchronological order, preferring instead a psychological order characterized by a dream-like aesthetic. Furthermore she makes an important observation regarding Rautavaara's hierarchic use of instruments and their connections with the characters of his operas; this will become one of the key issues of this book.

The most significant sources relating to Rautavaara's aesthetic and outlook can be found in his autobiography *Omakuva* (Autobiography) (1989), Hako's popular book about the composer *Unien lahja. Einojuhani Rautavaaran maailma*,[5] and a chapter about Rautavaara's operas in *Finnish Opera*.[6] In *Unien lahja*, which is based on interviews with the composer Hako discusses a number of interesting ideas such as the composer's attitude towards being a musical medium, his childhood interests and obsessions that later become an important source of inspiration, and his meta-artistic attitude to be at once a composer, writer, and painter. All of these areas form starting points for the fourth chapter on aesthetics.

The analyses of Rautavaara's music in the second part of this book draw on Tiikkaja's study of the Seventh Symphony *Angel of Light*;[7] Donald Gregory Lovejoy's analysis of the Organ Concerto *Annunciations* (2000);[8] and Klavier Luut's study of *Playgrounds for Angels*.[9] The analysis of the orchestral *Angels and Visitations* is indebted to important insights offered by

---

[4] See also Samuli Tiikkaja, "Einojuhani Rautavaara – Postmodern Intertextualist or Supermodern Intratextualist? On Auto-Quotations in Rautavaara's Oeuvre," *Musiikki* 2 (2004): 39-60.

[5] Pekka Hako, *Unien lahja. Einojuhani Rautavaaran maailma* [The gift of dreams. The world of Einojuhani Rautavaara] (Helsinki: Alatus, 2000).

[6] Pekka Hako, *Finnish Opera* (Helsinki: FIMIC, 2002), 96-109 (chapter "Rautavaara").

[7] Samuli Tiikkaja, "Einojuhani Rautavaaran seitsemäs sinfonia Angel of light: materiaali-ja muotoanalyysi," M.A. thesis, University of Helsinki, 2000.

[8] Donald Gregory Lovejoy, "Annunciations: The Wind Music of Einojuhani Rautavaara," dissertation, University of Washington, 2000.

[9] Klavier Luut, "Einojuhani Rautavaaren vaskipuhallinmusiikin tausta ja analyysi," M.A. thesis, University of Helsinki, 2008.

Introduction xvii

Aho,[10] while in the analysis of the last component in the piano suite *Icons*, "Archangel Michael Fighting the Antichrist," there contains occasional references to Eila Tarasti's ideas.[11]

Although the issue of spirituality in Rautavaara's music has not to date been the main subject of a monograph, two important works in this area are Siglind Bruhn's chapter about Rautavaara's opera *Thomas*,[12] and Tarja von Creutlein's interesting dissertation on Rautavaara's choral work *Vigilia* and its correspondences with Orthodox services and religious practices.[13] Hako offers some thoughts about the composer's interests in psychology;[14] further ideas can be found in Tiikkaja's master's thesis.[15]

The significance of Rainer Maria Rilke's poetry for Rautavaara's music is investigated by Kaisu Nikula[16] and also to a lesser extent in the doctoral dissertation of Fredrick Lokken,[17] although neither offers comparisons of the similarities between Rilke and Rautavaara's artistic aesthetic. It is essential to understand the signification of angels in Rautavaara's compositional aesthetic, and this will be the subject of the final chapter of this study.

Surprisingly, the topic of "angels" in music has not to date been the subject of any comprehensive study, and therefore this book collects and synthesizes many theories from various sources to demonstrate how the tradition of angelic music was shaped before and during Rautavaara's time. There is only one interesting book concerning the musicological study of angels by Michael Poizat[18] which considers the angelic as an attribute of

---

[10] Kalevi Aho, *Einojuhani Rautavaara as Symphonist* (Helsinki: Sibelius-Akatemia/Edition PAN, 1988).

[11] Eila Tarasti, "Icons in Einojuhani Rautavaara's *Icons,* Suite for Piano," *Musical Semiotics Revisited* (Imatra/Helsinki: International Semiotics Institute, 2003): 549-562.

[12] Siglind Bruhn, *Saints in the Limelight: Representations of the Religious Quest on the Post-1945 Operatic Stage* (Hillsdale, NY: Pendragon Press, 2003).

[13] Tarja von Creutlein, *Einojuhani Rautavaaran 'Vigilia Pyhän Johannes Kastajan muistolle" ortodoksisen kirkkomusiikin kontekstissa'* (Joensuu: Joensuun yliopisto, 2006).

[14] Pekka Hako, "Music Has a Will of Its Own," *Nordic Sounds* 3 (1998): 18-21.

[15] Tiikkaja provided the first account of Rautavaara's obsession with mandalas – those symbols of spiritual perfection that will be the object of investigation in the third part of this study.

[16] Kaisu Nikula, *Zur Umsetzung deutscher Lyrik in finnische Musik am Beispiel Rainer Maria Rilke und Einojuhani Rautavaara* (Jyväskylä: Jyväskylän Yliopisto, 2005).

[17] Fredrick Lokken, "The Music for Unaccompanied Mixed Chorus of Einojuhani Rautavaara," dissertation, University of Wisconsin, 1999, 185-200.

[18] Michael Poizat, *The Angel's Cry: Beyond the Pleasure Principle in Opera*, A. Denner, trans. (Ithaca, NY & London: Cornell University Press, 1992).

voice and timbre. The author significantly ascribes the term angelic to both vocal and instrumental music, paying particular attention to the brass as the most spiritual of instruments. There are important passages about angels in Jamie James's book[19] which is used in order to explain the significance of angels in works by St. Augustine, Thomas Aquinas, and Arnold Schoenberg. Angels do not receive much attention in the mythical contexts provided by Victoria Adamenko,[20] appearing only in the discussion of George Crumb's *Black Angels*. In order to describe angelic conceptions in music, the first part of this study draws on monographs and studies about the following composers and their compositions: Hildegard von Bingen by Błażej Matusiak, Johann Sebastian Bach by Albert Schweitzer, Alban Berg by Anthony Pople, Paul Hindemith and Olivier Messiaen by Bruhn.

A study about angels in music must begin by explaining the concept of angels in various religious and cultural contexts. This is done by drawing on various sources. Among them are different encyclopedias and dictionaries devoted to particular religions but also one very important collection of essays about angels which can be considered the summation of angelic knowledge: *Księga o Aniołach*.[21]

Rautavaara has provided an abundance of commentaries on his music, to be found in CD booklets, program notes, interviews, prefaces, and also in articles in music magazines. It also was a great honor for me to be allowed to interview the composer on several occasions. His own reflections on his music suggested new and interesting paths in this research that were developed in both the aesthetic and interpretative chapters. Together with minor articles in newspapers and musical magazines (particularly the *Finnish Music Quarterly, Faber Music News, Highlights, Gramophone, Fanfare, Tempo, Choir & Organ* and others) these are the most important sources of information about the composer's aesthetic and offer significant interpretative codes with which to explain the angelic figure in his music in the last chapter.

This study is divided into three parts. The first part is devoted to methodological considerations, demonstrating various approaches to angels in music and Rautavaara's aesthetic in order to provide a background for the study. The second part analyzes Rautavaara's five instrumental compositions

---

[19] Jamie James, *The Music of the Spheres: Music, Science, and the Natural Order of the Universe* (London: Abacus, 1995).

[20] Victoria Adamenko, *Neo-Mythologism in Music. From Scriabin and Schoenberg to Schnittke and Crumb* (Hillsdale, NY: Pendragon Press, 2007).

[21] Oleschko, ed., *Księga o Aniołach* [A book about angels] (Kraków: Wydawnictwo WAM, 2003).

referring to angels, and the final part summarizes the most important analytical observations and interprets them in their wider cultural, extramusical, and semantic contexts. Chapter 1 is devoted to the hotly-disputed question of semantic categories in music and traced the history of semantic attitudes from the Ancient Greek theory of ethos through to contemporary hermeneutic theories. It discusses the problem of representation in music by presenting various theories of representation which are the methodological tools for an investigation of Rautavaara's compositions: affects, actors and musical persona, mythical models, the uncanny, topics, and musical ekphrasis.

Chapters 2 and 3 are devoted to the signification of angels, firstly in various religions and secondly in music. Descriptions of angels in sacred texts and scriptures are studied in order to provide both a background and a set of interpretative codes with which to better understand the religious and spiritual symbol of the angel in music. Chapter 2 therefore presents the most important conceptions of angels in Judaism, Christianity, and Islam, for the symbol of Rautavaara's angel relates to the poetry of Rilke in which the two last mentioned conceptions of angels are present. It discusses angels of the New Age movement in order to examine Rautavaara's works in the context of the socialcultural-religious movement that was born in the 1970s and '80s when the compositions about angels were composed.

Brief demonstrations of various approaches to angels in music in Chapter 3 provide an important means of understanding how and by which tools music throughout history has tried to portray angels, and the consequences of this for the interpretation of Rautavaara's music. The question is whether the composer reinterpreted previous angelic theories for his music or whether he constructed his own approach to angels. In order to answer this question and provide a modern conclusion to the historical survey of musical angels this chapter focuses on those twentieth-century composers who have written instrumental compositions either before or contemporaneously with Rautavaara's five works, and who created their own personal musical approach to angels. Moreover the music of Berg and Hindemith had a strong influence on Rautavaara's style and probably the Finnish composer unconsciously adopted some ideas from their compositions with titles concerning angels. The conclusion to this chapter critiques the popularity of angels in pop music and their destructive influence on the understanding of the religious dimension of angels, and tries to refute the popular tendency that treats Rautavaara's compositions as part of the music of the New Age Movement.

Chapter 4 moves away from these various approaches to angels in music in order to discuss Rautavaara's aesthetic, paying special attention to his mystical attitudes. The role of the composer as a musical medium is discussed by tracing the spiritual message of his music that is communicated by means of obsessive myths, dreams, visions, and through his breaking of temporal and chronological time in his operas. This helps to demonstrate the composer's attitude towards spirituality and his status as a metareligious composer, writing the same work throughout his whole life.

The introduction to Chapter 5 observes how the figure of the angel can be found not only in Rautavaara's instrumental works but also in his vocal music, and particularly with characters in his operas. The composer uses similar techniques in his instrumental compositions as he does when writing for the characters in his operas. The subsequent analyses of the five instrumental compositions referring to angels together with the unwritten work *Monologue with Angels* show how the composer uses similar musical elements in all of the works to portray the figure of the angel. The analyses are not detailed since the intention is to determine common elements in form, instrumentation, and choice of musical material. While important scales, rows, and harmonic strategies are discussed, major segments of the analyses are limited to offering general overviews of the works. Specific attention is paid to instrumental interactions in the orchestra, and in particular to the roles of soloist and accompanists.

If the first part of the study outlines the theoretical, methodological and aesthetic background necessary for understanding both angels in music and the composer's aesthetic, and the second is analytical, the third part can be perceived as a synthesis of the two, insofar as the analyses are read through interpretative codes derived from the first part of this study. To achieve this synthesis, the most important angelic features in Rautavaara's instrumental compositions are categorized in terms of various distinctive features: *disturbance technique*; *musica automata/senza espressivo*; signification of instruments; musical brightness and light; and mandala form. In Chapter 6 these features are discussed in the context of musical mythologems, for angels can be treated as the composer's personal myth. In particular, binary oppositions and repetitiveness are connected with Algirdas Julius Greimas's theory of mythical actants in order to create the textural dichotomy of hero contra opponent. The third part of the study also examines the role of musical brightness both in the musical material and in the titles of Rautavaara's compositions. This examination demonstrates not only the mythical attitude that informs Rautavaara's works but also how the figure of the angel is made to correspond with particular instruments, timbres, and other musical materials.

The aim of Chapter 7 is to point out the extramusical associations of the common musical elements in the compositions referring to angels in the light of Bruhn's theory of musical ekphrasis. Here the composer's commentaries

Introduction

quoted in the fifth chapter are treated as sources for the interpretation of his figure of the angel. The focus is on those associations between Rautavaara's music and Rilke's *Duino Elegies*. Attention is paid to the role of these poems in Rautavaara's work, their philosophical message, and their signification of the figure of the angel. In other words, the poem is treated as an interpretative code in order to understand Rautavaara's angels. Moreover the chapter develops codes in reference to Carl Gustav Jung's theory of archetypes. Surprisingly these two codes are related to each other, and reveal the basic attitude of Rautavaara's figure of the angel to be its terrifying aspect. This aspect is investigated using Sigmund Freud's theory of the uncanny with reference to those musical elements that are characteristic of the compositions described in Chapter 6. The conclusion of that chapter touches on Rautavaara's amateur painting *Angel of Dusk* and its connection to the title of the Double Bass Concerto *Angel of Dusk* and the interrelations between them.

PART I:
THEORETICAL BACKGROUNDS

Chapter 1:
Musical Syntax or Semantics?

> The essential hermeneutic problem about music is usually put by saying that music is all syntax and no semantics, or that music lacks denotative or referential power, or, to revert to Hanslick's much quoted aphorism, that "[...] sounding forms in motion are the one and only content of music."[1]

The first stage of this study will be to discuss the problem of musical syntax and semantics, since the methodological tools employed are based on theories of musical representation. The controversy starts in the nineteenth century when the first studies about music aesthetics are written and musicologists consider the problem of musical symbolization. Their essential question is: does music refer to, represent, or express something beyond the music itself, or does music have only a purely musical meaning?

If adherents to the notion of absolute music were able to return to ancient times, their views would probably be met with perplexity, for no ancient philosopher argued that music was absolute and expressed only itself. Music of those times is treated as syncretic art, very often connected with ritual and spiritual practices, and the idea of music for and of itself is unknown. Music is recognized as an important educational tool and has a special role in maintaining the law of the country; the best example of this can be found in Plato's dialogue *The Republic*. According to Plato, rhythms, scales, and musical instruments are symbols of the psyche and have a profound impact on the human soul. The ancient Greeks believe that music can mimic the state of the human soul; some melodies are desirable and of great value in moral education, whereas others are forbidden, since they are too emotional and have an orgiastic character. In fact, music is divided into the moral dichotomy of good or bad, and this affects musical thought for the subsequent millennium. As James writes, "In *The Republic* Socrates tells us that the Mixolydian and the Hyperlydian modes are dirgelike and ought to

---

[1] Lawrence Kramer, *Music as Cultural Practice, 1800-1900* (Berkeley, CA: University of California Press, 1990), 2-3.

be done away with, for they are useless 'even to women'. The Ionian and certain Lydian modes, on the other hand, are relaxing and convivial [...]. That leaves the Dorian and Phrygian modes, which he allows: the former because it emboldens warriors and helps them accept and cope with setbacks, the latter because it has potent persuasive powers to induce temperance, moderation, and law-abidingness."[2] The particular focus of Plato's philosophy of music is the essential role given to rhythm, which he feels should mimic the manner of a nobleman's speech. Centuries later, and in accordance with this idea, the rhythms of Gregorian chant are strictly based on those of sacred texts, making it non-metric in comparison with the greater metricality and dance-like nature of secular music. The influence of the theory of Greek ethos can also be observed in the practice of avoiding the tritone—the *diabolus in musica*—in medieval polyphony. The mathematical proportions of the tritone are compared to the perfect fifth and hence the former is regarded as a false fifth—a "musical devil."

Analogies between music and speech are made throughout the ages, but this tendency increases thanks to Renaissance madrigals, which also informs the development of the Baroque theory of affects. Such music is recognized as a mysterious form of speech subject to the art of rhetoric, first intended for a small group of musical connoisseurs (so-called *musica reservata*) but rapidly understood by everyone. It is not an accident that the group that develops this kind of musical speech is the Florentine Camerata, which venerates the traditions of the ancient Greeks. The genesis of opera is directly linked with the attempt to imitate ancient drama with music in which the idea of catharsis is restored.[3] For this reason, the style initiated by the Camerata is an imitation of Greek monody, which very quickly evolves from simple *recitativo* to *rappresentativo*, the aim of which is to represent various kinds of affects. By the end of the eighteenth century, Jean-Jacques Rousseau and Jean-Baptiste le Rond d'Alembert claim that music is a kind of speech, a language that expresses the various sensations of the human soul. They claim also that not only vocal music but also instrumental music can represent various feelings, ideas, and visual sensations.

The individualism of the Romantic era brings to an end the socially-understood concept of musical speech, for every composer starts to create his or her own unique theory of music, approached in completely different and sometimes oppositional ways. As Alfred Einstein suggests, the lack of a

---

[2] James, 57.

[3] Girolamo Mei discovers the Hellenic *Hymns of Mesomedes*; Vincenzo Galilei edits them in his treatise *Dialogo della musica antica e della moderna* (1581) in which he tries to rediscover the musical practice of the ancient Greeks.

Musical Syntax or Semantics? 5

common musical language means that composers start to write commentaries and program notes in order to explain verbally what they wish to express in music.[4] The Romantic interest in poetry and other art forms creates the movement of programmatic music that, as a non-autonomous art form, can be comprehensible in a wider cultural context. Surprisingly, some composers from the nineteenth century begin to develop a contrary tendency in musical aesthetics, one that considers music as an autonomous and absolute art. In their opinion music is the most symbolic art for it has no semantic connotations and does not represent anything in the natural world. For this reason, it is treated as the most ambiguous art and the most spiritual. Arthur Schopenhauer's philosophical ideas dominate nineteenth-century music and have a great impact on subsequent generations of twentieth-century composers. The idea of absolute music is proclaimed by the most famous aesthetician, Eduard Hanslick, an admirer and supporter of Johannes Brahms's works. In his writings he returned to the concept of classical beauty and shared the formalist view established by Kantian philosophy.[5] Hanslick claims that music has no particular extramusical signification; rather, "[...] sounding forms in motion are the one and only content of music."[6] In fact, this tendency to accept only musical syntax as a source of musical meaning influences the study of music from previous epochs, classicism in particular, and is extended to twentieth-century and contemporary musical movements. It seems that the problem of absolute music and programmatic music is still present today, and concerns the primacy of musical syntax over musical semantics. It may be said that there are two schools: formalists who follow Hanslick's categories of musical beauty and referentialists for whom music can be investigated in the light of wider cultural practices. The opposition is also easy to recognize in the work of music analysts: those belonging to the first school prioritize musical structures and the relationships between sounds, grouping events according to linguistic, psychological, and mathematical theories (Heinrich Schenker, Eugene Narmour, Fred Lehrdahl, Ray Jackendoff); the second, "hermeneutic" school tries to find musical signification by drawing on biographical, historical, philosophical, and other extramusical data in order to support interpretations (Hermann Kretzschmar, Arnold Schering, Scott Burnham, Tibor Kneif, Hans Heinrich Eggebrecht,

---

[4] Alfred Einstein, *Die Romantik in der Musik* (Vienna: Berglandverlag, 1950), 28.

[5] See Kramer, *Music as Cultural Practice*, 3-4.

[6] Eduard Hanslick, *Vom Musikalisch Schönen. Ein Beitrag zur Revision der Aesthetik der Tonkunst* (Leipzig: Rudolph Weigel, 1854), 32.

Constantin Floros, Lawrence Kramer).[7] According to Raymond Monelle, some scholars dispute the idea that "[...] music cannot refer to anything because its reference can only be known from a verbal text of title."[8] Even in the mainstream of semiotic approaches to music, musicologists engage with the notion of musical referentialism, which has been aptly summarized by Tarasti thus: "[...] during its various stylistic periods, music has always been more or less related to extramusical reality, and has been semantic by its very nature of transmitting messages."[9] This book adopts the point of view conveyed in Susanna Välimäki's convincing argument that:

> We have no reason to consider music as more abstract, more without content, and less representative than some other art forms. For all sign systems are naturally abstract, and no sign system can exist without representation. Needless to say, musical representation differs from literary or visual representation because it is musical, i.e., because the medium is different. But even if we experience music as more abstract, we cannot conclude that music is less representative. On the contrary, it thus seems to represent "non-representativeness" most successfully.[10]

Stefan Jarociński raised essential questions about signification in music and distinguished between two problems: music in itself (*en soi*) and music in the perception of listeners (*pour nous*).[11] It seems that the problematic issues of musical syntax and semantics are not mutually exclusive but rather complement each other like two sides of a coin. Although some musicologists believe that music is referential, they find its referential aspect in expressions of feelings rather than in representations of visual forms and objects.[12]

---

[7] Hermann Kretzschmar was the pioneering scholar of hermeneutics who wanted to revive the eighteenth-century doctrine of affections. Arnold Schering used "poetic ideas" for his study of Ludwig van Beethoven.

[8] Raymond Monelle, *Musical Topics: Hunt, Military and Pastoral* (Bloomington, IN: Indiana University Press, 2006), 20.

[9] Eero Tarasti, "Music Models through Ages: A Semiotic Interpretation," *International Review of the Aesthetics and Sociology of Music* 17/1 (1986): 26.

[10] Susanna Välimäki, *Subject Strategies in Music. A Psychoanalytic Approach to Musical Signification* (Imatra/Helsinki: International Semiotic Institute, 2005), 42.

[11] See Stefan Jarociński, *Debussy: Impressionism and Symbolism* (London, UK: Eulenberg, 1976).

[12] Kendall Walton, "Listening with Imagination: Is Music Representational?," *Journal of Aesthetics and Art Criticism* 52/1 (1994): 47-61 and Susanne K. Langer, *Philosophy in a New Key. A Study in the Symbolic of Reason, Rite and Art* (Cambridge, MA: Harvard University Press, 1957), 204-245.

Theories of Musical Representation as Methodological Tools

In Baroque music, the *stile rappresentativo* (representative style) is an affective style. It can be translated into English as "theatrical style"[13]—in other words the style that represents the dramatic action and characters. The term first appears in print in 1600 both on the title-page of Giulio Caccini's *Euridice*: (*"composta in stile rappresentativo"*) and in Emilio de Cavalieri's drama *Rappresentatione di Anima, et di Corpo*, which follows the long tradition of *sacra rappresentatione*—stage performances of religious topics with music and dances. The term is taken up next by Claudio Monteverdi, who writes about the *stile rappresentativo* in the preface to his Eighth Book of Madrigals, *Madrigali guerrieri, et amorosi* (1638). The style rapidly influences all the important forms of instrumental music, particularly sonatas and concertos, and as a result it gives rise to enormous catalogues of rhetorical figures (see the next subchapter about rhetoric and music). It is the first embodiment of representation in music since the ancient Greek category of mimesis. Rousseau uses the ancient term *mimesis* when he discusses music that imitates extramusical things, and according to him music "[...] is no less capable of emulation than its sister arts."[14] Kramer claims that "[...] musical representation is one of the basic techniques by which culture enters music and music enters culture, as communicative action." Representation is less a relationship between a sign and a referent than "[...] a dynamic, culturally conditioned process of affirming and deploying such a relationship."[15] Musical signs can represent something when there is an intentional likeness between them and the referents that they represent. Here, it is important to note Charles Sanders Peirce's classification of signs in relation to their object as icon, index, or symbol.[16] Iconic musical signs are based on an isomorphism between music and the external world: in such cases, the musical representation has to imitate visual, aural, and formal aspects of the

---

[13] However, as Claude Palisca explains, the style was not reserved only for stage music but more generally for *seconda practica*—the emotional and dramatic style that, according to the Camerata, should imitate the emotional power of ancient dramas. See Claude Palisca, "Stile Rappresentativo," *The New Grove Dictionary of Music and Musicians* 18 (London, UK: Macmillan, 1980), 145.

[14] Siglind Bruhn, *Musical Ekphrasis. Composers Responding to Poetry and Painting* (Hillsdale, NY: Pendragon Press, 2000), 13.

[15] Lawrence Kramer, *Classical Music and Postmodern Knowledge* (Berkeley, CA: University of California Press, 1995), 68.

[16] See Naomi Cumming, *The Sonic Self. Musical Subjectivity and Signification* (Bloomington, IN: Indiana University Press, 2000), 86-95.

object. An index "[...] stands in a relation of contiguity with its objects,"[17] and "[...] points and invites a viewer to look actively in the direction indicated."[18] Finally, a symbol is always a sign according to a specific convention in which the relationship between the sign and object is arbitrary.[19]

In order to understand what is being represented in music, one must know the relevant interpretative codes. For this reason, it is important to discuss the musical designator that "[...] identifies what is being represented."[20] Music can possess various designators such as programs, titles, texts, composer's commentaries, epigrams, and expression markings; Kramer calls these textual inclusions.[21] Together, these textual inclusions form the first of three categories of hermeneutic windows: musical events that do not give themselves to understanding but rather must be made to yield to understanding. The second of Kramer's windows is that of citational inclusions, which comprise titles that link a work of music to a literary work, visual image, place, or historical moment, as well as musical allusions to texts, styles, inclusions, or parodies. Here music can be explained in reference to other works of art in terms of correspondence or musical ekphrasis. The third window is that of structural tropes, which can be understood as a procedure capable of various practical realizations, and which can function as a typical expressive act within a certain cultural framework. In this category one can include musical topics, along with baroque rhetorical figures. Kramer compares the three hermeneutic windows to categories of metaphors:

> The interpretation of such a metaphor involves the correlation of its discursive affiliations with the characteristics of the representation it informs—in this case with musical figures and processes.[22]

Such metaphors are well known from the work of Leonard B. Meyer as connotations: "[...] associations made between some aspect of the musical organization and extramusical experience."[23] As in literature, metaphors in music are ambiguous, and sometimes it is difficult to find definite reference

---

[17] Eero Tarasti, *A Theory of Musical Semiotics* (Bloomington, IN: Indiana University Press, 1994), 54.

[18] Cumming, 89.

[19] See Eero Tarasti, *Signs of Music. A Guide to Musical Semiotics* (Berlin/New York: Mouton de Gruyter, 2002), 11.

[20] Kramer, *Classical Music*, 69.

[21] This paragraph relies on information found in: Kramer, *Music as Cultural Practice*, 6-10.

[22] Kramer, *Classical Music*, 71.

[23] Leonard B. Meyer, *Emotion and Meaning in Music* (Chicago, IL: University of Chicago Press, 1956), 258.

Musical Syntax or Semantics? 9

to external realities. Bruhn creates two lists concerning musical representation, the first of which presented their various functions and the second their extramusical references. Musical representation can therefore be a signal, an emotional symptom, a mimetic image, an abstract trope denoting a thought, or a composite symbol referring to an entire concept.[24] Surprisingly the first list corresponds to Nikolaus Harnoncourt's categories of musical representation.[25] For him a signal is an acoustic imitation, for example bird song (in Peirce's theory an icon), an emotional symptom is a representation of thoughts and feelings (in Peirce's theory an index), a mimetic image is a representation of pictures,[26] and the last two of Bruhn's categories can correspond to musical speech and the theory of musical rhetoric. Bruhn's catalogue of the best-known extramusical references lists:

1) the figures of musical rhetoric [...],
2) the 'affective types' developed as an extension of the rhetoric-of-music tradition, and the influential system of categorizing the connotations of intervals [...],
3) the affective connotations linked with keys, tonalities, and modes,
4) the semantic interpretation of brief musical units as 'gestures' on the basis of their kinesthetic shape,
5) the tracing of a visual object [...] in the pitch outline,
6) the letter-name representation of, or allusion to, persons [...].[27]

This review of some of the most famous theories of musical representation is not exhaustive but creates an important platform for the discussion of angelic representation in the following chapters. It will establish a theoretical background and provide methodological tools for the investigation of Rautavaara's compositions referring to angels. Some of them, such as Greimas's theory of mythical actants, Edward Cone's theory of musical persona, Lévi-Strauss's mythological theories as transmitted in Adamenko's work, Freud's notion of the uncanny, and Bruhn's musical ekphrasis, are fundamental for this study and determine the area of methodological interest.

---

[24] Bruhn, *Musical Ekphrasis*, 10.

[25] Nikolaus Harnoncourt, *Baroque Music Today: Music as Speech: Ways to a New Understanding of Music*, M. O'Neill, trans. (Portland, OR: Amadeus Press, 1988).

[26] See Maria Rzepińska, *Historia koloru w dziejach malarstwa europejskiego* [The history of color in European painting] (Warsaw: Wydawnictwo Arkady, 1989), 606-629.

[27] Bruhn, *Musical Ekphrasis*, 16-17.

The Art of Musical Rhetoric

> After all, Baroque music always means to make a statement, to represent and evoke at least a general feeling or *Affekt*.[28]

The tradition of music as speech is established around 1650 and lasts for about two centuries. Theoreticians of that time (Johann Mattheson, Johann Joachim Quantz) conform to the notion that music is nothing but ingenious speech. The impetus comes from the Renaissance art of *madrigalism*: illustrative devices of poetic text used particularly in madrigals. Over the course of time vocal forms assume instrumental shape and madrigal techniques penetrate instrumental music as figures of affect. Baroque opera, which spread all over Europe, creates a musical vocabulary that is also used in the instrumental accompaniment of arias and recitatives. Harnoncourt suggests that the earliest instrumental works that directly imitate the rhetorical art of speech are used in funerals and *tombeaux*; both genres are thus related to the death of a person. The form of such compositions follows the rules of rhetoric for farewell speeches consisting of an introduction, a section in which to express opinions (personal response), an intensification from sorrow to despair, consolation, and finally a conclusion.[29] By the end of the seventeenth century the catalogue of affects is generally established. Since rhetoric is a common discipline taught in every school, its musical figures are probably understood by almost every educated, cultured man of this epoch. In this way, composers can communicate some affects not only by means of vocal music, but also though instrumental compositions with or without titles. It is a matter of discussion as to whether rhetorical figures in music are a kind of representation or whether they are a form of expression. Some figures imitate kinesthetic shapes as gestures, such as when weeping is represented as falling chromatic figures; some others are based on conventions, that is, cultural tropes, with probably the most spectacular example being the figures of *cathabasis* and *anabasis* which are interpreted as death and resurrection, Hell and Heaven. Figures can certainly be ambiguous, but this is not sufficient proof to conclude that music lacks semantic content since speech is also full of ambiguity.

---

[28] Harnoncourt, 118.

[29] Harnoncourt, 119.

Musical Syntax or Semantics? 11

Actor, Actant, and Musical Persona

Baroque music demands speech; Galilei argues that the composer should listen to people talking. It seems that the art of music in the Baroque is humanized, for it reflects human expression. Hence it is possible to accept the idea that instruments and voices are similar and that an instrument can substitute for the voice. It is true that instrumental music in some way seems to imitate the theatrical gestures of opera. The rhetorical art of the Baroque influences classical music and develops into musical topics. In contrast to earlier periods, Romantic music finds its own way of producing extra-musical references through the use of programs, titles, notes, and composer commentaries. Some of them, such as Hector Berlioz's *Symphonie fantastique* (1830), tell a narrative story comparable to literary works.

In Classical works, the opposition between the two main themes of sonata form has been interpreted by drawing on categories of literary analysis. Márta Grabócz attempts to connect rhetorical devices in music with the theory of narrative transformation through her exploration of the binary opposition of two themes.[30] Her theory is based on Greimas's theory of narrative grammar, which is well known as a theory of mythical actants or actors. The Russian formalist Vladimir Propp first uses the term actant in his analysis of characters in folk fairy tales. Greimas expands his model to six actants: subject, object, sender, receiver, helper, and opponent. Later, he limits the model to only the two actants of subject and object. The primal mythical situation is given when the subject is disjunct from or conjunct with an object.[31] In the first case, the starting point is the lack of object, and the whole story is about searching for and finally gaining it.

In his book *The Composer's Voice* (1974) Cone demonstrates with examples from Berlioz's music how instruments can fulfill the role of actors in conjunction with a programmatic title. In Cone's opinion, in the "Scène aux champs" from the *Symphonie fantastique*, "[...] the oboe and the English horn represent two shepherds in friendly dialogue."[32] These two instruments assume roles as virtual characters or virtual agents, which means that they do not represent real characters, but are rather like messengers of these characters. If they are to maintain their leading role throughout a movement or whole composition, such solo instruments can be called *permanent agents*.

---

[30] Márta Grabócz, "Affect and Narrative Transformation in 18th Century Sonata Forms: The First Movement of Mozart's Symphony in C major K.338," Eero Tarasti, ed., *Musical Semiotics Revisited* (Helsinki: International Semiotics Institute, 2003), 40-59.

[31] Tarasti, *Signs of Music*, 14-15.

[32] Edward Cone, *The Composer's Voice* (Berkeley/Los Angeles, CA: University of California Press, 1974), 87.

Such permanent agents include solo instruments in concertos, although if the instrument shifts its function to ornamentation, for example, it becomes a *temporary agent* and is no longer considered permanent. Cone argues also that themes and particular instruments can symbolize different aspects of the same thing. This happens in the *Symphonie fantastique*: when the theme representing the Beloved is played by the clarinet, it is taken to symbolize the real Beloved, in other words a character; but when it is transferred to other instruments, it becomes an idea of the Beloved in the titular artist's mind, as outlined in the composer's program. In this context it is necessary to mention also the *idée fixe* of Berlioz's next symphony, *Harold en Italie*. The symphony is written with an obbligato viola part and both the main theme and the viola as solo instrument represent the character Harold. However Cone maintains that "[...] the viola is not restricted to the theme; the theme is not restricted to the viola. If the viola represents Childe Harold himself, the theme is probably intended to emphasize one facet of his nature."[33] Although Berlioz seems to offer unique examples of instrumental representations such as these, it appears that his approach is not exceptional. Elliot Carter's music is based on a very similar idea, in which an instrument as character depends on instrumental character.

Mythical Narration

The subject of myths and music is addressed by Tarasti in his *Myth and Music* (1978) in which he investigates mythical structures in vocal-instrumental music by Jean Sibelius, Richard Wagner, and Igor Stravinsky.[34] More recently, a more extensive study has been provided by Adamenko in her *Neo-Mythologism in Music* (2007). This important work draws together philosophical considerations (Langer), ethnology (Lévi-Strauss), semiotics (Greimas, Tarasti, Yuri Lotman), psychology (Freud, Jung), and composers' writings (François-Bernard Mâche, Georg Crumb, Karlheinz Stockhausen). Adamenko adapts for music Lévi-Strauss's concept of basic mythical structural ideas that produce mythological forms. She lists the five types of structural ideas that can be found in music: binary opposition, repetitiveness, variability, symmetry, and numerical organization. Tracing these structural ideas in twentieth-century music, Adamenko classifies Alexander Scriabin, Stravinsky, Alfred Schnittke, Mâche, Crumb, Stockhausen, and Steve Reich as neo-mythological composers. It is vital to look closely at these five types

---

[33] Cone, 92.

[34] Eero Tarasti, *Myth and Music. A Semiotic Approach to the Aesthetics of Myth in Music, especially that of Wagner, Sibelius and Stravinsky* (Helsinki: Acta Musicologica Fennica, 1978).

Musical Syntax or Semantics? 13

of mythologems in music, for the analyses of Rautavaara's compositions employ these categories. Although binary oppositions can be found in Propp's and Greimas's models of mythical actants, the term as applied here is broad-ranging and does not need to be limited only to actors. Lévi-Strauss's primal mythical oppositions of life and death, male and female, and day and night, can be expressed in music through a variety of different relationships: "[...] regular and irregular, sound and silence; dynamic and static; high and low,"[35] chromatic and diatonic, rapid and slow, tonal and atonal, black keys and white keys, but also in terms of qualities such as dark and light. Repetitiveness is connected with mythical cyclic time in which every natural cycle is repeated (for example the cycle of the four seasons). A reflection of this type of time can be found in highly repetitive music by some twentieth-century composers, which is very often reminiscent of ritual or magic incantations.[36] In music, repetitiveness occurs most noticeably in the form of *ostinato* figures: short melodic, rhythmic, and harmonic patterns that are repeated several times in various configurations. Most often the repetition is limited to one or two notes or chords, which gives the music a primitive, shamanistic, ritualistic, and hypnotic character. It seems that the category of repetitiveness in music also introduces aspects of mechanicalness, which, drawing on Carolyn Abbate's theory of *musica automata*,[37] will form an important part of the analysis of Rautavaara's music offered below. Aspects of variability and symmetry are typical features of Rautavaara's aesthetic and appear in almost all of his compositions.[38] Chapter 6 is reserved for a close examination of the use of repetition in Rautavaara's music and its symmetrical aspects in reference to the mythical form of the *mandala*.

The term variability is linked with another (combinatoriality) and is the central feature of every mythical story. As Lévi-Strauss noticed, every myth is in some way a variant of the same story: "[...] there is nothing 'new' in the mythic world, which is fundamentally uniform: everything that exists only repeats, with slight variation, the initial order of things."[39] If the myth is the same story that recurs in different forms throughout various times and cultures, it is obvious that its structure is repeated; hence one myth consists

---

[35] Adamenko, 29.

[36] In the Catholic Church this kind of repetitiveness persists in the text of several prayers, of which the most famous are litanies and rosaries.

[37] Carolyn Abbate, *In Search of Opera* (Princeton, NJ: Princeton University Press, 2001).

[38] During Rautavaara's studies in America, Vincent Persichetti introduced him to symmetrical properties of music and gave him a great deal of advice in this area.

[39] Adamenko, 65.

of all its variants. Adamenko traces the idea of variability with reference to twelve-tone technique and Schoenberg's idea of melodic transformation. Here it is important also to discuss *bricolage*, a term that Lévi-Strauss used for the technique of recycling mythical themes.[40] Sivuoja-Gunaratnam notes that Rautavaara's music can be considered a typical transposition of *bricolage* into the field of music, for the composer mostly uses auto-citations in his music, from his earliest works to the latest ones, sometimes reusing one idea several times.[41] Such a procedure can be called self-mythical, for the composer actively produces his own "musical myths" and "musical mythologies." It may be said that throughout his career Rautavaara writes the same work in different ways, that his music when considered in its entirety forms a macrotext that can be read in any given individual composition. Such a macrotext is not a patchwork, it is rather a kind of meta-mythologem: a *mandala-text* that one reads in a circular rather than linear fashion. It is reminiscent of those scores of Stockhausen and Crumb that are written in the form of circle.[42]

The numerological tendency refers to the cosmological order in which numbers symbolize God and devils (order and disorder) and play an important role in incantations and rituals. It can be found in works which underline the important symbolic role of numbers such as through the use of specific numbers of repetitions, measures, seconds, minutes, semitones in particular intervals, and chords (a good example can be found in Crumb's String Quartet *Black Angels*, see Chapter 3).

The Uncanny

The term uncanny derives from Freud's essay *Das Unheimliche* (The Uncanny) and refers to something frightening that "[...] leads back to what is known of old and long familiar."[43] The thing is at the same time very familiar and completely alien for observers or subjects, which renders the uncanny object disorienting, ambiguous, and paradoxical. Among the most typical examples listed by Freud are human corpses, skeletons, parts of bodies, ghosts, and animated spirits. Freud explains the human tendency to produce the uncanny as a repression of the familiar in the psyche that must

---

[40] Claude Lévi-Strauss, *The Savage Mind*, G.Weidenfeld, trans. (Chicago: University of Chicago Press), 17.

[41] Sivuoja-Gunaratnam, *Narrating with Twelve Tones*, 240.

[42] See Adamenko, 201-240.

[43] Sigmund Freud, "The Uncanny," *The Standard Edition of the Complete Psychological Works of Sigmund Freud*, J. Strachey, trans., 17 (London, UK: Hogarth Press, 1981), 220.

Musical Syntax or Semantics? 15

be emanated consciously in a completely strange de-familiarized form. An example of this can also be found in Jung's theory of archetypes, particularly that of the shadow. The shadow is an archetype representing the dark and evil side of the human personality that is hidden in the attic of the psyche (the unconscious) but which emerges in instinctive patterns in dreams or symbols. According to Jung's theory, people try to protect themselves from the evil shadow and project it onto others, thereby turning them into scapegoats. In religions, the projection of the evil side of one's personality is replaced by its embodiment as bad spirits or demons that in different cultures receive various names and are represented symbolically in the arts.[44] In this way, the Jungian concept of the shadow followed Freud's uncanny as "[...] a key reference point in discussions of art and literature, philosophy, film, cultural studies, and sexual difference."[45]

Some musicologists (Abbate, Richard Cohn, Välimäki) have successfully applied the notion of the uncanny to music that represents or depicts topics such as ventriloquism, automatism, doubles, and repetitive compulsion.[46] The most privileged area for such scientific exploration is opera, in which the appearance of a dead person (in Wolfgang Amadeus Mozart's *Don Giovanni* and Alexander Dargomyzhsky's *Stone Guest*), bad spirits and magic (in Carl Maria von Weber's *Der Freischütz*, Giacomo Meyerbeer's *Robert le Diable*, Arrigo Boito's *Mefistofeles*, and Anton Rubinstein's *The Demon*) and animated toys (in Maurice Ravel's *L'enfant et les sortilèges*) are essential for the plot and the musical narration. The theory has also been applied to music with titles, composer's commentaries, or programs that had those uncanny qualities discussed by Välimäki in *Subject Strategies in Music* (2005), including processes whereby the familiar is transformed into the unfamiliar, features such as death, mechanicalness and automatism, doubles and multiplication, magic and "magnus like," infantile thinking (music boxes), repetition compulsion, repression, horror, dimness, and extreme nostalgia.[47] According to Välimäki, something can be regarded as an instance of the musical "uncanny" only if there is a combination or an overlapping of two or more of the aforementioned categories.

---

[44] See David Fontana, *The Secret Language of Symbols-A Visual Key to Symbols and Their Meanings* (San Francisco, CA: Chronicle Books, 1994), 14-17.

[45] Nicholas Royle, *The Uncanny* (Manchester, UK: Manchester University Press, 2003), 12-13.

[46] See Richard L. Cohn, "Uncanny Resemblances: Tonal Signification in the Freudian Age," *Journal of the American Musicological Society* 57/2 (2004): 287.

[47] See Välimäki, 275.

Topics

Some of the categories in Välimäki's list overlap with those of topic theory, which certainly has a place in the study of Rautavaara's music. The term *topic* comes from the Greek *topos*, meaning "commonplaces." Topics in music can be understood as "[...] a kind of vocabulary of standard expression"[48]: musical subjects that refer to conventional codes. For this reason they can only be understood as a result of knowing these conventions, be they historical, social, compositional, technical, stylistic, or generic. The theory was well known in the past; in modern times Leonard Ratner has reformulated the idea, distinguishing between three general topics that existed in eighteenth-century music: dance measures, styles, and word painting.[49] Scholars have built on Ratner's work to extend these ideas to the music of the Romantic generation,[50] to twentieth-century music, and to popular music.[51]

"Topics refer to definite semantic themes that are recognizable to a culturally competent listener."[52] Mozart had to know what effect he wanted to create in the audience when he used Turkish music in the opera *Die Entführung aus dem Serail* (1782).[53] Topics relate directly to social-cultural practice and in fact are recognizable as long as some aspect of this practice remains recognizable. Nowadays listeners can easily recognize the topic of waltz music, but only competent listeners who are familiar with features of seventeenth- and eighteenth-century dances will recognize the minuet. Some topics remain in current usage, the three most prominent being the pastoral, the hunt, and the military march, although their meanings have evolved over

---

[48] Välimäki, 119.

[49] Leonard G. Ratner, *Classic Music: Expression, Form, and Style* (New York, NY: Schirmer Books, 1980), 9.

[50] Monelle writes that "[...] such an understanding may be important for a much wider range of music, including romantic and modern repertoires," see Monelle, *Musical Topics*, 4.

[51] For studies on topics in Romantic music see Charles Rosen, *The Romantic Generation* (Cambridge, MA: Harvard University Press, 1995); for 20th-century music, see Kofi Agawu *Playing with Signs. A Semiotic Interpretation of Classic Music* (Princeton, NJ: Princeton University Press, 1991); Raymond Monelle, *Musical Topics: Hunt, Military and Pastoral* (Bloomington, IN: Indiana University Press, 2006); for popular music, see Philip Tagg, *Kojak-50 Seconds of Television Music: Toward the Analysis of Affect in Popular Music* (Göteborg: Göteborgs University, 1979); Susanna Välimäki, *Subject Strategies in Music. A Psychoanalytic Approach to Musical Signification* (Imatra: International Semiotics Institute, 2005).

[52] Välimäki, 119.

[53] See Agawu, 3.

time. Hence the topic of the hunt, which uses sounds of brass instruments not only to imitate the scene of the hunt but also as a fanfare that announces the entrance of the King, can also evoke the sound of nature, as well as having connotations of the military, of death, of the Apocalypse, and of religious music.

Topics can be used separately or in combination in order to create a wide network of musical symbols. Such juggling of different topics is particularly significant when a composer wishes to use music in a pictorial way. Possibly the most famous use of such topics can be found in Ottorino Respighi's "La Befana," the final movement of *Roman Festivals* (1926), in which he gives an impression of a popular fun-fair in Rome through the use of topics such as fanfares, music-boxes, Circus music, Italian popular songs, and *saltarello* dance.

As new dances, genres, styles, and signals developed in the twentieth century, composers began to incorporate them in their music. In fact contemporary musical practice is more pluralistic than that of the eighteenth and nineteenth centuries, since musical practice today is sometimes divided into oppositional genres and styles. This observation does not invalidate of the use of topic theory in the study of twenty-first-century music, but rather shows its universalism and ambiguity.

Ekphrasis

The word "ekphrasis" derives etymologically from an antique form of rhetorical exercise in which one was to communicate particular descriptions very clearly. Over the centuries the term came to refer to "[...] the literary practice of verbally representing sculptures and paintings,"[54] and according to Théophile Gautier the words *"une transposition d'art"* can be understood as the transposition of one art through means of a different art. This raises the issue of intertextuality because the reference need not be to a single poem or image but can be to a set of texts and images (with the cooperation of other musical texts): this is particularly true for twentieth-century music. Not every instance of illustrative music is an example of musical ekphrasis: Bruhn has argued that three conditions must be met for a musical composition to qualify as ekphrastic. What must be present is a three-tiered structure of reality and its artistic transformation: (1) a real or fictitious scene or story, (2) its representation in a visual or a verbal text, and (3) a rendering of that representation in musical language.[55] As with other arts,

---

[54] Bruhn, *Musical Ekphrasis*, xix.

[55] Bruhn, *Musical Ekphrasis*, 8.

music can refer to another work of art by means of transposition, supplementation, association, interpretation, and finally playfulness; each of these means of reference move gradually further from their original source. Transposition is thus a kind of re-creation "[...] through other means [than] what is expressed in the primary art work"[56]: here, either the content or form (or both) may be transposed. At the antipode is "playfulness," a kind of game that is played with the original work of art, very often freely, in which the artist need only choose one element and put it in completely different context. Bruhn describes this category as "the most light-hearted one." It is possible to see the original work of art as a pattern that the composer wishes to imitate (objectively, by not adding anything), supplement (by adding a personal commentary), interpret (by transforming it through one's personal aesthetic), associate (by referring to particularly interesting aspects), or play with (when the composer treats the original work of art in an ironic or humorous manner, or chooses some element from it).

While the end result of the transposition of a work of non-musical art into music differs from the source of inspiration, the composer nevertheless does not want to present his or her own ideas, but rather to step onto the same path of artistic expression begun by the original. Frequently a composer will admire a poem, painting, or sculpture so much that he or she feels the need to express the same idea in music. This is the case in Schoenberg's *Pelleas und Melisande* op. 5 (1903), in which motivic transformation imitates the development of the protagonists in Stéphane Mallarmé's drama.[57] In the case of supplementation, the composer adds those details that the poem or painting only mentions or is not able to express directly. This is particularly true of sensory experiences such as sound, smell, taste, and touch; the composer can also add particular situations that are connected with the work of art. The best-known example is that of Claude Debussy's *Prélude à l'après-midi d'un faune* (1894) in which the composer adds to Mallarmé's poem the sound of the Faune's flute which in turn becomes the work's main thematic actor. The category of association is much freer than that of supplementation, since the composer chooses some elements of the original work of art in order to develop them in a personal way, whereas in the case of interpretation a composer focuses on ideas relating to the work of art and to which he or she may add completely new elements. In the case of playfulness, the composer ironically presents elements from the original work in a so-called distorting mirror in which some elements are deformed

---

[56] Bruhn, *Musical Ekphrasis*, 58.

[57] See Bruhn, *Musical Ekphrasis*, 576-577.

for comic effect. The five forms of musical ekphrasis reveal the process of increasing subjectivity, from objective transposition that is without additional musical commentary to playfulness, which is only a pretext to showcase the composer's attitude. While in transposition, the non-musical work of art is the source of a composer's admiration, playfulness may express a composer's irony, and with it an ultimately negative attitude toward the referential work of art.

Rautavaara's music is full of associations, interpretations and correspondences to literature, philosophy, and paintings, allowing it to be investigated with reference to the theory of musical ekphrasis. For the presentation of the composer's interpretative codes and their signification in musical topics and uncanny categories in Chapter 7, the theory of ekphrasis will be used to demonstrate the connection between his compositions referring to angels and extramusical references such as Rilke's *Duino Elegies* and Jung's theory of archetypes.

Chapter 2:
Angels in Religions and Beliefs[1]

The word "angel" comes from the Greek word *aggelos* (ἀγγέλος), itself a translation of the Hebrew *mâlāk* (messenger),[2] which appears also in Ugaritic, Arabic, and other Semitic languages.[3] Although the angel is most often linked with the Judeo-Christian tradition and faith, many different religions that predate them also have divine messengers who intermediate between the visible and invisible worlds (the profane realm and the realm of the sacred), between Gods (deities) and man, and the living and the dead.[4] One can hypothesize that the model of the Christian angel-messenger was formed over the ages in various and fluctuating ancient cultures such as the Syrian, Mesopotamian, Hindi, Chinese, Egyptian, Greek, Roman, Mazdaic, as well as pagan mythologies.

The plethora of scientific, para-scientific, or popular items on angels suggest that one can talk of the discipline of angelic science (angelology).[5] The development of this quasi-science can be observed from the starting point of the notion of angelic choirs in the Middle-Ages through to the magical function of angels in contemporary occultism and the popularity of angels in the New Age Movement.

---

[1] This chapter is based on the summary of angels throughout the ages in different cultures, religions, poetry, and spirituality given in Oleschko's *Księga o aniołach*.

[2] In the Hebraic tradition, angels were given a variety of names, such as '*abbîrîm* – mighty, '*ĕlohîm* – gods, *bene 'elohîm* – sons of God, and others. See T. L. Fallon, "Angels in the Bible," *The New Catholic Encyclopedia* (Detroit, MI: Gale, 2003), 416.

[3] Geoffrey Wigoder, ed., *The New Encyclopedia of Judaism* (New York, NY: New York University Press, 2002), 61.

[4] Wendy Doniger, ed., *Merriam-Webster's Encyclopedia of World Religions* (Springfield, MA: Merriam-Webster, 1999), 55.

[5] See A. A. Bialas, "Angelology," *The New Catholic Encyclopedia* (Detroit, MI: Gale, 2003), 414-415.

Pre-Christian Angels

From the outset angels were grouped into ranks or hierarchies in accordance with the astrological theory of planetary spheres. Through the centuries and cultures there have been various representations of angels in the fine arts, but within these exist many elements in common with later Christian representations. They often appeared in an anthropomorphic form that emphasized their mission to humanity, with wings symbolizing their spiritual, ethereal, and celestial nature.

In the ancient Hindu religion, there were invisible creatures with the function of divine messengers called *agni* (sacrificial fire), *angiras* (demigods), *aditiows* (twelve spiritual deities that fight evil forces, and reward the good), and *maruts* (storm deities that rule over life energy and help fight demons). The Veda tells of guardians of the good called *gandharvas*. Ancient Chinese religions knew two kinds of spirits, the *celestial*, who were represented anthropologically or animalistically and who maintained the natural order, and the *terrestrial*, who took care of family life and agriculture. Egyptian sphinxes guarded temples and palaces and were visualized as winged lions with a woman's head; these had a rapidly increasing influence on Assyrian, Jewish, Phoenician, and Greek cultures. This symbol had a negative connotation, for those who tried to get into guarded places were punishable by death in a variety of ways.[6]

The religion of Ancient Mesopotamia had a significant influence on the later Judeo-Christian development of angelic representation. The Babylonians believed that planets and celestial objects were living spirituals beings, and towns as well as individuals had spiritual guardians that were comparable to the later Christian concept of guardian angels. They were often represented anthropomorphically, with a single or double pair of wings, a human or eagle's head, and a small bag of herbs of life on the waist.[7] The Jewish period of captivity in Babylon probably influenced the representation of angelic visions in Ezekiel's and Daniel's prophecies.

In Greek mythology, the god Hermes was not only a divine messenger but also a *psychopompos* who led the souls of the dead to the underworld; he was thus portrayed with a caduceus (a herald's staff), small wings on his hat, and sandals. He also acted as a guardian god who took care of travelers, inventors, poets, merchants, and thieves. Besides Hermes, various other

---

[6] The rediscovery of sphinxes took place in the late nineteenth and early twentieth centuries in the symbolist movement in art, in which the sphinx and vampire symbolized the demonic feminine nature: the *"femme fatale"* (see the works of Gustave Moreau, Ferdinand Khnopff, and Edvard Munch).

[7] The guardian spirit of Lamassu was portrayed as a winged bull with a human head.

deities were responsible for their particular natural kingdoms, such as dryads, nymphs, sileni, and typhons. In both Mesopotamia and Greece there were numerous demonic hosts who informed the later development of the symbols of evil spirits in the Judeo-Christian traditions: the devil and his servants (demons). In the Greek tradition demons did not have the negative connotations that they were later to accrue, for everybody had a *daimonion*, a guardian spirit who according to Plato consisted of ether, air, and water. The Greeks inherited sphinxes from Mesopotamian and Egyptian cultures; they appeared in various myths, and most famously in the tale of Oedipus.

Roman mythology adopted that of the Greeks, changing only the names of Gods and deities along with certain parts of particular myths. For instance, Hermes was renamed Mercury, and the *daimonion* became a *genius*. The idea of the *genius* was different from the Greek guardian spirit, becoming a divine element in human nature that accompanies one throughout one's life. With the passing of time, the Greeks began to distinguish good spirits that took care of particular places, nations, and social groups from bad spirits.

In Iranian Mazdaism, every human soul had a related spiritual being, the *favarti*, who leads them throughout their whole life; a sort of second transcendent "I" in which God reveals Himself to people. It was believed that on the third day after the body's death the soul would meet its celestial "I" and go to Divine Judgment. The highest God, Ahura Mazda, had a celestial host, in which an important place was given to *jazats* (good spirits) that carried out the orders of *amsaspands* (immortal saints). Mazdaism was later reformed by Zoroaster, and in the subsequent Zoroastrian religion, angels fulfilled very important functions and created an extended hierarchy.

In other mythologies, guardian spirits had peripheral roles. In Celtic beliefs the world of spirits coexisted with the human world, while German mythology had *fylgie*, one's spiritual double, which during sleep left the body but had to return as the human awoke. Valkiries transported slain warriors to Valhalla, and there was a world of other creatures: dwarfs, gnomes, trolls, and goblins. In Slavic beliefs, the *rodzanice* made decisions about the fate of newborn children, and there were also other spirits such as the *dziady* or *uboża*.

Pre-Christian angelic representations link zoomorphism with anthropomorphism for the purposes of hybridism; by giving an angel an animal head or form the ancients wished to ascribe to the angel attributes of that animal, such as velocity in the case of eagles or power in the case of a lion. Sometimes guardian spirits were gods themselves, as in the case of Hermes/Mercury. They formed a hierarchical society based on what they took care of. Unlike in Christian theology, the good spirits of ancient beliefs had no fundamental influence on the fate of an individual after death: a man is predestined from the start to salvation or damnation. Ancient representations of spirit messengers had a strong impact on the developing Jewish and later Christian angelology. It is also possible that individual ancient religions inspired and interacted with one another so that it is difficult now to find the origins of the Judeo-Christian conception of angels.

Jewish Angelology and the Kabbalah

Jewish angelology was influenced by beliefs held in neighboring cultures, in particular the Assyrian, Mesopotamian and Egyptian traditions. The representation of good spirits in the Old Testament is reminiscent of the Assyrian-Babylonian angelology, although the Jewish spirits did not have the godlike attributes that can be found in polytheistic ancient religions. The Old Testament contains many passages concerning angels and describes their impact on human life. Apart from the word "angel" one finds terms such as Sons of God, Messengers, Emissaries from Heaven, Saints, and Glories as well as the most famous kinds of angels: archangels, Seraphim, and Cherubim. The ban on images in Judaism prevented its angelic iconography from surviving; as a result, Jewish angels remain pictorially undefined and has never become a central concept or received systematic theological study. Jewish sources distinguish between two kinds of angels: messengers who deliver a message from God to an individual and praising angels, among whom can be counted Seraphim, Cherubim, Hayyot, and Ophanim.[8] In addition, Jewish texts employ the term "angel" for exceptional human beings, thus describing prophets or a "human messenger acting as the agent of another human."[9] The most famous Biblical passages including angels are Isaiah's vision, the Books of Job, Ezekiel, Zechariah, and the Book of Daniel. The non-canonical First Book of Enoch mentions seven archangels, the four most important of them being Uriel (leader of the heavenly host), Raguel (the avenger of God against the world of lights), Michael (the guardian of Israel), and Gabriel[10] (the ruler of paradise). In the mystical book of Zohar it is said that every human being has two angels, one good, one bad, and that these can be masculine or feminine. The most interesting and extended conception of angels appeared in the Gnostic Kabbalah. Its

---

[8] The popular Jewish song *Shalom Aleikhem* is addressed to the two angels that accompany each person (see Wigoder, 63).

[9] Wigoder, 61.

[10] See Doniger, 56.

adherents cited the secret knowledge contained in the Torah, but for them it was only a poetic background on which they created their own theories. In fact, for traditional rabbis and Christian theologians, the Kabbalah was a classical heresy. Cabbalists believed that between God, who is unity and infinity, and the visible world there are other intelligences known as Sephirots.[11] These were not created by God but rather arose from Him as a kind of representation of his attributes and faces. Ten Sephirots were treated as archetypes of being, each of them responsible for the order of a realm. This created a hierarchy in every realm of seven Heavens inhabited by angelic hosts. The lower the realm is in the hierarchy, the further it is from the ideal deity, and the more material both it and its angels are. Good spirits help people, and also take care of things, while others create objects. The lowest world is inhabited by demons—fallen creatures commanded by Samael. The Book of Kabbalah was written down in the thirteenth century and had a great influence on symbolism in European art; it was rediscovered by occult movements in the nineteenth- and twentieth-century New Age Movement.

Christian Angels

Christianity took from the Jewish tradition not only its liturgy and the Old Testament, but also a series of theological conceptions. On the basis provided by Judaism, the new religion developed numerous theories of angels in which the most important thinkers considered the nature of angels, their hierarchy, and their influence on the human soul. The Church Fathers in the first centuries of Christianity accepted the presence of angels as a truth of Faith, a belief that remains current in the *Catechism of the Catholic Church*.[12] Rejecting the idea that angels were a Christian counterpart of the pagan messengers of the gods or protective deities, they imitated Judaism by focusing primarily on the message angels convey rather than on angelic nature. In the Middle Ages, following Origen (who claimed that angels had ethereal bodies), St. Augustine provided the best definition of an angel: "'Angel' is the name of their office, not of their nature. If you seek the name of their nature, it is 'spirit'; if you seek the name of their office, it is 'angel': from what they are, 'spirit', from what they do, 'angel'."[13] Generally the angel was an invisible spirit who sometimes assumed a visible body. The

---

[11] Alternative spellings include Sephiroths and Sefiroths.

[12] See Frank L. Cross, ed., *The Oxford Dictionary of the Christian Church* (Oxford: Oxford University Press, 1997), 62.

[13] See *Catechism of the Catholic Church* (Vatican: Libreria Editrice Vaticana, 1993), verse 329.

Bible describes characteristics of angels in both the Old and New Testaments. These characteristics usually follow two general conventions. The first is anthropomorphic: the angel appears as a young, handsome man, well-dressed or almost naked, with one of the following in hand: a sword, keys, chain, trumpet, crown, cranium, or cane. In such cases angels were so similar to people that biblical persons (Tobias, Abraham, and St. Peter) did not recognize their presence. The second convention is symbolic: a fire, cloud, light, shining body, or a fantastic winged creature with a human or animal face, sometimes reminiscent of a moving hewn-out bronze or copper statue emitting a strange voice. The appearance of such an angel was a frightening experience for every biblical figure.[14] Such visitations were well described in the Bible as well as in various Holy Scriptures. The function of angels is a matter of secondary importance: descriptions concentrate instead on matters between humans and God. It is possible to categorize the mission of angels depending on their relation to God and to humans. The first function of angels is the adoration and praise of God;[15] the second is protection, a mission in which they are called soldiers, guardians of Paradise, and messengers. The relationship with humanity is broader, and here angels fulfill various functions as guardian spirits, angelic translators of God's will ("*Angelus interpres*"), observers that supervise and punish sovereigns and rulers, and as *psychopompoi* that lead the souls of the dead from Earth to Heaven.[16] The most important missions are reserved for the three archangels: Raphael, Gabriel, and Michael.[17] From the fifth century onwards, ideas about angels developed swiftly, based upon two lists of orders from Ephesians 1:21 and Colossians 1:16 written by the most influential philosophers and thinkers of the age: Pseudo-Dionysius the Areopagite, St. Augustine, Hildegard von Bingen, and Thomas Aquinas.[18] The first systematic overview of angelic orders, which gave rise to the notion of angelic choirs, was established in the fifth century by Pseudo-Dionysius the Areopagite in his treatise *De coelesti hierarchia* (Celestial Hierarchy). He grouped angels into three hierarchical orders, each consisting of three types of angel, known as

---

[14] See Judges 6:23; Tobit 12:16-17.

[15] Seraphim were mostly portrayed in the visual arts as musicians with instruments or as God's singers.

[16] In an analogous function to that of Hermes in Greek mythology, the apocryphal texts describe the Archangel Michael in the role of a *psychopompos*, a role that is still mentioned in Christian funeral ceremonies and is expressed in the text of the *Chorus angelorum*.

[17] Milton in his poem *Paradise Lost* added the fourth archangel, Uriel.

[18] The theory of angels proposed by Pseudo-Dionysius the Areopagite was further developed by Peter Lombard in his commentaries on the Sentences from the thirteenth century.

Angels in Religions and Beliefs 27

angelic choirs. In the first hierarchy he included Seraphim, often in red and surrounding the throne of God; the golden or blue cherubs who knew and worshiped God; and Thrones, who wore judges' robes, supported God's seat, and represented divine justice.[19] The angels of the second hierarchy were named Dominions, Virtues, and Powers. They governed the stars and the elements and lit up the third hierarchy with the glory of God. Dominions have crowns, scepters, or orbs in order to represent the power of God, Virtues have white lilies or red roses, and Powers are military figures that fight devils. The third hierarchy, consisting of Principalities, archangels, and angels, maintain contact between Heaven and Earth, and execute God's will. While Principalities oversee territories, archangels and angels transmit the word of God to humanity. The most commonly depicted archangels, also described in the Old Testament, are Gabriel, who appears especially in the representation of the Annunciation, and Michael, the bearer of the heavenly host, who is often depicted as a warrior leading the host against Satan and the fallen angels. Hildegard von Bingen probably did not know Areopagite's theory of the hierarchy of celestial spirits, for in her descriptions of her visions, she distinguishes not Areopagite's three but nine angelic choirs, arranged like circles surrounding God and symbolized by one of two perfect figures, a sphere or a ring. In her hierarchy the highest angels were Cherubim and Seraphim, followed by Thrones, Dominations, Principalities, and Virtues; the lowest were Archangels and Angels. The angelic choirs emanated energy, shining so much that some Gnostic theories spoke of angels as God's emanations; Hildegard naturally understood it in different way. The angels closest to God, Cherubim and Seraphim, emanate a special radiation that twinkles. Hildegard's conception is easily recognizable in illuminations from her treatise *Scivias* (Plate 2).

The most important conception of angels can be found in the extensive and sophisticated *De angelis*, the second part of Thomas Aquinas's *Summa theologica* (Compendium of Theology).[20] Aquinas says that angels are intelligences destined never to be united to a body, not composed of form and matter, beings that are both immortal and incorruptible, having neither extension nor dimensions.[21] From the time of Aquinas until the seventeenth century, angelology was limited to studies of scholastics.

---

[19] See Jack Tresidder, *The Complete Dictionary of Symbols* (San Franciso, CA: Chronicle Books, 2004), 33.

[20] Thomas Aquinas is sometimes called the Angelic Doctor because the problem of angels was central to his philosophy.

[21] See Cross, 62

Chapter 2

PLATE 2: Hildegard von Bingen, the hierarchical order of angels, from *Scivias*

The idea of the guardian angel also has its place in Christianity. As in Judaism, Christian tradition has it that every man has at his side a good and a bad angel, the first acting as his guardian and the second as his demon.[22] Guardian angels can be found in the children's prayer: "Angel of God, My Guardian Dear to whom God's love commits me here. Ever this day be at

---

[22] J. Michl "Angels. Theology," *The New Catholic Encyclopedia* (Detroit, MI: Gale, 2003), 420.

Angels in Religions and Beliefs

my side to light and guard and rule and guide. Amen."[23] The guardian angel is probably the most popular angel, frequently portrayed in devotional paintings and children's pictures. Both Catholics and Orthodox Christians believe that angels take part in the divine service and particularly the Holy Mass. For Catholics, believers and angels join together in one chant, the Sanctus, whereas in the Orthodox Church, the whole liturgy is considered angelic, for both the church and its liturgy are designed to imitate Heaven. There are particular feasts devoted to archangels in the liturgy of both churches, the most famous being the one for the Archangel Michael.

Together with the philosophical and theological considerations of angelic nature, the iconography of angels developed over the ages. The representation of angels was taken from oriental sources and ancient deities such as the Greek winged Victory, Nike, and Hermes (or Mercury). At first angels were represented as young men wearing a long tunics, a pallium (woolen cloak), or even a Roman toga, together with items such as a diadem, a scepter, or a codex. Female angels and playful angelic infants (*putti*) were invented during the Renaissance and continued to be represented in later periods, particularly in the Baroque.

Islamic Angels

Islam inherited the Christian theory of angels, though it developed and changed certain ideas[24] The Arabic words for angel are *malak* (a messenger of God that conveys prophecies) and *rasul* (the light of revelation and a stimulus, or inspiration).[25] In Islam angels are both God's emanations and beings with an existence in their own right. Tradition had it that they were created from light to bring this light to some of the chosen people, in particular to prophets. As in Christianity, they can take various forms, but they often have single, double, or triple pairs of wings. Compared to Christian angels, those of Islam have a much more important role, for the

---

[23] The Orthodox prayer is different from that of the Catholic version: "O Angel of Christ, my holy Guardian and Protector of my soul and body, forgive me all my sins of today. Deliver me from all the wiles of the enemy, that I may not anger my God by any sin. Pray for me, sinful and unworthy servant, that thou mayest present me worthy of the kindness and mercy of the All-holy Trinity and the Mother of my Lord Jesus Christ, and of all the Saints. Amen."

[24] Some angels have similar names: Gabriel – *Jibrîl*, Michael – *Mikâ'îl*; others are called by their functions (see Gisela Webb, "Angel," J.D. McAuliffe, ed., *Encyclopedia of the Qur'ân* 1 (Leiden: Brill, 2001), 84.

[25] D. B. Macdonald, "Malâ'ika," P. J. Bearman, ed., *The Encyclopedia of Islam* (Leiden: Brill, 1990), 216-218.

sacred book of Islam, the Quran, was dictated to Mohammed by an angel. Maurice Gaudefroy-Demombynes maintains that the first of Mohammed's revelations took place without angelic participation.[26] For a couple of years thereafter, Mohammed did not experience any revelations, until the moment when he felt the divine presence and surrendered to it. An angel came to him in the night,[27] and according to Muslim tradition, he tussled, howled, foam flowed from his mouth and sweat from his body. After this event Mohammed continued to roam on Hira's mountain, and when the angel ordered him to read a scroll he answered that he can not do it. As a consequence the angel shook him, repeating the command three times. He showed Mohammed the Holy Book and taught him how to recite it. Through its passages the prophet experienced his revelation and memorized it.

Islamic tradition claims that the archangel Michael, who is the leader of the angels from the sixth heaven, carries God's throne.[28] Although the Islamic hierarchy of angels is comparable to that of Christianity, it is much more mystical insofar as angels can come in winds and clouds. The counterpart of Satan is Iblis, who enters Paradise in the form of fog. Angels guard people and record their deeds, both good and bad, in books; every man has his good angel on his right-hand side and his evil angel on the left. Resulting from the influence of the Judeo-Christian tradition, demons watch over hell, the place of eternal damnation.[29]

New Age Angels

Beginning with the Enlightenment, in which the philosophy of rationalism gave priority to the sciences, angels were gradually and increasingly relegated to the sphere of legends, fairy tales, and children's stories.[30] The nineteenth century gave renewed importance to spirits, not strictly in accordance with particular religious beliefs, but rather coming to them through older beliefs as preserved in folk stories and legends that were revived and mixed with traditional religions. As a consequence, the

---

[26] See Maurice Gaudefroy-Demombynes, *Mahomet* (Paris: Albin Michel, 1957).

[27] The night when the angel visited Mohammed is called the Night of Power or Destiny. Muslims believe that if they spend this night in worship, angels will come down from Heaven to Earth. Traditionally Muslims celebrate the Night of Power on the twenty-seventh night of *Ramadan*.

[28] Doniger, 56.

[29] See Webb, 84-92; Macdonald, 216-219.

[30] See Michl, 422.

Romantics indulged in occultism on a large scale. Angels appeared in Tarot cards, in the Book of Kabbalah, and in the belief in the magic of crystals; finally, they began to be treated like certain deities from ancient religions or as pagan spirits. The most prominent branch of occultism was created and developed by Rudolph Steiner in his spiritual philosophy, which he called anthroposophy. According to Steiner, "Anthroposophy is a path of knowledge, to guide the spiritual in the human being to the spiritual in the universe. [...] Anthroposophists are those who experience, as an essential need of life, certain questions on the nature of the human being and the universe, just as one experiences hunger and thirst."[31] In the nineteenth and early twentieth centuries this philosophy provided the starting point in different European countries from which to create several societies. These gathered many followers from the different sciences and arts, including music. The most famous society, whose origins predate Steiner, is the Theosophical Society, established by Helena Blavatsky in New York in 1875. The ideas of Blavatsky were disseminated in several books—*The Secret Doctrine: The Synthesis of Science, Religion, and Philosophy* (1888), *The Voice of the Silence* (1889), and *The Key to Theosophy* (1889)—and inspired artists such as Jean Delville and Scriabin.

Theosophy and anthroposophy were two important sources for the spiritual movement that emerged in the middle of the twentieth century, variously called the New Age Movement, New Age Spirituality, or Cosmic Humanism. The term was first used by William Blake in 1809 and adopted by Blavatsky in her book *The Secret Doctrine* to refer to esoteric and occult traditions, astrology, magic, alchemy, and the Kabbalah. The New Age Movement includes elements of older spiritual and religious traditions, ranging from atheism and monotheism through classical pantheism and naturalistic pantheism to polytheism combined with science and Gaia philosophy; particular emphasis is variously placed on archaeoastronomy, astronomy, ecology, environmentalism, the Gaia hypothesis, psychology, and physics. In our days, the New Age Movement is primarily perceived as a cultural phenomenon, a hotchpotch of various elements deriving from sometimes contradictory cultures and tinged with the idea of a new spiritual dimension. In this kind of meta-religious thinking or "popular religions," angels do not seem to be the messengers of God but rather a substitute for God, posing as they do as the highest spiritual being helpful in daily human life. In fact, the symbol of the angel in the New Age Movement seems increasingly far removed from its original religious source and increasingly

---

[31] Rudolf Steiner, *Anthroposophical Leading Thoughts*, G. and M. Adams, trans. (London: Rudolf Steiner Press, 1973), 13.

multicultural, thereby losing its connections to the Jewish-Christian tradition. Some scholars suggest that if the New Age Movement can be treated as contemporary gnosis (a so-called neognosis), the popularity of the angel within it may become comprehensible.[32] There are plenty of New Age websites devoted to angels and their ultra-powerful influence on private life, testimonies of people who have received angelic visitations and advice on how to meet one's personal angel.

This survey of the significance of angels in particular religions and beliefs provides the essential theological and spiritual background to enable a discussion in the following chapter of how music and composers have portrayed or represented the symbol of the angel throughout history. Musical representations of angels strictly follow the spiritual doctrines, for until the twentieth century the angel was a religious and spiritual symbol and belonged to the semantic world of sacred texts: the Bible, the Quran, or the Gnostic Kabbalah.

---

[32] See Oleschko, 340-341.

Chapter 3:
Musical Approaches to Angels

The Jewish and Christian religions and beliefs are the richest source for representations of angels in music since these two religions created the most coherent and interesting ideas about angels. The best examples of angelic topics in music can be found in those vocal-instrumental compositions in which the texts are drawn from Biblical sources. The following list outlines some of them:

a) Old Testament
1. The creation of the world (Genesis 1-3) as paraphrased in John Milton's *Paradise Lost* (1674): Joseph Haydn's oratorio *The Creation* (1798), Rubinstein's oratorio *The Lost Paradise* (1875), Krzysztof Penderecki's opera *The Lost Paradise* (1978), and Darius Milhaud's ballet *La Création du monde* (1923).
2. Tobias and the Angel (Book of Tobit 5:4-23; 6, 1-19; 12:1-22): Haydn's oratorio *Il ritorno di Tobia* (1774-75), Arthur Bliss's television opera *Tobias and the Angel* (1960).
3. *Jacob wrestling with the angel* (Genesis 28:12-16): Arnold Schoenberg's oratorio *Jacob's Ladder* (1917/22), Penderecki's orchestral composition *The Awakening of Jacob* (1974).
4. Elias and the Angels (1st and 2nd Book of Kings); Felix Mendelssohn's oratorio *Elijah* (1846).

b) New Testament:
1. The annunciation of the archangel Gabriel to the Virgin Mary (Luke 1:26-38): every vocal composition which uses words from the popular prayer to the Virgin Mary, *Ave Maria* ("Hail Mary"); the Gregorian antiphon *Ave Maria* and its various polyphonic or choral settings by Josquin Desprez, Giovanni Pierluigi da Palestrina, Giulio Caccini, Charles Gounod, Brahms, Anton Bruckner, and contemporary composers such as Tavener and Górecki.
2. The birth of Jesus (Matthew 1:20-24; 2:13-14; Luke 2:9-14): Luke's verse 14 was used to create the Hymn of Glory ("Glory to God in the Highest") which appears as a Common Mass (*Gloria*); the whole of Matthew's and Luke's text's are sung in medieval

liturgical dramas, Christmas histories (Heinrich Schütz), cantatas and oratorios (Bach, Handel).
3. Christ's Resurrection (Matthew 28:2-7, Mark 16:5-7, Luke 24:4-7, John 20:11-13)[1]: music engaged with this topic from the very beginning, first in the 11th-century Wipo of Burgundy's Easter sequence *Victimae paschali laudes*, then as the trope *Quem quaeritis?* (Whom do you seek?), which developed into the Latin drama *Visitatio sepulchri* (The visit to the tomb). The text was used also in several cantatas, oratorios, and histories, notably in one work by Tavener: *Fall and Resurrection* for soprano, contra-tenor, baritone, mixed choir and orchestra (1997).
4. The Apocalypse (Book of Revelation 8:2-13; 9:1-11, 13-15; 10:1-10; 11:15-19): some passages of the text were used in the popular sequence *Dies irae*, which in turn became a component in *requiem* composition such as those written by Mozart (1791), Berlioz (1837), Giuseppe Verdi (1874), Gabriel Fauré (1888), and Antonín Dvořák (1890); compositions based on larger portions of the text include Jean Françaix's *L'Apocalypse selon St. Jean* (1942), Gian-Carlo Menotti's symphonic poem *Apocalypse* (1951), and Tavener's *Apocalypse* (1993). In the field of opera, two explicit interpretations of the topic are R. Murray Schafer's *Apocalypsis: John's Vision* (1977) and Wolfgang von Schweinitz's *Patmos* (1989).
c) Hagiographies:
see, e.g., Stefano Landi's opera *Sant'Alessio* (1634), and Olivier Messiaen's opera *Saint François d'Assise* (1975-83).

The list contains only vocal-instrumental compositions that refer to the most popular Biblical texts in which angels appear as characters. However, the situation is different when one considers instrumental compositions referring to angels. Without knowledge of a literary source, it is difficult to recognize if the symbol of a spiritual messenger refers to the Christian faith, Islam, or some ancient belief. Composers frequently avoid biblical texts but rather draw on some general idea, be it philosophical or poetic, which they develop in a very personal manner. How is it possible to identify the musical symbol of an angel in instrumental compositions whose titles suggest their presence? Do composers use the same kind of angelic representation in vocal and instrumental music, or do they create different approaches for these two musical genres?

---

[1] Beethoven's oratorio *Christus am Ölberge* ("Christ on the Mount of Olives") includes the moment in which an angel appears during Christ's prayer and supports him.

The following examination of representations of angels in music will show how music throughout the ages has tried to portray them by means of different approaches. It will particularly focus on those angelic representations that have relevance to the subsequent investigation of the symbol in Rautavaara's instrumental works referring to angels.

Musica coelestis: the Theory of Angelic Choirs

It is difficult to think of the symbol of the angel in secular music of the past, which had a strict relationship with rituals and liturgy. Spirits, the souls of the dead, or demons appear in the music of every ancient religion. Moreover, all ancient religions except for Judaism are polytheistic, making it hard to distinguish between spirits and particular deities. In the most primitive religions the cult of spirits was the most important element of belief systems, and the main function of shamans was to summon spirits through music. Music had a strong orgiastic character intended to drive demons from the village, the community, or the individual. Music was a secret door to heaven and God and hence was sacred: songs and dances were important forms of thanksgiving to tutelary deities and spirits, who (among other tasks) led the souls of the dead to eternal life. Angels first appeared in the liturgical music of Judaism; of the hymns that praised God, the most ecstatic was the *Song of Angels*.

In antiquity music was treated as a mediator between two planes, a concept later developed in ancient Greece, particularly in Platonic philosophy. Plato writes about two kinds of music: orphic music, which he believed leads to order, and ecstatic music connected to the cult of Dionysus, which he claims results in chaos. Plato also formulates the basic foundation for the theory of ethos, in which music can have a good or bad impact on people, including the capacity to heal, and hence has an important role in education. He argues that each Greek mode has a different spiritual effect, which can be good or bad, i.e., which can have the capability to heal or harm. Music according to Plato is the key to both the human soul and the universe. The early church assimilated these Platonic conceptions; "Clement of Alexandria used music as a principal metaphor in his *Exhortation to the Greeks*, a treatise written in the late second century that revealed the errors of paganism and the perfect truth of Christianity."[2] As the first medieval scholars tried to reconcile the idea of Greek philosophers with Christianity, they identified the celestial musical ratios with the Greek *logos*: "The Heavenly Intelligences, which motivated the cosmic spheres in Aristotle's cosmic

---

[2] James, 69

scheme, are transformed in the Christian era into angels."[3] The question of angels was a matter of heated debate until Thomas Aquinas:

> That the celestial bodies are moved by spiritual beings, I cannot think of one philosopher or saint who would have denied it; and if we admit that the angels move the spheres, no official source, that is, no saint could deny this proposition [...]. Therefore the conclusion is: Everything that moves in nature is moved by the Ruler; the angels transmit the motion to the spheres.[4]

In the hierarchy of angels created by Pseudo-Dionysius the Areopagite in his *De coelesti hierarchia*, the primary function of angels is to praise God. Each kind of angel praises God in a different manner: Seraphim, for example, dance around God and sing songs of praise to him. It was believed that these hymns were beyond human comprehension so the Seraphim's task was to transmit these songs down "[...] until the musicians of the terrestrial church, discerning the faint echo of the heavenly songs, convey them, in the form of a now audible music, to human ears."[5] This is one of the reasons why music is so important in Christianity. Vocal music has a particularly special significance because here word and music are united.

In the Middle Ages, Gregorian chants were an attempt to imitate angelic music through the means of vocal music. Although liturgical texts very often included mention of angels, there were no musical representations of angels through the use of special melodic motifs and rhythm. In contrast to words such as "Jesus" or "Christ," "angel" was placed in the category of "ordinary" words. In the thirteenth century, Franciscans collected eighteen masses in separate cycles. Cycle VIII includes a work listed as *Missa de angelis*. This title, however, was taken from the original text and does not indicate extramusical references to angels. Two parts of the ordinary mass (*Ordinarium missae*) can be described as angelic songs: the *Gloria*, according to evangelists, are the words of glory sung by the angels accompanying the shepherds on the day of Jesus' birth, and the *Sanctus*, the song of praise to God sung by angels around the throne of God (from Isaiah 6:3). Despite the angelic provenance of the *Gloria*, for the most part it was only the *Sanctus* that was called the "angelic hymn." According to church scriptures, it is an acclamation that concludes the *prefatio* (the essential prayer of the celebrant) by speaking of the glory and joy of the angels that believers should join in following the *Sanctus*. Pseudo-Dionysius the Areopagite writes that Seraphim, who have multiple faces and six pairs of

---

[3] James, 70-71.

[4] James, 71.

[5] Poizat, 127.

Musical Approaches to Angels

wings, sing with voices "similar to the swoosh of the many waters" in the incessant hymn of praise "*Sanctus, sanctus, sanctus, Deus Sabbaoth, pleni sunt caeli et terra gloria tua.*" He assumes that the highest angels sing, although there is nothing in the Bible to suggest that they sing before the throne of God in Heaven. It was a custom in choral masses that the word *sanctus* was emphasized by long ornamental melismas that belong to the category of choral *concentus* (Ex.1). In later ages some composers continued this practice: the most spectacular example can be found in the *Vespro della Beata Vergine* (1610) by Monteverdi in his "Duo Seraphim" (Ex.2).

EXAMPLE 1: Three beginnings of the Sanctus from Masses VIII, IX, and XI

EXAMPLE 2: Monteverdi, long melisma on the word "Sanctus"

The visionary, mystic, and composer Hildegard von Bingen (1098-1179) devotes an extended passage from her *Scivias* (passage 1,6) to the singing of the angels. The theory of angelic choirs was further disseminated through the work of Thomas Aquinas and influenced Renaissance music. For this reason, choral music was treated as the imitation of angelic singing and instruments were excluded in the Christian liturgy until the Reformation (with the exception of the Renaissance Venetian School); in the Orthodox Church this rule is still enforced.

Angelic Modes and Scales

The history of the symbolic use of key signatures and scales is very long and dates from ancient Chinese, Egyptian, and Indian music.[6] The Greek theory of *ethos* developed by Aristotle in the fifth century formulated principles for different scales and instruments and ascribed an educational role to them. Plato in his *Dialogues* lists scales within particular moral and aesthetic categories.[7] The theory of *ethos* strongly influenced medieval music; theoreticians such as Boethius applied "mechanical" Greek modes to medieval modes, giving them the same names as the Greek modes and attributing to them the same properties. Several theoreticians (Guido d'Arezzo, Hermannus Contractus, Johannes Cotton, and others) later formulated their own theories of characterizing church modes.[8] Although the religious music of the medieval period is on the whole considered to be "angelic," Guido d'Arezzo believes the Mixolydian scale to be particularly so.[9] There are no examples in music demonstrating how this scale may manifest these properties, but this way of thinking developed over the following centuries.

For instance, one can find traces of such notions in Athanasius Kircher's treatise *Musurgia universalis* (1650), which influenced Baroque theories of scales. The establishment of the well-tempered system allowed Gioseffo Zarlino, in his treatise *Istitutioni harmoniche* (1558), to formulate aesthetic

---

[6] See Rita Steblin, *A History of Key Characteristics in the Eighteenth and Early Nineteenth Centuries* (Rochester, NY: University of Rochester Press, 2002).

[7] See James, 56-57.

[8] See Gustave Reese, *Music in the Middle Ages: With an Introduction on the Music of Ancient Times* (London, UK: Dent, 1940), 159.

[9] The theoretical character of modes provided by various medieval thinkers did not always have practical implications in music, although in some staged drama in the medieval church, scales can characterize the role of actors. See Dunbar H. Ogden, *The Staging of Drama in the Medieval Church* (Newark, NJ: University of Delaware Press, 2002), 188-190.

Musical Approaches to Angels

differences between the major and minor scales and to argue that in general major scales are joyful, in opposition to minor scales, which were deemed sad and sorrowful. This semantic distinction between major and minor was in common use until to the end of the seventeenth century, but no specific characteristics were ascribed to individual keys.[10] Although there are several later Baroque theoreticians who provided interpretations of various key signatures (for instance, Rousseau, Marc-Antoine Charpentier, Mattheson, Jean-Philippe Rameau), nobody identified specifically angelic scales. Classical music very often employed Zarlino's oppositional practice in which modulation from the minor mode to the major (and vice versa) became the most important strategy in compositional technique. The most famous example can be found in Ludwig van Beethoven's Ninth Symphony in which the motion from D minor to D major can be interpreted as a motion from doubt and darkness to faith and light. There is a cherub in the finale of the symphony who announces the Ode to Joy: after the line "[...] und der Cherub steht vor Gott" (and the cherub stands before God) is sung, there is a half measure of silence, the tonal center changes to D major, and the Ode begins.[11] The appearance of an angel is thus very often connected with minor and major scales. To illustrate the fall of Satan from good to evil in the second number of his oratorio *The Creation*, Haydn shifts from A major to C minor.[12] Such techniques of passing from minor to major and vice versa can be interpreted as the theory of light in music wandering from dark to light or light to dark.

Of the theorists who classified the different semantic roles of keys in the Classical period, only one, Johann Jakob Heinse in 1795, ascribes angelic connotations to E major,[13] calling it heavenly;[14] others such as Mattheson (1713) and Christian Friedrich Daniel Schubart (1789) interpret it as demonic. In Weber's *Euryanthe* (1823), E major is used as a symbol of jealousy and moreover the tendency remained in at least one late-romantic

---

[10] See Steblin, 31.

[11] See Poizat, 123.

[12] See H.C. Robbins Landon, *Haydn: The Years of "The Creation," 1796-1800* (London, UK: Thames and Hudson, 1977), 399-400.

[13] C major was interpreted by various theorists (Georg Joseph Vogler, Schubart, Heinse) as innocent and pure; others found it noble (André Grétry). It is difficult to accept C major as a scale that portrays angelic attributes for it was one of the most popular and also most vulgar key signatures (see Mattheson's statement, quoted in Steblin, 226).

[14] "Heavenly; it is the highest to which beautiful nature climbs. Exalted heavenly life." Steblin, 252.

opera, Engelbert Humperdinck's *Hänsel und Gretel* (1893), in which the scale is used in the representation of the witch. Nevertheless as the nineteenth century progressed, E major gained both spiritual and amorous connotations. For instance, in the fourth movement of his Fourth Symphony, Mahler uses the song "Das himmlische Leben" in E major to represent a child's vision of Heaven. Schering relates the second movement in E major of Franz Schubert's *Unfinished* B-minor Symphony (1822) to the composer's short prose work "My dream" in which Schubert discusses "celestial thoughts" and "eternal happiness."[15] For Schering, the key signature of the movement becomes a symbol of the glorification of eternal life and bliss, but some scholars have claimed that such an interpretation goes too far; such readings are very controversial. In the last movement of Brahms's *German Requiem* (1868), the composer uses an odd progression from F major to E major, surprisingly returning to F major. The significant return of the key signature creates a strong symbolic effect as if "the door of Heaven was opened for a moment." Alfred Lorenz argues that E major in Wagner's *Tristan and Isolde* (1857-59) is the central key signature that symbolizes the idea of love. In late romanticism E major is interpreted by various scholars as luminous: Ernst Pauer (1877) regards it as bright, light, and splendid; Paul Ertel (1896) describes it as the most luminous and bright of all key signatures. The connection to light relates to the theory of angelic choirs in which angels are shining, twinkling, and surrounding God's throne; in this way, E major can be a symbol of the reflection of God's light, Heaven, and Paradise.

The argument of Schubart (1806) regarding the characterization of keys is supported by many famous composers.[16] His theory strongly emphasizes the metaphysical symbolism of different key signatures, as he argues that some of them evoke religious or demonic connotations. Among the former he counts A major and E-flat major, and also A, B and C-sharp minor; to the latter E-flat minor. Furthermore, Schubart highlights B-flat major as a key that can transport one to Heaven, a function that is close to that of the angel. For this reason B-flat major may be called angelic since its function seems to follow the medieval theory of uniting *musica instrumentalis* and *musica coelestis*. Certainly the composers from the Romantic generation link the minor key signature with demonic characters and death, particularly in the keys of F and B minor, as in Heinrich Marschner's *The Vampire* (1828), *Hans Heiling* (1833), and Richard Strauss's *Die Frau ohne Schatten* (1919).

---

[15] See Peter Pesic, "Schubert's Dream," *Nineteenth Century Music* 23/2 (1999): 137.

[16] See Steblin, 103-133.

The same is true for C minor, the key signature Beethoven chose to represent fate. The best example for the use of symbolic key signatures is probably the scene "Milch des Mondes fiel aufs Kraut" from Weber's *Der Freischütz* (1821). In the late nineteenth century, composers start to use key signatures with numerous sharps and flats to which they ascribe a symbolic spiritual role. This is in accordance with the writings of Wilhelm Christian Müller (1830), a scholar from the early romantic period, who argues that D-flat/C-sharp major symbolizes a celestial enlightening while F-sharp/G-flat major indicates an ambiguous irresolution between Heaven and Earth. Jarosław Mianowski argues that in Wagner's *Ring Cycle*, key signatures such as D-flat major reflect a divine sphere, in contrast to C major which he interprets as symbolic of the human sphere.[17] Wagner also uses the typical romantic polarization between major and minor to signify antinomies such as the hero and his death, or knowledge and its negation, which are essential for the musical structure and dramaturgy.

In fact, in classicism and romanticism, the opposition of minor versus major signifies the transition from the level of the earth to the spiritual realm, according to the rule that major keys have positive connotations while minor keys suggest something negative. This dichotomy contributes to the opposition between diatonic and chromatic passages, which similarly have connotations of positive and negative. As a consequence, composers using minor "demonic" keys frequently use dissonant harmonies. Although the theory of consonances and their contrasting dissonances dates from ancient times, they are understood differently through the ages. In the twentieth century, the symbolization of intervals changes in accordance with individual composers' musical languages.

The *Diabolus in Musica*: Angelic and Demonic Intervals

The anonymous ninth-century treatise *Musica enchiriadis* was the first to discuss two kinds of early organum: *organum diapente*, based on parallel perfect fifths, and *organum diatessaron*, in which two voices that begin on the same tone move a fourth apart, proceeding in parallel motion until the final close in unison. The underlying principle of both of these kinds of *organum* is to avoid the tritone that appears as a diminished fifth or

---

[17] Jarosław Mianowski, *Semantyka tonacji w niemieckich dziełach operowych XVIII-XIX wieku* [The semantics of keys in German operas from the 18th to the 19th century] (Toruń: Adama Marszałek, 2000), 140.

augmented fourth in the progression of parallel perfect fourths and fifths. As early as the thirteenth century, the tritone is called the *diabolus in musica*[18] and regarded as an unstable interval: *discordantia perfecta*.[19] Hence this interval represents for the medieval listener a portrayal of the fallen angel: the devil, who disturbs the natural order of music. The theory is developed over time in accordance with the rules of counterpoint, and the tritone's association with evil angels can be found in the work of composers as late as Stockhausen. During the Renaissance, the theory of affects interprets the tritone as a strong affect, suitable for the *saltus duriusculus*, which has a strong emotional connotation when it appears in a melodic line. Bach frequently uses the tritone in the harmonic structure of vocal works in major keys, and particularly in the Passions, in which the diminished chord as a mixture of two tritones symbolizes Judas believed to have acted in collaboration with the devil. (The second measure in Ex. 3, at the words "Judas aber," shows the diminished chord G / B-flat / D-flat).

EXAMPLE 3: Bach, *St. John Passion*, no. 2, recitativo, mm. 4-6

In classical and romantic music, and particularly in German romantic opera, the tritone is regularly used to portray the evil side of humans, bad spirits, or some ominous event.[20] In *Der Freischütz* Weber uses the tritone to characterize the evil spirit Samiel, the demon who helps the main character Casper prepare the magic bullets in return for his soul (Ex. 4).

---

[18] There is debate over when the term *diabolus in musica* appeared; some scholars claim that it was introduced in the eighteenth century on the basis of historical tradition, others that it was coined by Guido d'Arezzo. See Joseph Smith, "Some Aspects of the Tritone and the Semitritone in the Speculum Musicae: The Non-emergence of the Diabolus in Music," *Journal of Musicological Research* 3 (1979): 63-74.

[19] See William Drabkin, "Tritone," *The New Grove Dictionary of Music and Musicians* 19 (London, UK: Macmillan, 1980): 154-155.

[20] See Drabkin, 155.

EXAMPLE 4: Weber, *Der Freischütz,* Act II, no. 10, mm. 43-47

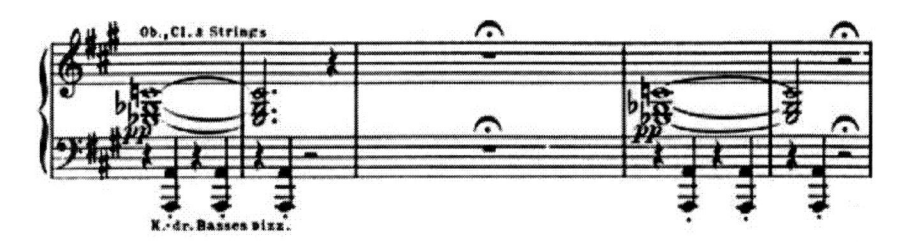

Even in the twentieth century dodecaphonic composers frequently use the tritone as a symbol of evil or of Satan; the most spectacular examples can be found in the scores of Alban Berg and Stockhausen. In his first opera, *Wozzeck* (1921), Berg uses the tritone as a foundation of the composition from the very beginning to anticipate the tragic finale in which Wozzeck murders Marie, where the tritone appears for the last time.[21] In Stockhausen's gigantic cycle of dramas *Licht: Die sieben Tage der Woche* (1977-2003) Lucifer is portrayed by the tritone that signifies the distortion of the perfect fourth that is the symbol of the Archangel Michael. This can be proof that the medieval distinction between perfect fifths or fourths and the tritone are still used by contemporary composers.[22]

The Angel as a Number

Angelic and demonic intervals can directly refer to the numerology that formulated the metaphysical and esoteric relationship between numbers and the physical world. Numerology has a long tradition first established by the school of Pythagoras; it was treated as a secret knowledge in astrology and occultism and also plays a role in early Christianity and other religions. In the Bible numbers are often symbolic, particularly in the books of Daniel and in St. John's Book of Revelation. Not only God, but also angels and demons are represented over time with different numbers and symbolizations.[23]

Prior to the twentieth century, Johannes Ockeghem's and Johann Sebastian Bach's works were already recognized as being replete with

---

[21] See Poizat, 82-84.

[22] The tritone is also used in popular music as a symbol of the devil: the song *Black Sabbath* by the metal group Black Sabbath may be the most famous example.

[23] See Annemarie Schimmel, *The Mystery of Numbers* (Oxford: Oxford University Press, 1994).

numerical signifiers.[24] In the twentieth century, Schoenberg is prominent in applying the system to music.[25] His belief in the magical power of numbers is most evident in his opera *Moses und Aron* (1927-32), in which the dichotomies of Moses-God and Moses-Aron are portrayed by the harmony of the infinity and the disharmony of finiteness.[26]

Three spectacular examples of how angels were treated as numbers can be found in Crumb's String Quartet *Black Angels* (1970), Stockhausen's cycle of operas *Licht*, and Messiaen's orchestral work *Éclairs sur l'au-delà...*(1988-92). Although Crumb's intention is to present fallen angels and not God's angels, it is important to discuss his conception in comparison with Stockhausen's and Messiaen's. In the Quartet *Black Angels*, Crumb intends to portray the symbolic polarity of the Devil contra God; to this effect, he applies the numbers 7 and 13 to musical passages which characterize fallen angels. While in the biblical tradition, the number 7 often stands for the cosmos and spiritual perfection, Crumb draws on its original symbolization as a number of conflict, pain, and complicated union, endowing it with demonic connotations. Another such number is 13, which is the most common number used to symbolize disharmony, catastrophe, death, ruins, curses, and betrayal; it is also regarded as a number that can destroy the cosmic harmony. These two numbers are the foundation of the structure of Crumb's composition, which consists of 13 short parts; in addition both numbers participate in the creation of melodic, rhythmic, harmonic, and temporal structures, such as irregular 7th- and 13th-note motifs, repetitions of trills, motifs, intervals (occasionally including the tritone in its function as "diabolus in musica"), and syllables (particularly the frequent *ka-to-ko*). Some motifs and passages last for 7 or 13 seconds; time signatures also make use of these two numbers; musicians whisper and shout the numbers from one to thirteen in different languages, including German, French, Russian, Hungarian, Japanese, and Swahili; and motifs and chords consistently number thirteen semitones. Apart from this demonic sphere of numbers, there is also the divine number 5 (Christ's number), which appears in the three final parts of the work. The whole quartet therefore seems like a numerological *étude* for the composer, although the composer recognizes that such structures are not easily perceptible:

---

[24] See Ruth Tatlow, *Bach and the Riddle of the Number Alphabet* (Cambridge, UK: Cambridge University Press, 1991).

[25] Schoenberg also experienced the fear of the number 13, which possibly began in 1908 with the thirteenth song of the cycle *Das Buch der Hängenden Gärten* op. 15. See Hans H. Stuckenschmidt, *Arnold Schönberg*, E. T. Roberts and H. Searle, trans. (London, UK: Calder, 1959), 96.

[26] James, 223.

> The numerological symbolism of Black Angels, while perhaps not immediately perceptible to the ear, is nonetheless quite faithfully reflected in the musical structure. These "magical" relationships are variously expressed; e.g., in terms of length, groupings of single tones, durations, patterns of repetition, etc. An important pitch element in the work—descending E, A, and D-sharp—also symbolizes the fateful numbers 7-13. At certain points in the score there occurs a kind of ritualistic counting in various languages, including German, French, Russian, Hungarian, Japanese and Swahili.[27]

One composer who is even more devoted to numerology than Crumb is Stockhausen, who in his monumental operas uses a complicated codified system. His attention focuses on two numbers in particular, which he employs to represent two opposite realms: 12, as a number of fullness, represents the Archangel Michael, whereas 13, as a number of destruction, stands for the Fallen Angel Lucifer. Moreover these two conceptions follow the symbolization of intervals: the fourth as a signifier of Michael and the tritone as a signifier of Lucifer. Just as the tritone is not perfect but a distorted fourth, the number 13 is a deformed imitation of Michael's perfect 12; Lucifer is thus portrayed as a "false" version of the divine.

Messiaen used numbers to convey the theological message of his Catholic faith throughout his career. In accordance with Biblical symbolism, the number seven occurs many times in his work with reference to angels in general and the seven angelic trumpets of the Apocalypse announcing the end of time and the world in particular (Book of Revelation 8:2). Although the title of "Danse de la fureur, pour les sept trompettes" (Dance of fury, for the seven trumpets) from *Quatuor pour la fin du Temps* (1940-41) contains the word "seven," the composer does not use the number to inform the musical argument. The opposite is true for "Les Sept Anges aux sept trompettes" (The seven angels with the seven trumpets) from *Éclairs sur l'au-delà...*, in which 7, as the number of the angelic trumpets and the symbol of God's perfection, appears on the rhythmic level in various formulations of notes in groups of seven. The main melodic theme is given to horns, trombones, and bassoons as an imitation of the angelic trumpets with an independent accompaniment of percussion that beats out the rhythms based on the number seven.

---

[27] George Crumb, commentary on the String Quartet *Black Angels*, in the booklet accompanying the recording Elektra-Nonesuch 7559-79242-2 (1990).

The Angel as an Actor

Historically, vocal music was understood as a transmission of the angelic choir to the earth, whereas instrumental music was forbidden as something secular and orgiastic. The first representation of angels in Renaissance music occurs as part of the theory of affects. In madrigalism, which influenced Baroque music, spirits appear for the first time on stage as actors, dancers, and singers. This happens at a time when humanistic philosophy and the rediscovery of the art of the ancient Greeks makes a strong impact on the arts, and angels begin to be painted mostly in anthropomorphic forms as young men, rather than in the symbolic guises of the Middle Ages. In opera and in ballet, good spirits are cast both as God's messengers and as the spirits of the dead. The Baroque sees the creation of many different forms of religious music such as oratorios, cantatas, histories, and ecclesiastic concertos in which angels are frequently cast as characters in Biblical stories. Composers also introduce a considerable number of good and bad spirits from the ancient Greek and Roman religions as well as those from pagan cultures, whose representation had been prohibited during the Middle Ages.

An important appearance of angels occurs in the early religious opera *Sant'Alessio* by Landi. For the first time, angelic connotations of good and evil are expressed in specific human voices: the part of the demon is sung by a bass, that of an angel by a high soprano. The ascription of a high voice to an angel and a low to a devil is a general tendency which begins in the early Renaissance. The question of angelic singing is raised in sentences that claim that angels dwell "in heaven on high." Scholars relate this "on high" to the "high" voice and by way of contrast assign the demonic part to the "low" voice. Poizat hypothesizes that as in the Islamic tradition, where only high voices can be called angelic, the voices of children and castratos are considered angelic for they are sexless, one of the principal attributes of angelic nature.[28]

In opera the tendency to present good spirits and positive characters through the use of high voices is present from the beginning. In Jacopo Peri's *Euridice* (1600) and Monteverdi's *L'Orfeo* (1607), the parts of Pluto and Charon are sung by basses with accompaniments of dark, unpleasant timbres; the regal part of Orpheus is given to the high voice of a tenor or countertenor, accompanied by a lute or lyre. From the outset, then, instruments contribute to the presentation of operatic characters. The Passions, in which the part of Jesus is traditionally sung by a bass voice and the choir of Jews and soldiers by high voices, constitute an apparent exception, as the tradition goes back to from the Middle Ages in which low voices were

---

[28] Poizat, 114.

considered more noble than high voices. These oppositional features combine in the new form of the oratorio, so that angels can no longer be considered good and evil based on register alone; this is true in Handel's oratorios and also in Haydn's and Mendelssohn's works. Hence the role of angels in operas and oratorios occasionally harks back to ideas from previous ages. In two of Haydn's oratorios, *Il ritorno di Tobia* and *The Creation*, the composer uses archangels as narrators in recitatives, virtuoso arias, and ensembles. As a result, *The Creation* features three narrators, Uriel (tenor), Gabriel (soprano), and Rafael (bass), who do not receive any special "angelic" musical characterization. Mendelssohn's oratorio *Elijah* tells the story of the Prophet Elijah's visit by an angel who revealed to him God's will. Mendelssohn follows the model of Handel's oratorios and Bach's cantatas by using dotted rhythms for the symbolic illustration of angelic presence (see the trio of angels from its second part "Hebe deine Augen auf zu den Bergen," the angel's recitative "Stehe auf, Elias, denn du hast einen grossen Weg," and its aria "Sei stille dem Herrn und warte auf ihn"). The angelic choir is represented in the final chorale, "Heilig, heilig, heilig ist Gott der Herr," the text of which is based on the Seraphim's acclamation *Sanctus*, thereby relating to the theory of heavenly choirs in the Middle Ages.

The angel as a supporting character rather than a narrator plays an important role in two of Mozart's operas, *Idomeneo* (1780) and *Don Giovanni* (1787). In the latter, the character of *Il Commendatore* may, as a spirit of the dead, be interpreted as an angel; in the former, the voice from Heaven heard in the scene of the prince's intended sacrifice together with an accompaniment of brass and wind instruments announcing the divine will, is the voice of an angel.[29] In both cases the angelic appearance interrupts the musical action and plot, stopping Don Giovanni's supper and Idomeneo's sacrifice respectively, and introducing contrasting musical materials that disturb the narration.

The Angel as an Instrument

From its roots in the Renaissance Venetian School, instrumental music spread across the whole of Europe and found its way into the Catholic liturgy.[30] Although the sixteenth-century Council of Trent forbade the

---

[29] See Siglind Bruhn, "Wordless Songs of Love, Glory, and Resurrection: Musical Emblems of the Holy in Hindemith's Saints," in S. Bruhn, ed., *Voicing the Ineffable. Musical Representations of Religious Experience* (Hillsdale, NY: Pendragon Press, 2002), 171-172.

[30] Ogden describes the practice of using instruments during the performance of staged drama in the medieval church. See Ogden, 190-191.

practice of instrumental accompaniment of liturgical songs, for only vocal music was felt to be angelic, Renaissance iconography begins to show angels as musicians playing on various instruments such as trumpets, lyres, and viols. The choice of high instruments for angel musicians corresponds with the use of high voices; low instruments such as the trombone and double bass were associated with demonic forces. For instance, in Handel's early oratorio *La resurrezione* (1708), the fallen angel Lucifer is represented by a bass voice together with a brass ensemble, whereas the angel is a soprano accompanied by violins and oboe.[31]

As instruments begin to represent angels or demons, the composers who write for them and musicians who play them also take on angelic or demonic connotations. This is joined with the notion of heavenly beauty (that is, Hildegard's conception of God as the Highest Beauty). Thus those composers who in the opinion of their contemporaries compose extremely beautiful music, or those performers who perform works gently and subtly, are called angelic; those who perform works incorrectly or overly expressively are felt to be demonic. This distinction is clear in case of the Baroque violist Marin Marais who is said to play like an angel (*comme un ange*) because of his delicate and introverted style, in contrast with his rival Antoine Forqueray who plays like a demon (*comme un diable*) in the expressive Italian style. During the Baroque era, performances can be deemed angelic or demonic according to the degree of their perfection and expressive qualities. Later epochs develop this way of thinking, and the Romantics in particular glorify great performers such as Niccolò Paganini, the so-called "Devil of the Violin," and Franz Liszt, the "Angel of the Piano."

In addition to the angelic associations of instruments and musicians detailed above, there are a few instruments whose names refer to angels and heaven, and which were probably constructed with the intention of imitating the celestial harmony. One such instrument is the double-necked lute, the so-called "angel lute" or *angélique* (in Italian *angelica*), with ten single strings on the lower head and six or seven on the upper. It is played like a harp; its sound is delicate and suitable for slow and grave music.[32]

In 1886, Auguste Mendel invented the *celesta*, giving it a name that reflects its celestial association. This instrument, intended to portray heavenly, angelic music, has a timbre comparable to a glockenspiel or music-box,

---

[31] See Percy M. Young, *The Oratorios of Handel* (London, UK: Dennis Dobson, 1949), 36-42.

[32] See Ian Harwood, "Angel Lute," Stanley Sadie, ed., *The New Grove Dictionary of Musical Instruments* 1 (London/New York: Macmillan Press, 1984), 60. Alec H. King describes also the angelic organ: musical glasses invented by Richard Pockrich in 1741. See Alec H. King, "Musical glasses," *The New Grove Dictionary of Musical Instruments* 1 (London/New York: Macmillan Press, 1984), 59.

but its sound is much more "heavenly" because of the delicacy associated with little bells.[33]

The *Ondes Martenot* is another important angelic instrument, developed in 1928. Although it is one of the first electronic instruments, its soft timbre imitates the human voice. Messiaen " [...] gave a prominent part to the instrument in the *Trois petites liturgies de la présence divine* (1943–4) and the *Turangalîla-Symphonie* (1946–8), where the unmistakable association of the instrument with the human voice creates the impression of a goddess-like figure, without the human limitations of range or power."[34] Even more significant is the use of this instrument in Messiaen's opera *Saint François d'Assise*, where the heavenly music played by God's angel to give the pious Francis the foretaste of heaven for which he has prayed, is dominated by a melodic cantilena in the *Ondes Martenot*.

The *Dies irae* and Apocalyptic Angels

According to the biblical description in the Last Judgment from Book of Revelation (verses 8:2-13; 9:1-11, 13-15; 10:1-10; 11:15-19), the angels blowing into seven trumpets announce the end of the World and start the sequences of catastrophes and plagues. The image of angelic trumpets playing in the divine presence of Christ, announcing the end of time, accompanying the opening of tombs and the resurrection of bodies, was the most popular subject for artistic representation.[35] Sometimes the angelic trumpets are also interpreted as horns, relating to the Jewish *shofar*[36] and medieval *olifant*, or as trombones, reflecting the translation of *shofars* as trombones in German and French versions of the Bible. These three different modern renditions of the ritual Jewish instrument, employed as musical icons of apocalyptic angels, are the only angelic instruments mentioned in the Bible. Composers throughout the ages have used these brass instruments in vocal-instrumental works such as oratorios, operas, cantatas, and

---

[33] Apart from the *celesta* there are also two further instruments whose names are derived from "celeste"—the *celestina* and the *celestinette*.

[34] Richard Orton, "Ondes Martenot," *The New Grove Dictionary of Musical Instruments* 2 (London/New York: Macmillan Press, 1984), 816.

[35] The best example is Michelangelo's *The Angel's Trumpet and the Books of Good and Evil Deeds* from his *Last Judgement* fresco painted on the ceiling of the Sistine Chapel.

[36] "The Jewish shofar in the Temple in Jerusalem was generally associated with the trumpet, and both instruments were used together on various occasions." F.L. Cohen, "Shofar," I. Singer, ed., *The Jewish Encyclopedia* 11 (New York/London: Funk and Wagnalis, 1905), 301.

histories.[37] The Requiem Mass and the Sequence *Dies irae* (Day of Wrath) are also privileged places in which to use trumpets, horns, and trombones: the most spectacular examples include the trombone in Mozart's *Requiem,* in the *Tuba mirum,* and the brass instruments in Verdi's *Requiem* in the *Dies irae.* Some Romantic composers also use brass instruments in works in which the plainchant *Dies irae* is quoted in order to represent the angel of death, death itself, or its *danse macabre*: for instance, Liszt's *Totentanz. Paraphrase on Dies irae* (1849), Berlioz's "Songe d'une nuit de sabbat" from *Symphonie fantastique.*

In addition to texts from the Apocalypse and the *Dies irae* sequence (and its parody), there are also other works in which brass instruments symbolize the appearance of spirits or angels. In the first movement of Hindemith's Symphony *Mathis der Maler* (1934), the chorale "Es sungen drei Engel ein süssen Gesang" first appears in the trombones and represents a concerto of the three archangels Michael, Gabriel, and Raphael. Bruhn argues that it establishes "a context in which man is someone to be judged," and the use of these instruments reminds us that the angels of the Last Judgment are "powerful creatures who pronounce their verdicts over human conduct."[38] Mozart had intended to use three trombones in his opera *Idomeneo* (1780) in the scene in which the voice from heaven tells the main hero not to sacrifice his son. According to Bruhn, "Mozart was adamant, finding the sound of trombones absolutely essential for a moment in which a higher verdict is given with regard to the morality of Idomeneo's actions."[39] The passage was so important for Mozart that he wrote four versions of it, but he finally replaced the three trombones with horns, clarinets and bassoons because the court at Munich did not allow for the intended instrumentation (Ex. 5).

In Stockhausen's cycle of operas *Licht,* the good angel and the fallen angel are represented by instruments from the brass group: Michael is portrayed by a trumpet, Lucifer by a trombone. The composer probably draws on the biblical vision of the Apocalypse as well as the old Baroque practice begun in Monteverdi's *L'Orfeo,* in which trumpets were simultaneously understood as belonging to the supernatural and earthly worlds, whereas trombones belonged to the underground world of Hades.

---

[37] The most famous is George Frideric Handel's bass aria with baroque trumpet "The trumpet shall sound" from his oratorio *Messiah* (1742).

[38] Siglind Bruhn, *The Temptation of Paul Hindemith: Mathis der Maler as a Spiritual Testimony* (Stuyvesant, NY: Pendragon Press), 290.

[39] Bruhn, *The Temptation,* 290-291.

EXAMPLE 5: Mozart, *Idomeneo*, Act III, scene X, no. 28c, mm.1-5

[musical score: Trombone alto, Trombone tenore, Trombone basso, Corno I,II in Do/C, LA VOCE — "Ha vinto A - mo - re..."]

The apocalyptic topic also appears frequently in Messiaen's music, notably in compositions such as the *Quatuor pour la fin du Temps*, *Éclairs sur l'au-delà...*, and *La Transfiguration de Notre Seigneur Jésus-Christ* (1965-69). As will be shown in more detail below in the section *Messiaen's Theology of Angels*, Messiaen developed a special technique in which he combines brass instruments with those of the percussion group in unison.

The Angel as a Rhetorical Figure

The Baroque practice of rhetorical art results in special musical figures that represent angels as symbols of joy, glory, and praise of God. Examples abound in Bach's oratorios and cantatas as well as in Handel's oratorios. In his analysis of Bach's music, Schweitzer notes a special rhetorical motif in accompaniments that occurs every time angels appeared in the text.[40] Characterized by dotted rhythms in triple meter, the motif can be found in the flute and string parts of the Sinfonia from the *Weihnachts-Oratorium* (1734) (Ex. 6), in its final choral, "Wir singen dir in deinem Heer," as well as in the cantata composed for the day of St. Michael, "Es erhub sich ein

---

[40] This section relies on information found in Albert Schweitzer, *J.S. Bach* II, E. Newman, trans. (Neptune: Paganiniana Press, 1961), 78-81.

Streit" (1726), particularly in the aria "Bleibt, ihr Engel, bleibt bei mir." Interesting examples of this rhythm occur also in the compositions devoted to the birth of Jesus, in which angels join shepherds in praise of the Lord (referred to in the medieval angelic hymn "Gloria in excelsis Deo"), such as Bach's tercet from "O wohl uns!" from the cantata no. 122 *Das neugeborene Kindelein* (1724) and Handel's chorus "Glory to God in the highest" from his oratorio *Messiah*.

EXAMPLE 6: Bach, *Christmas Oratorio,* Sinfonia, flutes and violins

As with angels, the devil as a "fallen angel" is portrayed in Bach's cantatas by means of a special rhetorical figure in the melodic line that by virtue of its crawling motion signifies the snake (the animal which represents Satan in the Bible). The most spectacular example can be found in the cantata *Dazu ist erschienen der Sohn Gottes* no. 40 (1723) in the bass aria "Höllische Schlange! wird dir nicht bange?,", in which writhing melodic lines that portray the devil are given to violins (Ex. 7). Others examples occur in the chorus "Es erhub sich ein Streit (no. 19) from the cantata devoted to St. Michael and in the verse "Und wenn die Welt voll Teufel wär" from the cantata no. 80 *Ein' feste Burg ist unser Gott* (1724).

EXAMPLE 7: Bach, Cantata no. 40,
bass aria "Höllische Schlange! wird dir nicht bange?"

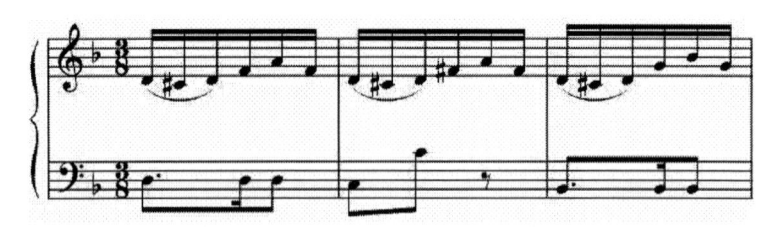

Schweitzer draws some remarkable analogies between Bach's angelic motif and the *putti* angels of the Baroque, particularly with reference to the chorale preludes for Christmas, *Allein Gott in der Höh' sei Ehr* (VI no. 5), claiming that Bach shows the angelic choirs "hovering in the clouds in charming disarray." According to this analogy, some organ cadenzas are representations of "peace on Earth."

The music of the Baroque begins to represent angels not only by different human voices (high and low), but also through the use of special instrumental motifs that are developed in subsequent eras; the oratorios of Haydn and Mendelssohn are perfect prolongations of such tendencies.

Angels and National Spirits

Prior to Romanticism the idea of angels in music appears only in the context of the Christian religion and faith. This changed in the nineteenth century. As part of the search for national identity, artists begin to return to ancient religions and primitive national beliefs; in this light Romanticism can be considered as an era in which spirits entered all the arts, including music. In opera, composers start to develop an interest in fantastic creatures from fairy-tales and fairy stories, representing pagan spirits, deities, and demons that simultaneously support both magical and national topics. The Romantic tendency is to shift the focus from the real world to unreal experiences by providing strong oppositions between the human and earthly world on the one hand and the world of magic and fantasy on the other; the interactions between the two frequently prove tragic for the people involved.[41] It is customary for composers to differentiate these two worlds by using different musical material, although the connection of the fantastic characters with good or evil spirits is not always clear. Even Satan as a fallen angel finally appears as a character in opera, notably in Rubinstein's *The Demon* (1871) and Giacomo Meyerbeer's *Robert le Diable* (1831). Generally speaking, Romantic music idolizes the devil; the era's fascination with Johann Wolfgang von Goethe's *Faust* gave us compositions like Berlioz's *The Damnation of Faust* (1846), Gounod's *Faust* (1859), Boito's *Mephistopheles* (1868), and the folk opera *The Devil and Kate* (1889/98) [42] by Dvořák. In all the aforementioned works, in addition to the principal demonic character, a supporting role is given to angels, who sing in a choir constituting the oppositional, heavenly world of God. Such a conception of angelic choirs is a direct descendent from the medieval theory of *musica coelestis* and the hierarchy of angels by Pseudo-Dionysius the Areopagite and Thomas Aquinas.

---

[41] There are numerous examples which refer to various national mythologies: German sprites in Weber's and Marschner's operas, in Gustav Albert Lortzing's *Undine* (1845), and in Wagner's dramas; Scandinavian trolls in Edvard Grieg's music from *Peer Gynt* (1875); Czech spirits and water nymphs in Dvořák's *Rusalka* (1900); Russian spirits and witches in Nikolai Rimsky-Korsakov's *Mlada* (1890), *The Snow Maiden* (1881/95), *Sadko* (1896), the *Golden Cockerel* (1907), to name only some examples.

[42] Dvořák's folk opera can be regarded as a Czech version of the Brothers Grimm's fairy-tale *Hänsel und Gretel*, the text of which was used by Humperdinck.

It can be found also in choral symphonies: in Liszt's *Dante Symphony* (1857) the choir of angels is represented by a female choir whereas in his *Faust Symphony* (1854), the male choir in the third movement may be interpreted as an announcement of salvation in Heaven. In addition, instrumental music follows these general tendencies through the use of programs and titles.

However illustrative the titles are in pre-Romantic music, there is no doubt that the new generation of Romantic composers gives new emphasis to the programmatic role of titles in music. Nationalistic color in music is provided not only by texts about spirits or angels, but also through the use of programmatic titles and commentaries in instrumental music. Romantic composers who feature national spirits as characters in their operas and other vocal works tend to choose corresponding programmatic titles for their instrumental works. Instrumental music starts to portray and represent angels symbolically or to imitate angelic choirs performing heavenly music. Composers begin to use archaic musical effects from previous eras such as modes, the tritone, and particular registers, or they employ unique harmonic progressions and sophisticated instrumentation that make the works seem unreal, extraordinary, and uncanny. Berlioz is probably the first Romantic composer to make extensive use of such modern effects when portraying the witches' Sabbath in the final movement of his *Symphonie fantastique*; the most famous case includes the high register of the small E-flat clarinet, bowing *con legno* in the strings, and tumultuous passages using brass instruments. Subsequent composers follow Berlioz's path by portraying numerous good or bad spirits; examples include Mendelssohn's music to William Shakespeare's *A Midsummer Night's Dream* (1842) and his oratorio *The First Walpurgis Night* (1831/43), Modest Mussorgsky's *A Night on the Bare Mountain* (1867), Nikolai Rimsky-Korsakov's opera *Sadko*, César Franck's symphonic poem *Les Djinns* (1884), Dvořák's symphonic poems *The Water Goblin* (1896) and *The Noon Witch* (1896), Edvard Grieg's *March of the Dwarfs* from his *Lyric Suite* (1891/1904), Anatoly Liadov's symphonic poems *Baba Yaga* (1904) and *Kikimora* (1909), Sibelius's symphonic poem *The Oceanides* (1914) and others. Under the strong influence of Goethe's *Faust* the demonic, satanic topic is developed not only in opera but also in instrumental music; the majority of examples comes from Liszt's output, such as *Mephisto Waltzes* for symphonic orchestra and also for piano (1859-62, 1880–81, 1883, 1885) and the *Dante Sonata* (1849) in which the composer uses the tritone to suggest hell. Scriabin's sonatas *White Mass* op. 64 (1911) and *Black Mass* op. 68 (1912-13) are two further examples of the genre.[43]

---

[43] Scriabin did not give the title *Black Mass* to the Ninth Sonata; rather, he thought of his Sixth Sonata as demonic and nightmarish, and it was never played in public.

The fascination with spirits, devils, demons, fairies, magical creatures, astrologists, wizards, sorcerers, and witches is on the one hand a result of the turn to the world of emotion, beliefs, and feelings; on the other it shows the crisis of the Christian church, whose angelic topic no longer possessed the strength to inspire artists.

Angelic Dreams

The Violin Sonata in G minor (1749) *Il Trillo del Diavolo* (Devil's Trill) by Giuseppe Tartini is noteworthy as it is probably the first instrumental composition with a demonic program in music history. According to the French astronomer Jérôme de Lalande, the composer claims that the sonata was inspired by a dream:

> "One night in the year 1713," said Tartini, "I dreamed that I had made a pact with the Devil, and that he stood at my command. Everything thrived according to my wish, and whatever I desired or longed for was immediately realized through the officiousness of my new vassal. A fancy seized me to give him my violin to see if he could, perchance, play some beautiful melodies for me. How surprised I was to hear a sonata, so beautiful and singular, rendered in such an intelligent and masterly manner as I had never heard before. Astonishment and rapture overcame me so completely that I swooned away. On returning to consciousness, I hastily took up my violin, hoping to be able to play at least a part of what I had heard, but in vain. The sonata I composed at that time was certainly my best, and I still call it the 'Devil's Sonata,' but this composition is so far beneath the one I heard in my dream, that I would have broken my violin and given up music altogether, had I been able to live without it."[44]

The Sonata is in three movements, the first slow, the second virtuosic, and the third featuring the famous "devil's trill." The trill requires that the violinist play two voices simultaneously: the trill in the first and the melodic line in the second (Ex. 8). The work rapidly became famous and spawned a new development in which trills can be used to portray the devil's music, as they are in Crumb's String Quartet *Black Angels*.

---

[44] Walter Rowlands, *Among the Great Masters of Music* (London, UK: E. Grant Richards, 1906), 40-41.

EXAMPLE 8: Tartini, Sonata *Il Trillo del Diavolo*, mvt. III, mm. 30-34, solo violin

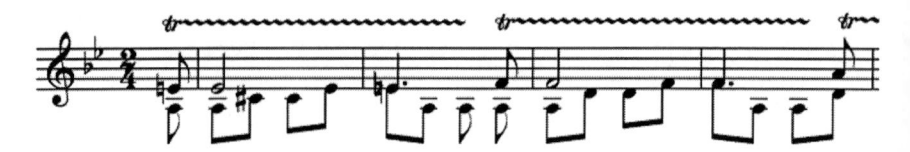

In addition to Tartini's sonata there are other works that were inspired by dreams in which supernatural agents—angels rather than the devils—dictate the musical theme to the composer. The most remarkable example is Robert Schumann's *Variationen in Es-Dur über ein eigenes Thema ("Geister-Variationen")* (1854), inspired by the composer's belief that an angel had visited him.[45] However, all these compositions have no clear features of "angelic music": their connotations to angels have their source in the composer's dreams and visions.

Representations of Angels in 20th-century Instrumental Music

Berg, Hindemith, Crumb, Messiaen, and Stockhausen wrote several instrumental compositions in which angels appear in the title, program, or commentary. Two of them, Berg and Hindemith, were particularly important for Rautavaara in his youth. Berg's music influenced his first opera *Kaivos* (The Mine) (1957-58/1960/1963) as well as instrumental works such as the Second String Quartet (1958), Canto I (1960), and Canto II (1961). Berg's conception of tonal dodecaphony and his romantic aesthetic affected Rautavaara's own idea of twelve-tone music. Hindemith's works showed the young Rautavaara how composing in a logical way can maintain coherence in compositions.[46]

Berg's Violin Concerto Dem Andenken eines Engels
The subtitle of Berg's Violin Concerto (1935), *Dem Andenken eines Engels* (To the Memory of an Angel) refers to Manon Gropius, the daughter of Alma Mahler Werfel and the architect Walter Gropius. Manon had contracted polio and died tragically at the age of seventeen. Berg felt an affinity with her mother, an intelligent and gifted woman whom he revered

---

[45] One year later Brahms composed his own variations on the same theme: *Variations on Schumann's theme* op.23 for four hands (1861).

[46] See Hako, *Unien lahja*, 57.

Musical Approaches to Angels 57

as the widow of his musical idol Mahler. Moreover, Manon's nickname "Mutzi" reminded Berg of a girl with whom he had had an affair and a child when he was seventeen. Berg's Violin Concerto was intended as a kind of requiem dedicated to Mutzi, who was in Alma Mahler's opinion "[...] a person of almost other-worldly spiritual beauty [..]. She was a fairy-tale being; nobody could see her without loving her [...]. She was the most beautiful human being in every sense. She combined all our good qualities."[47] To realize the idea of a concerto-requiem Berg decided to use two citations in the two-movement work: a Carinthian folk song and, in the final section, Bach's chorale "Es ist genug." The citation of the folk melody symbolized for Berg the lovely image of the girl by virtue of the dreamy and rustic character of the tune, whereas the solemn chorale symbolized her approaching death ("with bitter harmonies ends this sad farewell"). The concerto opens with a rising twelve-tone passage built from minor and major chords, starting from the open strings G-D-A-E. Pople believes that, as the theme spreads across all four strings of the violin, it seems like the essence of the violin and may therefore symbolize the "violin's soul."[48] In analogy to Cone's claim that the eponymous hero in Berlioz's *Harold en Italie* may be symbolized not only by individual themes but also by the instrument itself,[49] the solo violin in Berg's concerto can symbolize the tragic Manon or her spiritual soul, which at the end of the work goes to Heaven, represented perhaps by an ecstatic and sustained high note. In this way, the solo violin may stand for the "angel" in the title.

Hindemith's Symphony Mathis der Maler *and Marienleben*

The idea of angels as instruments is presented also in the first movement of Hindemith's Symphony *Mathis der Maler* (1934), which is entitled "Angelic Concert." Before finishing the opera *Mathis der Maler* (1934-35), Hindemith wrote this three-part Symphony containing the instrumental preludes from the opera; musically, these represent three panels from Matthias Grünewald's *Isenheim Altarpiece* (1512-1516). The title of the first movement, "Angelic Concert," refers to the left half of the central second-tier panel in which three angels play viols in praise of the new-born Jesus. To portray the angels, Hindemith adapts the old medieval German tune "Es sungen drei Engel ein süssen Gesang" and uses it as the

---

[47] Anthony Pople, *Berg: Violin Concerto* (Cambridge, UK: Cambridge University Press, 1996), 28.

[48] Pople, 32-33.

[49] See Cone, 91.

opera's main leitmotif. At first it is given to three trombones in *pianissimo*. Bruhn suggests that the reason why the composer used brass rather than string instruments, given that Grünewald's painting showed three angels playing viols, may be that Hindemith wanted instruments that "[...] raise the angelic musicians from the mainly decorative to a status of equality with humans."[50] For this reason, his instrumentation consisted of instruments such as the horn, trumpet, trombone, and bassoon that can imitate the biblical *shofar*.

In the opera, "Es sungen drei Engel ein süssen Gesang" is later sung by a young girl, Regina, and uses the original text: "Three angels were singing a sweet song, which resonated wide into the high heaven. They are joined by the heavenly choir, they perform in front of God and the saints." The scoring within the scene includes instruments other than those heard in the overture (and first symphonic movement): clarinets and flute are used as a prolongation of the Regina's voice as she falls asleep and dies. When she sings the words "into the high heaven," she is accompanied only by an oboe; the rest of the instruments are silent, preparing listeners for her death. Bruhn writes: "[...] this young girl, whom Mathis mercifully took in after his ill-fated participation in the Peasant War which cost her father's life, implicitly helps convey the message of worldly temptation and divine judgment."[51] In the context of the present study, the character of Regina may be interpreted as an angel-messenger that links the heavenly and earthly worlds.

In the song cycle *Marienleben* op. 27 for soprano and piano to poetry by Rilke (1922-23), Hindemith expands on his manner of symbolizing angels in music: the three notes of an augmented triad (D-flat, F, and A) represent the three archangels (Gabriel, Rafael and Michael) from the Grünewald's *Isenheim Alterpiece*.[52] Hindemith not only creates a musical symbol from the augmented triad, but also uses three transpositions by the same interval (a major third) to represent angelic perfection.[53] In the second version of the song cycle (1936-48), the composer relates the complex system of tonal relations to the three actors who appear in Rilke's text—the Archangel Gabriel, Jesus, and the Virgin Mary—ascribing to each a different symbolic key a perfect fifth apart. Jesus is signified by the tonal

---

[50] Bruhn, "Wordless Songs," 171.

[51] Bruhn, "Wordless Songs," 175.

[52] See Bruhn, *Mathis der Maler*, 241-242, 288-291.

[53] See Bruhn, *Musical Ekphrasis in Rilke's Marien-Leben* (Amsterdam/Atlanta, GA: Rodopi, 2000), 91

center E; the subdominant A represents the Archangel Gabriel, and the dominant B provides the tonal anchor for the Virgin Mary. The keys associated with Gabriel and Mary are thus the two polarizations of Jesus' key: a triangle that can symbolize the Holy Trinity. For the Angel of the Annunciation, Hindemith additionally intents a particular motif, which is taken up later in the cycle.

Crumb's String Quartet Black Angels

Crumb's String Quartet *Black Angels* (1970) is one of the most prominent examples of an instrumental work referring to angels. In her doctoral dissertation, Dolly Kessner explores the different juxtapositions of the two numbers on which, as mentioned earlier, Crumb bases his work, claiming that the number 7 represents seven half-steps (a perfect fifth) and symbolically represents "God and Life," whereas 13 as a "fatal number" stands for thirteen half-steps (a minor ninth) and represents the eponymous *Black Angels* and Death.[54] Crumb himself has argued that the number 7 in his quartet corresponds to the tritone, generating connections with the *diabolus in musica*. Although these two interpretations offer conflicting numerological readings of the number seven, they both emphasize the essential role of opposition in the quartet. This opposition is represented symbolically not only by the number of repetitions, seconds, sections, intervals, and irregular rhythms within the work, but also in its structure. The center of the composition is the seventh movement "Threnody II: Black Angels," which combines the numbers 7 and 13 as multiples, i.e., in the manner of 7 times 7 and 13 times 13. This movement functions like a structural mirror that symmetrically reflects both the first six movements and the next six movements.

Not only the symbolic numbers stand in opposition to one another, but also the three parts of the composition entitled "Departure," "Absence," and "Return." Semantically the first title is in opposition to the third, and the respective movements correspond to each other; for example, the fourth movement, "Devil-music," serves as a foil to the tenth movement, "God-music." The opposition appears structurally and in the choice of instruments that play the most important role: in the tenth movement, the composer introduced three sets of tuned glasses played with bows (glass harmonica), thereby creating a harmonic backdrop for the solo cellist's "aria." The

---

[54] See Dolly Kessner, "Structural Coherence in Late Twentieth-Century Music: The Linear Extrapolation Paradigm Applied in Four American Piano Compositions of Diverse Musical Styles (Martinů, Rzewski, Crumb, and Adams)," dissertation, University of Southern California, 1992, 114.

cellist's part acts as the *vox dei*, which in the eternal spiritual world is represented by the sounds of glasses. By contrast, the eleventh movement features a solo violin whose harsh sounds are emphasized by percussive articulations achieved with wooden plectrums, glass bars, and metal paperclips. The seventh movement features wild cadenza for the solo violinist, a *vox diaboli* reminiscent of Tartini's Sonata *Il Trillo del Diavolo*, Paganini's reputation as a devil of the violin, and the Devil's violin in Stravinsky's *Histoire du soldat* (1918). Thus the spiritual dichotomy is underlined by structure and articulation as well as instruments that emphasize the mythical opposition of God versus Devil. The oppositional practice in *Black Angels* can also relate to the category of light, for the title indicates black and dark coloristic qualities.[55]

Messiaen's Theology of Angels

Beside Berg's violin concerto, Hindemith's angelic movement from his Symphony *Mathis der Maler*, and Crumb's String Quartet *Black Angels*, the majority of instrumental compositions about angels can be found in Messiaen's rich *oeuvre*. From his earliest organ cycle *La Nativité du Seigneur* (1935) to his last orchestral work *Éclairs sur l'au-delà...*, the figure of the angel is featured in the majority of his compositions.

Like Rautavaara, Messiaen leaves an enormous collection of commentaries to his music; the majority of these appear in the scores, in which he cites passages from the Gospel, theological treatises, and other literary sources. As these verbal sources prove, his conception of the angelic follows the doctrines of the Catholic Church, although he developed it into a very personal poetic vision.

In Messiaen's instrumental and vocal works, angelic appearances fall into three general categories. The first of these relates to the angels of God's glory, as in "Les Anges" from the organ cycle *La Nativité du Seigneur*, "Amen des Anges, des Saints, du chant des oiseaux" from the cycle for two pianos *Visions de l'Amen* (1943), and "Regard des Anges" from the piano cycle *Vingt Regards sur l'Enfant-Jésus* (1944). The second category includes the angels of the Last Judgment, as in "Vocalise pour l'Ange qui annonce la fin du Temps," "Danse de la fureur, pour les sept trompettes," and "Fouillis d'arcs-en-ciel pour l'Ange qui annonce la fin du Temps" from *Quatuor pour la fin du Temps*, "L'Ange aux parfums" from the organ cycle *Les Corps Glorieux* (1939), and "Les sept anges aux sept trompettes" from the orchestral composition *Éclairs sur l'au-delà...*. The third category is the

---

[55] See Adamenko, 42-43.

most fascinating: in it, Messiaen combines the two previous categories and connects them through his *style oiseau*. While it would certainly be an over-interpretation to claim that each reference to bird song in Messiaen's compositions should be read as musical suggestions of angelic presence, works that feature both birds and angels seem to hint at a relationship between them. The most spectacular examples include their verbal combination in the movement title "Amen des Anges, des Saints, du chant des oiseaux" from *Visions de l'Amen* and their musical combination in the opera *François d'Assise*.

The first of Messiaen's angelic categories is related to the medieval theory of angelic choirs, in which angels praise God in Heaven through song or by playing instruments around Him. Songs of joy and adoration before the throne of God have direct links to the first sentences of the *Gloria* and *Sanctus*. In Gregorian chant, these liturgical songs were generally neumatic, in some instances with longer melismas that were reminiscent of the masterful medieval alleluias and particularly the extended *jubilus*. As a Catholic, Messiaen admired Gregorian chant and took up certain aspects of it, developing it in a very individual manner. In "Les Anges," the sixth of the nine organ meditations of *La Nativité du Seigneur*, Messiaen cited the following from St. Luke's Gospel, also used in the first line of the Gloria: "L'armée céleste louait Dieu et disait: Gloire à Dieu au plus haut des cieux" (The celestial army praised God and said: "Glory to God in the Highest"). The composer designed the entire work as an expanded instrumental song of God's glorification, built on short motifs repeated several times and based on symmetrical scales. One figure of ornamentation rises out of another figure in a manner reminiscent of the Gregorian *jubilus*. The higher layer, with its repetitions of minor third, may relate to an old Jewish ecstatic acclamation as well as the *Sanctus*.

EXAMPLE 9: Messiaen, "Les Anges," mm. 1-2

"Regard des Anges" for piano contains in its first four measures similar ornamentations to those found in "Les Anges"; here, Messiaen's musical representation of angels can be understood in its theological context. In the preface to the work, the composer wrote: "Sparkles, percussion effects, powerful breath into immense trombones; your servants are flames and fire ... 'then the song of birds that engulfs the blue', and the angels' astonishment grows: for it is not with them but with the human race that God has united Himself." Messiaen refers to the notion that angels radiate God's light, an idea postulated by Pseudo-Dionysius the Areopagite who used the word "claritas" to describe it; Hildegard von Bingen and Thomas Aquinas developed this notion further. According to this idea, the main feature of a spiritual being is its shining; the closer angels are to God, the more they glow. Hildegard argued in her *Liber divinorum operum* that when God created light, the angels were born as judicious lights, and in the hierarchy of angels one angelic group grows from another like rays of sunshine.[56] Messiaen gave this idea musical representation in "Les Anges" through the use of arpeggiated figures in contrary motion of five white notes against five black notes in the same register, creating the effect of "luminescence".

EXAMPLE 10: Messiaen, "Regard des Anges," m. 1, angelic sparkling

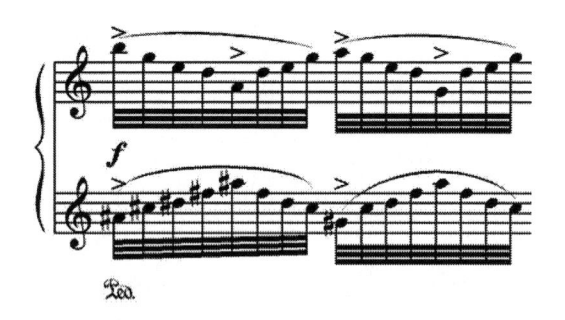

, The composer's commentary provides a much richer interpretation of angels, one that is not limited to angelic light. In his preface, Messiaen writes about the "powerful breath into immense trombones" of the apocalyptic angels. It is interesting to note that Messiaen does not divide the angels into a joyful group praising the glory of God and a terrifying group of apocalyptic messengers. The trombones are portrayed very simply

---

[56] See Błażej Matusiak, *Hildegarda z Bingen – teologia muzyki* [Hildegard von Bingen – The theology of music] (Kraków: Homini, 2002), 28-29.

Musical Approaches to Angels

through motifs in four double octaves, *fff*, in a low register (mm. 38-43). A similar use of unison to represent the seven apocalyptic trumpets occurs in the "Danse de la fureur, pour les sept trompettes," the fifth movement of the *Quatuor pour la fin du Temps*.

EXAMPLE 11: Messiaen, "Danse de la fureur, pour les sept trompettes," mm. 23-24

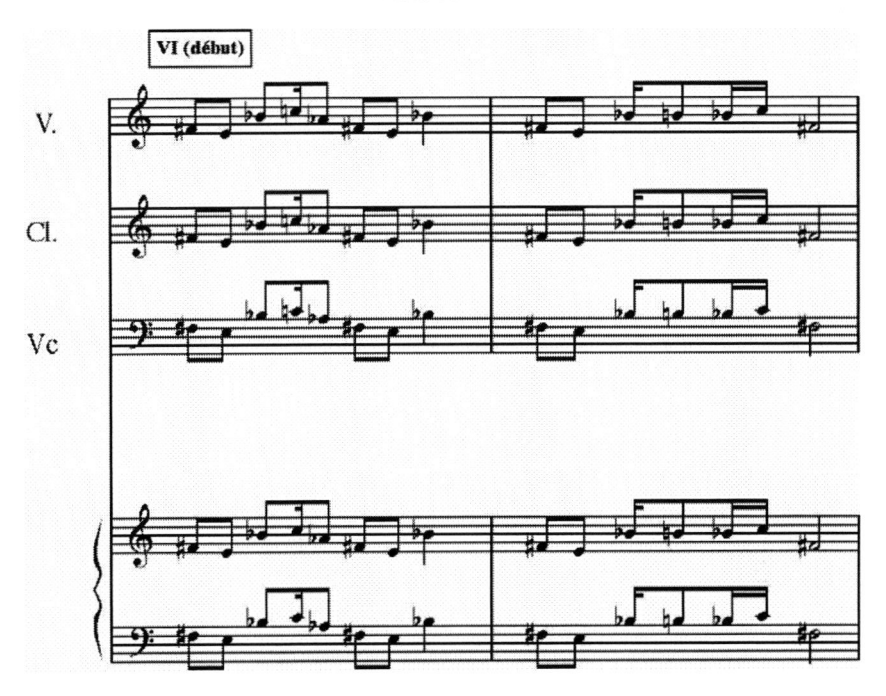

In "Les sept anges aux sept trompettes" from Messiaen's last orchestral work, *Éclairs sur l'au-delà...*, the effect is heightened by brass instruments in the foreground and gongs, tam-tams, slapstick, whip, and bass drum in the background. This creates a divine and mysterious atmosphere that also pervades many passages in *La Transfiguration de Notre-Seigneur Jésus-Christ*. Moreover, Messiaen symbolically represents the seven angelic trumpets by seven notes given to percussion instruments that interrupt the dramatic brass line in union. Such an effect is very picturesque and corresponds with the passage from Book of Revelation 10:1 cited by the composer in his commentary: "Then I saw another mighty angel coming down from heaven, He was robed in a cloud, with a rainbow above his head; his face was like the sun, and his legs were like fiery pillars [...] He planted his right foot on the sea and his left foot on the land, and he gave a loud shout like the roar of a lion." Elsewhere, Messiaen refers to the iconographic evocation of Michelangelo's *Last Judgement*: "These are athletic angels with human forms: eyes half-closed with the effort involved, they blow huge brass instruments which have a sonority akin to that of trombones or Tibetan trumpets above the intervallic augmentation emitted by these 'trombones', fragments of the Theme of Chords are heard."[57]

The second category of Messiaen's angels not only stems from the traditional apocalyptic vision of angels but is also of importance in discussions of Rautavaara's angels. Both Messiaen's and Rautavaara's musical visions are close to that of the poetic figure of angels in Rilke's *Duino Elegies*, in which the poet speaks of terrifying angels. These are not the blond fairy-like angels of devotional art and children stories, but independent, powerful, and shining beings that judge. Messiaen added in his commentary to "Regard des Anges" that angels are so independent that they can not understand God's plan to incarnate his Son in human form rather than angelic.[58] These surprised, confused, and astonished angels "struggle with their embarrassment," which is musically portrayed through the asymmetric bifurcation of the angelic trombones' lines in the piano texture. Messiaen emphasizes the angels' growing astonishment by gradually raising the dynamic level from *pp* to *fff* in what finally leads to a sharp contrast between two extreme piano registers.

In the light of these two categories, it is rather strange that the composer very often juxtaposes the figure of the terrifying apocalyptic angel with birdsong, as he does in his two great piano cycles: *Visions de L'Amen* ("Amen des Anges, des Saints, du chant des oiseaux") and *Vingt Regards sur l'Enfant-Jésus* ("Regard des Anges"). To deal with this problematic issue it is important to look first at the role of the angel in Messiaen's opera *François d'Assise*.

The opera features a single angel, who is represented on three levels corresponding to various aspects of its nature. The soprano voice symbolizes the angel as a messenger in accordance with anthropomorphic conventions; the angel as a spirit with colored wings is symbolized by chromatic clusters in strings and by glissandi performed by three Ondes Martenot together with a crescendo on the suspended cymbal concluded by claves and whip; finally, the viol on which the angel plays in answer to Francis's prayer

---

[57] Translated from Messiaen's commentary about *Regard des Anges,* in the booklet accompanying the recording of *Vingt Regards*. Erato 4509-91705-2 (1973).

[58] This paragraph relies on information found in Siglind Bruhn, *Messiaen's Contemplations of Covenant and Incarnation. Musical Symbol of Faith in the Two Great Piano Cycles of the 1940s* (Hillsdale, NY: Pendragon Press, 2007), 216, 237, and 241-242.

for a foretaste of heavenly bliss follows the old theory of *musica coelestis*. Moreover, the angel's harmonic background is based on Messiaen's two favorite modes: 2 and 3, both containing A-major triads. If on the first level the music seems to follow the beautiful melodic line, the second spiritual aspect of the angel is completely oppositional to the first one that, as Bruhn writes, it "[...] is beyond human comprehension."[59]

To demonstrate the significance Messiaen attaches to the role of the angel in the opera, it is enough to look at the titles of individual scenes: the angel appears in the third, fourth, and fifth tableaux, "The Kissing of the Leper," "The Journeying Angel," and "The Angel-Musician." When the score indicates that "the angel prepares to play the viol," the dramatis persona is usually seen raising a correspondingly instrument—in a more or less abstract form—while the melodic line heard from within the orchestra is played on the Ondes Martenot, occasionally accompanied or interrupted by string glissandos (all of this against a harmonic background of a major chord played by strings and choir singing *mormorando*). The single melodic line soaring above a static harmonic center is reminiscent of the *jubilus* and emphasizes the celestial nature of angels.

Writing about Messiaen's opera, Bruhn argues that there is an internal five-tiered hierarchy of realms that shows "[...] the progression of divine grace in the soul of a saint."[60] Birdsong may also be treated as angelic, for Messiaen thought that birds have features that link Heaven and Earth: "The birds represent the manifest realization of the marriage between both realms, participating in each insofar as their exquisite song brings to physical reality an otherworldly beauty while their little bodies are made from mortal stuff."[61] (Fig. 1 according to Bruhn)

FIGURE 1: Progression of realms in Messiaen's opera *François d'Assise*

```
            God        ⎤
          ↗           ⎥
         ↗  Angels    ⎦  DIVINE REALM
BIRDS ↗
      ↘
       ↘  Francis of Assisi      ⎤
        ↘                         ⎥
         ↘ God-fearing people    ⎦  HUMAN REALM
```

---

[59] See Bruhn, *Saints*, 379.

[60] Bruhn, *Saints*, 368.

[61] Bruhn, *Saints*, 368.

In Messiaen's opera the angelic symbol is announced by the song of the gerygone, which is associated with the divine messenger. In Messiaen's two piano cycles, *Visions de l'Amen* and *Vingt Regards*, birds are often combined with angels. Like the song of angels, birdsong praises God's glory, but on earth rather than in heaven. In *Visions de l'Amen*, birds exist alongside angels and saints and participate in the wide panorama of heaven: angels (divine), saints (human), and birds (animal). In *Vingt Regards*, the presence of *style oiseau* among sparkling and percussive effects expresses the pure natural joy experienced by angels in heaven.

Pop-angels: the Destruction of the Angelic Symbol in Popular Music

The New Age Movement created a new kind of music, the object of which is to provide the relaxing, serene, and calm atmosphere that is an important condition for meditation and spirituality. Such music is often used by listeners as a background sound to such activities as yoga, massage, meditation, reading, and thus as a method of stress management. The sometimes primitive melodic lines of New Age music have had a great impact on twentieth-century music that has dealt with angelic topics; this can be observed in the works of Crumb and Stockhausen. These two composers mixed diverse elements to create their own musical style in order to accent the spiritual function of music, a category that has generally been ignored in twentieth-century music. Some listeners have detected in Rautavaara's music some of the features of New Age music, for example when it is serene, meditative, and smooth. In particular, the Seventh Symphony *Angel of Light* is felt to belong to the repertoire of musical New Age. In order to stave off such criticism and unwelcome connections, the composer wrote a commentary to express his artistic position:

> It probably comes down to the spirit of the times, the Zeitgeist. After all, angels are popular now. I felt self-conscious about putting angels in the titles in the 1970s, when my colleagues were giving their works matter-of-fact titles such as Structures for Strings. Now, I feel self-conscious about the fact that angels have become popular in a banal sense with the New Age phenomenon.[62]

---

[62] Einojuhani Rautavaara, commentary on Seventh Symphony, in the booklet accompanying the recording Naxos 8.555814 (2003).

Like the composer Peter Michael Hamel,[63] Rautavaara desires to sever connections between his music and New Age philosophy. Nevertheless, there are instances of New Age multicultural phenomena in his oeuvre: reflections of different religions (the Orthodox faith in *All-Night Vigil* (1971-72/1996) and *Icons*, Catholic sensibilities in *Canticum Mariae Virginis* (1978), *Magnificat* (1979), *Credo* (1972), and *Lapsimessu* (1973); a fascination with Eastern cultures and aesthetics (*Nirvana Dharma*); an interest in the expansion of consciousness[64] and psychology;[65] as well as works of an ostensibly non-denominational spirituality. Although Rautavaara's outlook is informed by the Hellenic culture and old European traditions and the majority of his works refer to Christianity, the New Age scholar Kurt Leland describes him (together with Stockhausen) as a mystical composer. Leland's New Age credentials can be ascertained from the following passage, one of many such passages in his book:

> The evolving mystics are the great musical teachers in the yoga of listening. When we meditate upon the works of such composers, in the words of David Tame "the energies and states of consciousness necessary for spiritual attainment and initiation are transferred to us."[66]

It seems that New Age music, together with pop music, ends the long process of secularization of the symbol of the angel that began during the late Renaissance and Baroque eras, in which the angel began to be portrayed by a voice, actor, and/or instrument. There is a strict correlation between this musical secularization and processes observed in the visual arts of the time, when angels are presented anthropomorphically as children (*putti*) or as androgynous beings with instruments. As a result the border between sacred and profane art starts to blur.

In New Age music, the connotation of angels depends on categories of calmness and serenity that are appropriate for meditation and relaxation; such connotations appear generally in electronic and instrumental music. By way of contrast, in popular music angels can frequently be found in the

---

[63] Peter Michael Hamel, *Durch Musik zum Selbst* (Berg/Munich/Vienna, Scherz Verlag, 1976).

[64] See Martin Anderson, "Einojuhani Rautavaara, Symphonist. The Finnish Composer Talks to Martin Anderson," *Fanfare* 7/8 (1996): 66.

[65] See Einojuhani Rautavaara, "On a Taste for the Infinite," *Contemporary Music Review* 12/2 (1995): 114-115, and also "Choirs, Myths and Finnishness," *Finnish Music Quarterly* 1 (1997): 3-6.

[66] Kurt Leland, *Music and the Soul: A Listener's Guide to Achieving Transcendent Musical Experiences* (Charlottesville, VA: Hampton Roads, 2005), 350.

words to love songs. A few pop songs refer to the religious guardian angel (for instance, "Angels" by Coma, "Angel" by Massive Attack, and "There Must Be an Angel" by Annie Lennox), but the majority of singers and songwriters treat angels as symbols of a beloved person or very beautiful woman or man (for example, "Angel" by Aerosmith). Such a woman-angel is a mixture of sexual and spiritual fascinations, portrayed as a guardian angel who can help a man in love. These angelic beings are nothing but pop products, angels for everybody, the faithful and not-faithful, Catholics and Buddhists. They are claimed to be superficially extraordinary, but appear simultaneously banal, trashy, and in fact very material and earthy. The process of the deconstruction of the angelic symbol in art and music provokes a crisis for the angelic topic.

Chapter 4:
Rautavaara's Mystical Aesthetics

> Mysticism is only an exceptionally intensive way of experiencing reality.[67]

Rautavaara's output has gone through several stylistic periods: neoclassicism (up to 1957), a first serial period (1957-65), neo-romanticism (1967-83), a synthetic second serial period (1984-94), and a "mystical" style (since 1994).[68] These periods witnessed no change in the composer's aesthetic but rather broadened it. Rautavaara has described how modernism (or structuralism), mysticism, and Finnish-nationalism have been particularly important for his music and have found expression throughout his career.[69] Mysticism in particular has shaped his development for a long while, with his most recent "mystical" style representing the culmination.[70] Rautavaara claims that he has been fascinated by metaphysical and religious subjects as well as texts from childhood, and that this fascination has influenced his music and aesthetics.[71] Although he grew up in the Lutheran tradition and faith, he does not belong to any religion and church: "My background was Lutheran, but I never really worried about different 'creeds.' I fear that my ecumenical relationship to the various churches meant indifference to their dogmas and theology."[72] This unrestricted attitude allowed Rautavaara to compose works to texts from the Orthodox liturgy, the Roman Catholic Church, and the shamanistic Kalevala. Some of his instrumental compositions also received titles that point to religious sources, such as *Icons* for piano (1955), *Ta Tou Theou* for organ (1967), and *Laudatio Trinitatis* for organ (1969). Thus Rautavaara regards himself as an "ecumenical" composer, that

---

[67] Einojuhani Rautavaara, "Seven Questions for Einojuhani Rautavaara," *Highlights* 22 (2007): 7.

[68] See Kimmo Korhonen, *Finnish Orchestral Music and Concertos 1995-2005* (Jyväskylä: Finnish Music Information Centre, 2006), 53.

[69] See Rautavaara, *Omakuva*, 264.

[70] See Aho, "Einojuhani Rautavaara": 3.

[71] See Einojuhani Rautavaara, preface to *Orchestral Works* (Helsinki: Warner/Chappell), 5.

[72] Einojuhani Rautavaara, "On a Taste for the Infinite": 112.

is to say, one who believes in religiousness as a feeling for and affinity with infinity. He sometimes uses sources from various religions simultaneously, such as in his opera *Thomas*,[73] or gives his compositions titles that point at religious topics, characters, or symbols without reference to a particular religion, as in the Piano Sonata No. 1 *Christus und die Fischer* (1969), the Organ Concerto *Annunciations* (1976-77), the String Quintet *Les Cieux Inconnues* (1997), and the series of compositions referring to angels that is the subject of this study. He can be considered a mystical composer not because of such references to religious texts, subjects, and symbols, but rather because of his philosophy about music and his perception of the artist's role.

The term "mysticism" is used in various religions to express feelings beyond human experience: something that is the result of an inexpressible experience of contact with an ultimate reality, God, divinity, or spiritual truth. Mystics hold that there is a deeper or more fundamental state of existence beyond the observable world. In her book *Mysticism*, Evelyn Underhill lists five stages of the process of mystical union with the absolute: awakening, purgation, illumination, the dark night of the soul, and finally union with (the) God.[74] However, as Dana Greene has observed, Underhill "[...] does not mean that all those who lead the spiritual life have lives like those of the great mystics, but rather that the pattern of those lives is the same."[75] In particular, although illumination is very often reached by an artist through various visions, only some of them go further to the "dark night of the soul" —a term used by Carmelite mystics to refer to the "confusion, helplessness, stagnation of the will, and a sense of the withdrawal of God's presence."[76] Many elements of Rautavaara's aesthetic correspond directly with Underhill's five stages, suggesting that the composer's attitude is in some way mystical. Some elements of his aesthetic clearly reveal him to be a mystical composer: for instance, the way he treats his whole œuvre as a macrotext with autocitations, in which there is no linear development of his style; his very self-centered way of living; the way he regards the composer's role to be that of a midwife who helps his works to come into existence; his experience of dreams and visions; and his multiple artistic role as composer, writer, and painter. A short introduction to these elements will establish the theoretical background for analysis and further interpretations in the following chapters.

---

[73] See the analysis of the opera offered by Bruhn in *Saints*, 127-140.

[74] See Evelyn Underhill, *Mysticism: A Study in Nature and Development of Spiritual Consciousness* (Grand Rapids, MI: Christian Classics Ethereal Library, 2005 [1923]).

[75] Dana Greene, "Adhering to God: The Message of Evelyn Underhill for Our Times," *Spirituality Today* 39 (1987): 22-23.

[76] Greene, "Adhering to God": 22-23.

Rautavaara's Output as Macrotext

From the very beginning, Rautavaara sought to create his own "world of beauty": "I have always said that what I considered particularly interesting in composition at the beginning of my career was the opportunity to create a world of one's own, a 'world of beauty,' to quote Richard Strauss, and to act in that world."[77] The development of his aesthetics was not linear, for Rautavaara frequently turned back to his earlier works in order to revise or orchestrate them. Moreover, there are a great number of common melodic and harmonic motifs as well as other compositional techniques that recur across his works.[78] Rautavaara has compared this pluralistic musical tendency to sculpture, which exists in "simultaneous" rather than diachronic-linear time.

> When one has consciously set out to build for himself—no, rather around himself—a life as work of art, one's own escapist world, then time becomes spatial, it is transformed to an object, like a sculpture. And there is no chronology in sculpture, its author can revise and alter [the sculpture] as well [from] in fronts as from behind or on top and from below. It is present in spite of time.[79]

The aesthetic attitude can be described as a very personal form of Romanticism: "The Romantic has no coordinates. In time he is either yesterday or tomorrow, not today. In space he is over there or over there never here."[80] Rautavaara's romantic tendency began with his First Symphony and compositions from his first serial period. His Third Symphony in particular; a significant work in his output, is the first work in which he recognizes himself despite clear affinities with Bruckner's style.[81] At the same time, Rautavaara was strongly influenced by modernism, including the dodecaphonic practice. The modernist aesthetic blended with his Romantic attitude to create his idiosyncratic idiom and a technique manifested in compositions from his second serial period (1984-1994).

Musical pluralism can also be discerned in Rautavaara's tendency to re-use material from earlier compositions; these auto-citations can be

---

[77] Hako, *Unien lahja*, 53.

[78] See Anne Sivuoja-Gunaratnam, "'Narcissus Musicus' or an Intertextual Perspective on the Œuvre of Einojuhani Rautavaara," Tomi Mäkelä, ed., *Topics, Texts, Tensions. Essays in Music Theory* (Magdeburg: Otto-von-Guericke Universität, 1999): 16.

[79] Rautavaara quoted in Sivuoja-Gunaratnam, *Narrating with Twelve Tones*, 239.

[80] Korhonen, *Finnish Concertos*, 37.

[81] See Aho, *Einojuhani Rautavaara as Symphonist*, 82-88.

understood as Rautavaara "remaking" his own past.[82] The practice can be found in early works such as *Three Symmetrical Preludes* (1949-50), *Fiddlers* (1952), *A Requiem in Our Time* (1953), and the first two symphonies, and continues to inform compositions created throughout his career. It can be described as musical narcissism, an attempt to "make works live longer" and "emphasize their form in 'the now'."[83] For a listener, musical material from one work, re-orchestrated and in the context of another work, functions like a musical topic, an emblem of Rautavaara's style.

Alongside the practice of auto-citations, one finds the repeated use of certain basic plots, in which the fundamental conflict it the relation between an aging hero and the environment. These plots appear in Rautavaara's operas, from early works such as *Kaivos* and *Apollo and Marsyas* (1970) to the most significant mature ones, such as *Thomas* (based on events from the life of the first bishop of Finland), *Vincent* (recounting scenes from the struggles of the painter Vincent van Gogh), *The House of the Sun* (1989-90, telling of the sad, monotonous life of two Russian sisters), *Aleksis Kivi* (1995-96, portraying the celebrated Finnish author), and *Rasputin* (2001-03, about the Russian mystic and Tsar's confident).[84] The outcome of Rautavaara's operas is often the same: the hero fails and never reaches his goal during his life. As a result, these operas appear as one work presented in a variety of different literary and musical forms. Owing to this similarity between the operas and his use of auto-citations, the totality of his compositions can be considered as macro-text. As Sivuoja-Gunaratnam argues, this notion "[...] diminishes the uniqueness of a single composition, but on the other hand the internal coherence of the œuvre is reinforced."[85] All the auto-allusions function as a network joining all the compositions together and thereby creating Rautavaara's "world of beauty," his private reality.

> It appeared that here would be an entirely new kind of sign system which enables me to construct a world of beauty of my own. In such a world ... I would be the sovereign ruler, out of reach of anybody else's criticism, where nobody would command me and where I would not be responsible for anyone. There I would be safe from the rottenness and defeats of this world.[86]

---

[82] See Sivuoja-Gunaratnam, "Narcissus Musicus": 10-13.

[83] Tiikaja, "Einojuhani Rautavaara – Postmodern Intertextualist": 49.

[84] See Sivuoja-Gunaratnam, "Narcissus Musicus": 13-16.

[85] Sivuoja-Gunaratnam, " Narcissus Musicus": 16.

[86] Rautavaara quoted in Sivuoja-Gunaratnam, *Narrating with Twelve Tones*, 240.

The essential feature of Rautavaara's aesthetic allows to hypothesize that there must exist a system of signs: musical symbols that function as signifiers of a macro-textual identity. Given the great number of the composer's self-quotations, the system of symbols must be considered as coherent and understood in the context of works from the earliest to the latest, thus making it stable and persistent. Sivuoja-Gunaratnam draws on Lévi-Strauss's mythical terminology to label this technique as *bricolage*.[87] An analogy can be drawn with the work of a visual artist whom Rautavaara admires, Salvador Dali, whose overall output can also be understood as a huge macro-text with recurring colors, motifs, themes, and with symbols like walking sticks, burning giraffes, skulls, ants, lions, distant landscapes, and so on. In this sense, the composer's admiration of the surrealistic movement and of artists like René Magritte and Jean Delvaux is fully comprehensible.

On the assumption that the hero in the plot underlying Rautavaara's operas represents the composer's alter-ego,[88] his instrumental works might be read as reflecting his musical ego.[89] While the composer is aware of his musical self-sufficiency, he does not want listeners to focus on him or his life. Instead he hopes that his music may be an index of another reality.[90]

> It is my belief that music is great if, at some moment, the listener catches "a glimpse of eternity through the window of time." This, to my mind, is the only true justification for all art. All else is of secondary importance.[91]

In the context of the composer's self-sufficient way of living is easily explained by the notion that Rautavaara wants his music to be a messenger. He himself therefore becomes a kind of medium who helps the music to come into existence. Like other mystics he tries to isolate himself, to turn away from the world toward himself in order to focus exclusively on his compositional tasks. His compositions are not intended to be autobiographical, but rather music that points at eternity and infinity.

---

[87] See Sivuoja-Gunaratnam, *Narrating with Twelve Tones*, 240, and also "Narcissus Musicus": 17.

[88] See Anne Sivuoja-Gunaratnam, "Einojuhani Rautavaara as Opera Composer," *Finnish Music Quarterly* 3 (1993): 42.

[89] See Sivuoja-Gunaratnam, *Narrating with Twelve Tones*, 241.

[90] See Rautavaara, preface to *Orchestral Works*, 5

[91] Lovejoy, 13.

The Artist as a Medium[92]

The idea of the artist as a medium or messenger is an extension of ancient Platonic philosophy, where ideas are believed to exist somewhere outside and the role of the artist is to bring them into existence in the real world. According to Rautavaara's repeatedly suggested notion that he is not the mother of his music but rather its midwife,[93] he does not invent music but looks for it and tries to discover its exact ideas. In this sense he compares his role as a composer to that of a gardener and the process of musical composition to the growth of organic forms.

> I have no wish to be a musical architect; I should prefer the term "gardener" (though one in a garden laid out in the English fashion rather than the French). But the chaotic is to be avoided since it is aesthetically uninteresting, and improvising is equally undesirable, since it always stems ultimately from the improviser, and not from the subject. Nature does not improvise, nor is it chaotic; it follows strictly the directions of a genetic code, in mutual relation with environmental factors. Within musical material, within its constellations, there lies hidden such a genetic code, the amino acids of the music—all the necessary information is implanted there. The composer is not able to add anything of any significance to this. He must simply find it, and so must be interested in the tendencies of his material.[94]

In the composer's view, musical ideas are treated like plant seeds that he must first find, and then help grow and develop until they become compositions. Thus the musical material is very important in the compositional process, because it obeys rules that cannot be forced; all the composer can do is follow them. When Rautavaara taught at the Sibelius Academy in Helsinki, he very often gave his pupils only one instruction:

> Listen to what the music is trying to tell you, where it wants to go. It's not your job to be the maker of the music, its mother. Your job is to be the midwife who helps the music to live on its own terms. It occurs to me that I could never have produced anything like that. These works must always have existed, perhaps

---

[92] See Hako, *Unien lahja*, 58-75.

[93] See Robert Levine, "Taste for Eternity," *Classical Pulse* 4 (1996): 7; Pekka Hako, "Music Has a Will of Its Own," *Nordic Sounds* 3 (1998): 18.

[94] Einojuhani Rautavaara, "Thomas—Analysis of the Tone Material (An Experiment in Synthesis)," *Finnish Music Quarterly* 1-2 (1985): 48.

in some Platonic world of ideas. My skill lies in tying them down, not in forcing them to conform to my idea.[95]

In presenting himself as a kind of spiritual messenger who conveys a message from the ideal to the real world, the composer assumes a role similar to that of an angel bringing a message from Heaven to Earth. For Rautavaara, music is a kind of Jacob's Ladder, which makes it possible to bring ideas down to reality (through the act of composition) but that simultaneously helps one to climb up to the invisible world: "I do not 'use music' —music uses me, as a channel for coming into existence. It has, to quote Thomas Mann, 'a sort of metaphysical will of its own: it wants to be born'."[96] Composers must be dexterous craftsmen in order to select and develop the best musical material and sometimes write—and discard—a work several times: a time-consuming procedure. But as Rautavaara admitted to his pupils, "Be glad that there is something in music that you can cope with just by sitting and working hard; the main thing is something else together."[97]

Such a compositional attitude can be compared to the fifth and most intense of Underhill's states of mystical experiences. "Filled up with the Divine Will, it [the self] immerses itself in the temporal order, the world of appearances in order to incarnate the eternal in time, to become the mediator between humanity and eternity."[98] The state relates to a specific temporality which, together with the use of auto-citations and catalogues of literal symbols in operas such as "[...] knives, mystic appearances and door, allusion to birds, Jesus Christ, Mother Mary,"[99] creates the category of simultaneous time which is another hallmark of Rautavaara's mystical attitude.

Between Past and Present: Childhood Memories, Dreams, and Psychology

An important component of Rautavaara's librettos is the disruption of the plot's temporal level (its chronology) through retrospections, dreams, illusions, and mystical appearances. The present time intertwines with the past in the act of remembrance, thereby accentuating the essential role played by memory and imagination. Rautavaara explains the role of

---

[95] Hako, "Music Has a Will of Its Own": 18.

[96] Rautavaara, preface to *Orchestral Works*, 5.

[97] Hako, *Unien lahja*, 62-63.

[98] Greene: 30.

[99] Sivuoja-Gunaratnam, "Narcissus Musicus": 15.

psychological aspects and the term "projection" in the commentary to his opera *Vincent*: "Almost everything is or could be Vincent's dream or flashback. In one's memories everyone projects; consciously, when needed; an important person, an attitude, or a point of view (with its representatives) to a certain time, where they did not exist in reality."[100] In this context, the composer's auto-citations may also be understood as returns to his prior musical activity in the manner of remembrances: "Life is symphonic, you see: a journey through new landscapes, strange and sometimes incredible. The same motifs are involved from start to finish, albeit they change and grow, perhaps not reaching their full extent until the very end."[101] This is the reason why Rautavaara has a tendency to favor two musical genres, opera and symphony, reflecting his predilection for classical and romantic forms that show life as a journey. In operas, we glimpse only a fragment of this journey (an aging hero approaching death), but in the symphony a whole life is presented: "For me operas and symphonies have occupied, and continue to occupy, a prominent position in my œuvre."[102] The germ of this can be observed in *Kaivos*, but *Thomas* along with the subsequent *Vincent*, *Aleksis Kivi*, *The House of the Sun*, and *Rasputin* develop this topic extensively. In the case of his symphonies, Rautavaara maintains that his Third Symphony is his most personal work, in which for the first time he conceives of the musical ending as death.[103]

> I discovered that the finale is of course the same as death, the death of an individual, of a creature, an event, a story, or of a composition. I have seen people dying. They have lamented the physical pain or mental agony, and then they have died. Never have they declared anything. Maybe this is why every noisy finale makes me mutter, "now you are lying."[104]
>
> The return home is undoubtedly an archetype. But I expected more imagination and boldness from the prodigal son as a matter of course. The journey that does not lead into the great unknown is not worth making, at least in art.[105]

---

[100] Sivuoja-Gunaratnam, "Narcissus Musicus": 15.

[101] Rautavaara, preface to *Orchestral Works*, 3.

[102] Aho, *Einojuhani Rautavaara as Symphonist*, 75.

[103] Almost all of Rautavaara's later symphonies close with a diminuendo. The only exception is the Eighth (1999), whose title, *Journey*, suggests its programmatic character, which is related to Milan Kundera's philosophy. See Einojuhani Rautavaara, program note for the performance of his Third Symphony, 29 January 1970.

[104] Rautavaara quoted in Sivuoja-Gunaratnam, *Narrating with Twelve Tones*, 237.

[105] Rautavaara quoted in Aho, *Einojuhani Rautavaara as Symphonist*, 86.

The past plays a very important role in the composer's imagination, often in the guise of memories of his childhood experiences; in order to escape from difficult situations such as the tragic death of his parents, the young composer entered into the safety world of his dreams: "The dreams of Einojuhani Rautavaara's childhood and adolescence were such self-induced shamanistic trance states, his first tentative efforts at building a world of his own."[106] From that time onward, dreams have been a very important element of Rautavaara's aesthetic and of the music itself.

Dreams provide a special kind of musical expression that the composer describes as "dreamlike." Probably the best-known examples are the third movement of the Seventh Symphony with its expression marking *come un sogno*, and two of the movement titles in the *Manhattan Trilogy* (2003-05): "Daydreams" and "Nightmares." A translation of the adjective "dreamlike" recurs in the second movement of the Second Piano Concerto, "Sognando e libero," and in the subtitle of the Third Piano Concerto, *Gift of Dreams* (1998). The composer claims that "[...] the dream element is very important in piano music, above all with Romantic composers. [...] I feel that lyricism is an essential component of piano music."[107]

An obsessive dream sequence from Rautavaara's childhood briefly returned during his 50s, in imagery about a vast, gray, powerful creature that wanted to embrace him, making him fear he would suffocate:

> The one [angel] I met when I was a child of seven or eight. I was haunted by a dream. Night after night I would dream about a vast, gray, silent creature of no particular shape. I would walk slowly towards me and close me inside it. And I felt I was suffocating. These dreams only vanished when I eventually gave up and surrendered.[108]

This dream played an important role in the composer's decision to write the series of compositions referring to angels: *Angels and Visitations*, the Double Bass Concerto *Angel of Dusk*, the Seventh Symphony *Angel of Light*, and the chamber work *Playground for Angels*. It is a rhetorical question whether the dream or another stimulus initiated the composer's interest in psychology and particularly in the theories of Freud and Jung. More pertinently it seems that Rautavaara's fascination with psychology gave him tools to interpret his private reality (and particularly childhood experiences), becoming an important element of his outlook. Two of Jung's

---

[106] Hako, *Unien lahja*, 12.

[107] Hako, *Unien lahja*, 32.

[108] Rautavaara quoted in the documentary movie *The Gift of Dreams* (Leipzig: Arthaus Musik, 1997).

theories—those relating to archetypes (the collective unconsciousness) and synchronicity—were of particular interest to him in this context.

The theories of archetypes informed Rautavaara's outlook, particularly with regard to the topic of angels, and in some way explains the terrifying figure appearing in his dreams. The world of archetypes is linked closely with his conception of myth and its function in music. The Jungian theory of synchronicity allows him to understand his return to books or inspirations from his childhood and youth. Significant compositions in this category include *On the Last Frontier* (1998) based on Edgar Allan Poe's poem *Narrative of Arthur Gordon Pym*, which Rautavaara read when he was twelve, and the children's opera *The Gift of the Magi* (1993-94), based on the Christmas story by Olivier Henry, which the composer found in New York in 1955.[109] The composer repeatedly refers back to memories of a trip taken with his parents to Valamo,[110] which he maintains was a stimulus for his great interest in mysticism and infinity, and which inspired such works as *Icons* for piano and the choral work *All-Night Vigil*.[111]

Rautavaara's nostalgia for childhood became increasingly pronounced from the 1990s onwards. The first of his works devoted to the topic of memory and death was the opera *The House of the Sun*. This opera is based on flashbacks of the two main characters, the Russian twin sisters Riina and Noora, who live in Finland in the 1980s but dream of and long for the lifestyle of the Czarist Russia of their youth.[112] *The House of the Sun* initiated a series of works that explore absence and melancholy, such as *The Isle of Bliss* (1995), *Autumn Gardens* (1999), *Book of Visions* (2003-05), *Manhattan Trilogy* (2003-05), *Lost Landscapes* (2005), and *A Tapestry of Life* (2007).[113] This is a continuation of the romantic topic of absence, to be in the state between life and death, a state of melancholy and of lost paradise.[114] In some of these works Rautavaara recalls his studies in different countries, and particularly those in the United States (*Manhattan Trilogy*, *Lost Landscapes*); in others he represents death symbolically (*The Isle of*

---

[109] See Hako, *Finnish Opera*, 106 (chapter "Rautavaara").

[110] See Eila Tarasti, *Icons*, 549-562.

[111] See Rautavaara, "On a Taste for the Infinite": 110-111.

[112] See Sivuoja-Gunaratnam, "Einojuhani Rautavaara as Opera Composer": 42.

[113] At the time of writing this book, the composer was working on an opera about the life of Spanish poet Federico García Lorca, the best-known poet of death. See Rautavaara, "Seven Questions": 7.

[114] Charles Rosen finds exemplification of this cluster of emotions in Schubert's cycle *Winterreise*, in which each song is based on symbols of memory, longing, absence, and death. See Rosen, 116-124, and 194-204; Välimäki, 236-257.

Rautavaara's Mystical Aesthetics 79

Bliss, Autumn Gardens). It is important to look briefly at *The Isle of Bliss,* the orchestral interlude to the opera *Aleksis Kivi,* and the parallels with the historical Kivi's poem *Lintukoto* (Isle of Bliss). In his commentaries to both the opera and to *The Isle of Bliss,* Rautavaara suggests that *Lintukoto* may be regarded as a mythical poem in which the isle of birds is a symbol of safe haven and a lost paradise:

> The more I got to know Kivi, the more important and symbolical the Utopian world, the "isle of bliss," the image of the ivory tower, the ideal, the dream became. There are lines from the long epic *Lintukoto* (Isle of Bliss) both at the beginning and the end of the opera, and I think it was this poem more than any other that helped me to discover my own view of the poet's tragic life: a view of the dreamt-of ivory tower that is destroyed, of the squirrel's nest that nevertheless proves vulnerable.[115]

> The Finnish title of the composition [*Lintukoto*], however, is also associated in my mind with a personal memory of one of the outer islands in the Baltic Sea, where I often used to spend the summer. Once late at night I saw a large bird there, pacing solemnly back and forth along the rocky shore—the next morning it lay there, dead. And the fisherman told me that it was the custom for old seagulls, when they felt death approaching, to fly out to that solitary shore, the last home of the birds.[116]

Rautavaara's tendency to revisit childhood experiences can also be examined from the Freudian perspective of separation and loss. These themes can be found in Romanticism in the form of the alienation of the artist from society, as well as in the protagonists of Rautavaara's operas: Simon in *Kaivos* is a rebel, Thomas, Vincent, Aleksis Kivi are all characters who are not understood in their environments, Rasputin is a visionary, Noora and Riina are isolated from the real world. Each of them is an outsider, someone who is at the same time a prophet and a freak, sustained between reality and imagination, and between the past and the present. This is reflected in their dual personalities: Vincent, as a schizophrenic who has lost contact with the real world, is an extreme example of such an attitude, and his suicide seems to be an attempt to return to the ideal world. Cases of such dual identities in Rautavaara's work can also be understood as angelic, for the angel as a spiritual being links two planes, it is neither God nor human, and its form is both human and spiritual.

---

[115] Einojuhani Rautavaara, commentary on the opera *Aleksis Kivi*, in the booklet accompanying the recording Ondine 1000-2CD (2002).

[116] Einojuhani Rautavaara, commentary on *Isle of Bliss*, in the booklet accompanying the recording Ondine 881-2 (1997).

The Aesthetic of the Double

The aesthetic of the double (*"Doppelgänger"* in German literature) was probably born from the idea of the struggle humans felt within themselves between the contrasting qualities postulated by the Romantic Movement: light and dark, good and bad, emotional and rational. The psychological aspect of the double is described as a dual personality in which a single person has two different and often contradictory natures. In certain circumstances such persons can forget about their first nature and do something wrong, because the first nature has no control of the second, nor any recollection of its actions. In literature the best-known example of such a dual personality is the protagonist of the novel *The Strange Case of Dr. Jekyll and Mr. Hyde* by Robert Louis Stevenson (1886).

> In the novel (the idea for which came to Stevenson in a nightmare), Dr. Henry Jekyll, long interested in the problem of dual personality, has invented a chemical that can alter his character from that of a kind physician to that of the violent, criminally minded Edward Hyde. Gradually, Dr. Jekyll loses his ability to shift at will from one personality to another; at the same time, he loses control over Hyde's violent behavior, which leads to murder. In the end, lacking any chemical to transform him from Hyde back to Dr. Jekyll, the protagonist kills himself and reveals all by the means of a letter.[117]

The barbaric behavior of Mister Hyde is uncontrolled: he does not feel emotions and his actions are psychopathological by nature; in consequence, he has no human face. As Stevenson writes, "Edward Hyde, alone, in the ranks of mankind, was pure evil."[118] The novel shows the double as the evil side of a personality, corresponding to Jung's archetype of the "shadow." There are numerous characters in Rautavaara's operas who exhibit dual personalities: both Vincent van Gogh and Aleksis Kivi are schizophrenic and live in two planes (the real and the imaginary worlds); the Russian twin sisters Noora and Riina from *The House of the Sun* live physically in the present but mentally in the past; and Rasputin exhibits two different kinds of morality, one as a healer, the other as a heretic. Rautavaara often uses the technique of projection in both the music and the libretti of his operas: "In memories everyone projects (consciously, when needed) an important

---

[117] I.B. Nadel and W.E. Freedeman, eds., *Victorian Novelists after 1885* [*The Dictionary of Literary Biography* XVIII] (Detroit, MI: Gale Research Company, 1983), 293.

[118] Robert Louis Stevenson, *The Strange Case of Fables. Other Stories and Fragments* (London, UK: William Heinemann, 1931), 61.

person, an attitude or point of view (and the people embodying it) onto a certain time where they did not exist in reality."[119] The aspect of dual personalities is also very important for the composer's outlook and reflects his early interest in other realities:

> This is an idea that has been very central for me since I read a book by the scientist William James, who experimented with hallucinogenic drugs, LSD. He wrote that every time the person came out from the effect of the drug, the very first thing you wanted to say was that the hallucination was so real that it was the most real thing you have ever met, and that this reality is nothing compared to that. This happened over and over again to the subjects of his experiments. William James says it seems to be true that there are other realities around us, that there's only the thinnest of screens between this world and that, and that taking those drugs is one possible way to open the window to that second reality. Then we have to think: What is music, really? When we talk about music, when we go to hear a pianist playing classical repertoire, we may say, well, he has got the style, he has got the technique, but he does not really understand it. What is it that is missing? I can not tell you using any verbal means of expression. I can only do it by going to the piano and saying: "This is how it should be." So the information in music is very exact, but it is not expressible in words, in concepts. It is another reality, a very exact reality, but it has nothing to do with this reality, and it can not be expressed in terms of this reality.[120]

If music reflects another reality, and if a composer acts as a link between the two worlds as a messenger or midwife who helps music to come into existence, then he can be called an angel. Living in two realities he seems to be schizophrenic, having a dual personality, striving to be a kind of divine performer that aims to decipher an invisible musical text as perfectly as possible. From this point of view, the characters in the operas reflect Rautavaara's position as a composer and his heroes represent that which Rautavaara has discovered in himself.[121] The most significant are the two operas that portray artists: *Vincent* (a painter) and *Aleksis Kivi* (a poet). At the end of the 1970s the composer also wrote an autobiographical single-act chamber opera in Swedish, *En dramatisk scen* (A Dramatic Scene), in which he portrays himself as a composer by the name of Järnberg, using the

---

[119] Sivuoja-Gunaratnam, "Einojuhani Rautavaara as Opera Composer": 42.

[120] Anderson: 66.

[121] See Sivuoja-Gunaratnam, "Vincent–not a portrait": 6 and "Einojuhani Rautavaara as Opera Composer": 42.

Swedish name that is close to the Finnish "Rautavaara."[122] He later withdrew the opera, which remains unperformed to this day:

> Some time ago I had a look again at *En dramatisk scen* but decided to let it be withdrawn. This work was composed during a difficult time of crisis in my creative history and the music does not appeal to me at all. Also, the Swedish commissioner wanted a wind orchestra in the opera, and wind instruments always have a strong tendency to cover vocal parts. Also I wrote the libretto in Swedish, although it is not my first language. But mainly the reason for the withdrawal was the music. I do not think it is of value. Consequently nothing from that opera was used in other compositions.[123]

Even though it was withdrawn, the opera was nevertheless written, and can thus be treated as Rautavaara's first opera with an autobiographical element in which the composer explores the difficulties in the life of an artist. It complements the next two operas, *Vincent* and *Aleksis Kivi*, to create a triptych in which the crucial problem is the artist's mission. With hindsight we can even detect that this operatic trilogy represents the composer's own artistic abilities: his activities as composer, writer, and amateur painter.

FIGURE 2: The triple role of Einojuhani Rautavaara

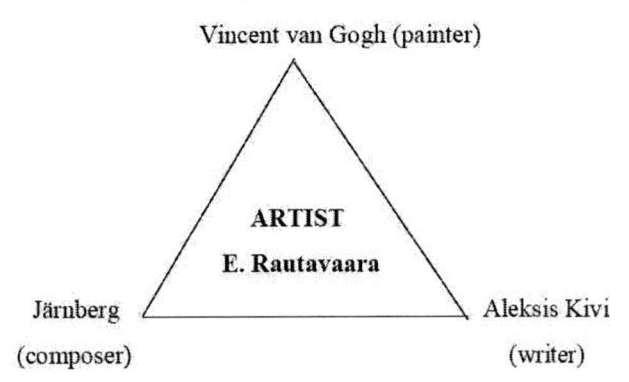

Vincent van Gogh (painter)

ARTIST
E. Rautavaara

Järnberg (composer)   Aleksis Kivi (writer)

---

[122] See Hako, *Finnish Opera*, 98. (The components of the composer's name are dictionary words: *rauta* is Finnish for "iron" while *vaara* means "danger, risk." The Swedish name *Järnberg* ("iron rock") comes close.

[123] Personal communication, 18 October 2007.

Literary and Philosophical Associations

Rautavaara's operas are not the only works in his output that involve absence, longing, and memory; the same is true of his instrumental works with titles. Interplay between literature and music can be found in Rautavaara's *œuvre* from his earliest works onwards, both in songs and instrumental compositions.[124] His admiration of literature and poetry stems from his family background and environment, as both his father and his cousin Aulikki Rautawaara were singers. While still at school, Rautavaara composed dozens of songs to various texts, a preference that has lasted throughout his life; his favorite poets were Shakespeare, Rilke, Lorca, and T. S. Eliot. Interesting for the purpose of this study is particularly the fact that he frequently uses material from his songs in his instrumental compositions[125]: the central movement of the Fourth String Quartet (1975) is an arrangement of the song "Die Liebende" from *Die Liebenden* (1958-59), a cycle based on poems by Rilke; the Third Piano Concerto *Gift of Dreams* is derived from a song to Charles Baudelaire's text *Le mort des pauvres* (1978). Later chapters will demonstration that in Rautavaara's music, the signification of the words remains present when vocal material is used in non-vocal compositions.[126]

Literature and philosophy is thus a major source of inspiration for Rautavaara; further examples include Canto III: *A Portrait of the Artist at a Certain Moment* (1972), the title of which is an allusion to James Joyce's novel *A Portrait of the Artist as a Young Man*; the Eighth Symphony *Journey*, which Rautavaara in his commentary relates to the meaning of journey in the writing of Milan Kundera; and also the symphonic fantasy *The Isle of Bliss*, which is related to the poem by Aleksis Kivi. The evocation of literature is not only passive (for example, in quotations from literary works, titles), but also active, in the composer's writings, as can be seen in the

---

[124] See Mikko Heiniö, "A Portrait of the Artist– Focus on the Composer Einojuhani Rautavaara," *Finnish Musical Quarterly* 2 (1988): 12, and Sivuoja-Gunaratnam, "Narcissus Musicus": 13.

[125] "Very often songs, and motifs that originated in them, served as the starting point for larger-scale orchestral works." Einojuhani Rautavaara in the booklet accompanying the recording of some of his songs BIS-CD-1141 (2003).

[126] Rautavaara even experimented with the text of two paragraphs from James Joyce's *Finnegans Wake* (1939), which he wanted to transform into music. He chose the notes E, A, and D as symbols of the words "Eve," "Adam," and "Paradise," and continued to compose it word by word. But during the composition of the second paragraph he realized that his music had to develop in a different way and finally he reworked it as the *Adoration of Aphrodite*; its title was later changed again to *Anadyomene* (1968), which manifests its hidden structure.

librettos to nine of his ten operas and in the texts to his songs, as well as in his non-musical works: his autobiography[127] and a collection of essays entitled *Mieltymyksestä äärettömään* (On a Taste for the Infinite) from 1998. These last two works give a perfect insight into the composer's world view, interests, and biography.

Titles as Mantras

Rautavaara's work titles frequently provide him with a starting point for the music: "The impulse for a work often comes from some text with a strong atmosphere. The text may be just a couple of words, like 'fire sermon,' 'angel of light,' or 'annunciation.' The words are often used as the title for the piece born around them."[128] The trigger may be a whole literary work, as was the case with Poe's novel *The Narrative of Arthur Gordon Pym* (1838), from which grew the choral fantasy with orchestra *On the Last Frontier* (1998); it may also be a short poem, a sentence, or only a few words. Rautavaara finds that a brief sequence of words often proves to be the best "inspiration" for his music; "It was actually the words which gave me the music! And those words are always in English."[129] In the composer's thinking, words give music, short words in English that keep repeating over and over like mantras radiate special energy that is turned into music. Rautavaara described this phenomenon thus: "But I feel that I owe those mantras for the inspiration, the idea and the energy for the music which resulted; it would be false to leave the mantra out of the title."[130] Titles referring to angels came to the composer in this way. The most famous case is that of the inspiration for the Double Bass Concerto *Angel of Dusk*:

> While returning to Helsinki I was reflecting upon this new challenge when, looking out of the window of the plane, I saw a strikingly shaped cloud, gray but pierced with color, rising above the Atlantic horizon. Suddenly the words "Angel of Dusk" came to mind. Those words remained with me and returned to me, like a mantra, when I heard the news of Olga Koussevitzky's death the following year and the project had to be postponed.[131]

---

[127] Rautavaara's *Omakuva* is highly valued in Finland as a literary work.

[128] Rautavaara, "Seven Questions": 7.

[129] Hilary Finch, "Guided by Angels," *Gramophone* 6 (1996): 24.

[130] Rautavaara, "On a Taste for the Infinite": 115.

[131] Rautavaara quoted in the booklet accompanying the recording on Finlandia Records 4509-99969-2 (1981) of the Double Bass Concerto *Angel of Dusk*.

In many cases, the titles were in existence prior to the first written note of the work, giving the composer the actual impetus to write and suggesting various aspects of the composition (color, timbre, character, and occasionally even components of the musical material). The majority of Rautavaara's compositions about angels had a title before the music came into being:

> In the case of *Angel of Dusk* and *Angel of Light*, the title was pre-existent; it was more or less an impetus for the music. In *Angels and Visitations* the title came later, after "analyzing" and interpreting my dreams. For *Playgrounds for Angels* also, I remember inventing the title during the composition of the first movement.[132]

Although titles and subtitles play an important role in Rautavaara's music, their significance for the compositional contents varies widely. Quite a few works have generic titles, like the First, Second, Third and Fifth Symphonies, the four numbered string quartets; the Violin Concerto, the Suite for Strings and so on. Some compositions have metatextual names that point to the musical structure or compositional technique: two examples are the Fourth Symphony *Arabescata* (1962) and the work *Regular Set of Elements in a Semi-regular Situation* (1971). Sivuoja-Gunaratnam has demonstrated the semiotic interplay between the musical structure of the former, ARA-BESC-ATA, and its name *Arabescata* in terms of symmetric interpolations.[133] But not all titles should be read like this: some are more arbitrary.

Most of Rautavaara's titles are thematic, referring to extramusical contents. Although the composer has emphasized that his music has no program, story, and fixed imagery, he has nevertheless provided a large number of commentaries to his works in which he explains their titles with reference to literature, paintings, and philosophy. They require an interpretation, thereby fixing the cultural code through which each work must be read. It is thus impossible to omit issues connected with these aspects.

In many cases, his "mildly programmatic"[134] titles require knowledge of his previous works, particularly where they resemble those of other compositions. Moreover, series such as Cantos I, II, III, and IV have been called the composer's private genres, suggesting a practice comparable to that of painters in the twentieth century who create their idiosyncratic, unique but

---

[132] Personal communication, 11 July 2007.

[133] Sivuoja-Gunaratnam, *Narrating with Twelve Tones*, 633-641.

[134] See Tiikkaja, "Einojuhani Rautavaara – Postmodern Intertextualist": 56: "Rautavaara's symphonies, too, are often at least mildly programmatic."

recognizable label by re-using certain themes, motifs, and colors.[135] The analogy with series of paintings such as Claude Monet's *Cathedral in Rouen, Grain Stacks, Poplars, Bridges*, and *Waterlilies* and titles of works by surrealist painters such as Magritte, Delvaux, and Dalí is thus undeniable. Rautavaara's most famous thematic series is the one comprising his works about angels, where titles highlight relations between music, colors, and iconic signs.

Pictorial Aspects of Music

In addition to being a composer and a skillful writer, Rautavaara is also an amateur painter.[136] His interest in the visual arts began when he was young, at a time when he had no contact with music. At that time he set out to paint music on paper with watercolors, displaying the resulting sheets in his bedroom in lieu of real musical compositions.[137] It was as if he was emphasizing to himself his destiny to be an artist. In 1955, while studying at the Tanglewood Music Center, he had an influential meeting with a painter. Talking to the artist at the beach, he learned that the process of painting is similar to that of composition.

> Perhaps what makes art individual is the method and procedure through which a work of art is created. Everyone has to find his own process for himself. After that, it does not really matter what one works with: words, colors, shapes or music. They are all materials to choose from.[138]

After years of alienation from the visual arts while at school he returned to painting in the 1970s. His first picture of this period, *Angel of Dusk*, shares its title with his later Double Bass Concerto. (The interplay between these two works will be explored some more in the section *Beyond Rilke: Rautavaara's Musical (Self-)Ekphrasis*.)

The important role played by dreams, visions, memories, fantasies, and the presence of high reality in Rautavaara's subtitles and commentaries demonstrates that the composer has an attitude toward the arts similar to that of the symbolists and surrealists. This is most obvious in those of his operas in which aspects of two realms are mixed and seem to have no boundaries; *Thomas* and *Vincent* in particular are perfect examples of Rautavaara's musical surrealism. Instrumentation plays an important role in such music,

---

[135] Sivuoja-Gunaratnam, *Narrating with Twelve Tones*, 240-241.

[136] See Sivuoja-Gunaratnam, "Narcissus Musicus": 13.

[137] See Rautavaara, preface to *Orchestral Works*, 3.

[138] Hako, *Unien lahja*, 24.

which when combined with special harmonization creates surprising effects comparable to certain techniques used by painters. (More on this below, in the section *Dark Versus Light*.) Unlike Messiaen, Rautavaara does not see colors when listening to or creating music and has no color associations with scales, harmonies, and instruments, but neither does he reject the existence of colors in music. He once tried to transpose colors into music when composing *Vincent*. He planned his orchestral overture and interludes as musical depictions of van Gogh's paintings and to this end used three different tone rows as "pigments." These rows can be compared to the three primary colors in a painter's palette—red, yellow, and blue—which when mixed provide all the others (Ex. 12 according to Sivuoja-Gunaratnam).[139]

EXAMPLE 12: The three rows from the opera *Vincent* as three basic colors

With these colors, the composer "painted" three of Vincent van Gogh's paintings that are representative of significant moments in his life: *Starry Night, Wheatfield with Crows*, and *The Church at Auvers*.[140] He also used a synthesizer to broaden the range of orchestral sounds in order to create the special and hypnotic atmosphere of his protagonist's visions. On the symbolic level, Rautavaara discovered himself as a musical painter: in composing *Vincent*, he felt he was painting his own portrait in music.

From his early works onward, Rautavaara signs his works with an artistic anagram that recalls the typical signatures of painters. It consists of three intertwined letters, EJR, and thus does not resemble a traditional composer's signature. Moreover, Rautavaara does not limit this signature to its written form, but uses it also as a musical motto within most of his serial

---

[139] See Sivuoja-Gunaratnam, "Vincent–not a Portrait," *Finnish Music Quarterly* 2 (1990): 7-9.

[140] See Rautavaara, preface to *Orchestral Works*, 3.

works.[141] This, too, is reminiscent of painters who portray themselves in some of the picture's character.

FIGURE 3: Einojuhani Rautavaara's handmade signature and its graphical version

A strong affiliation with painting is reflected in the important role of his titles; although the composer rejects their visual connotations, it is enough to look at such titles as *Angel of Light, Gift of Dreams, Dances with the Winds, Annunciations, Angels and Visitations, Playgrounds for Angels, Adoration of Aphrodite, Isle of Bliss, On the Last Frontier*, and *Autumn Gardens*, to ascertain that some of these works realize the impressionistic tendency to reflect one work of art in another. The two spectacular examples of this in Rautavaara's output are the symphonic fantasy *Isle of Bliss* and the orchestral work *Anadyomene – Adoration of Aphrodite*. The titles of these compositions refer directly to paintings: *Isle of Bliss* to Puvis de Chavannes's paintings of Arcadia, *Adoration of Aphrodite* to *The Birth of Venus* by Sandro Botticelli and by Alexandre Cabanel. Rautavaara probably did not plan to imitate such paintings in his music but rather to add something private to the notion of "painting in music" (as in Debussy's music, which he admires). The two examples were inspired by two different myths on the same topic—lost paradise (*Isle of Bliss*) and lost beauty (*Adoration of Aphrodite*)—and thus function as further exemplifications of mythological topics in Rautavaara's music.

Personal Myth as Universal Myth

The belief in archetypes is crucial to Rautavaara's aesthetic, who feels that old myths still fulfill an important role in contemporary society, despite the desire of modern people to reject them.[142] At the same time, myths like

---

[141] See Sivuoja-Gunaratnam, *Narrating with Twelve Tones*, 160-161.

[142] Rautavaara believes that in the culture of his native country national myths are still lively and the inspiration for his two choral operas: *Runo 42 'Sammon ryöstö* (Myth of Sampo) from 1974 and *Marjatta matala neiti* (Marjatta, the Lowly Maiden; 1975). The composer has explained that during work on a composition, he does not absorb aspects of concrete myth: "The metaphor, the image, the symbol emerged only afterwards, in performance. The myth and its ritual arrange themselves only when the story is told." Rautavaara, "Choirs, Myths and Finnishness": 4.

dreams belong simultaneously to the composer's private psyche. According to the theories of the French critic Mauron, the main representative of the Psychocritic School who studied the obsessive myths of Mallarmé and Baudelaire, the obsessive recurrence of the motif of angels needs to be investigated with reference to the composer's childhood.[143] The role of the nightmare that haunted the composer in his youth and came back forty years later is thus not to be underestimated: the 1970s were precisely the time when the first work in the series, *Angels and Visitations*, was composed.

The angel, however, is just one of several incessantly recurring motifs in Rautavaara's work. More than others, it shows the influence of literature, philosophy, religion, and psychoanalysis. Through angels, Rautavaara alludes not only to the Romantic synthesis of the arts but also to its incarnation as Symbolism at the turn of the twentieth century. In terms similar to those advanced by the symbolists, Rautavaara has suggested that "[...] words and concepts have the weakness of being able to inform of another reality, another form of consciousness, only through our everyday reality or form of consciousness, if at all. Music on the other hand, and myth along with it, passes the message along whole, 'in its original language.' That this does not happen by means of rational concepts is not necessarily a weakness, in fact quite the opposite."[144] For Rautavaara, myth and music are both able to present another reality, and together they create a more powerful and more influential spiritual message. For this reason Rautavaara often uses myths in his music. Central to Rautavaara's mystical beliefs is the conviction that the composer as a "messenger" helps the passage of messages from a realm beyond this world, concretizing it in his music, which is then transformed into a message for other people during performance.

It is tempting to hypothesize that if the composer perceives himself as a messenger, i.e., a kind of angel, then he in some sense conveys a message about himself in his works. Yet his philosophy of angels does not only derive from his childhood dreams but primarily from Rilke's myth of angels as exposed in the *Duino Elegies*. As will be shown in Chapter 7, both Rautavaara and Rilke use this mythical conception of angels to express their own philosophical and metaphysical attitudes.

---

[143] See Charles Mauron, *Introduction to the Psychoanalysis of Mallarmé* (Berkeley, CA: University of California Press, 1963).

[144] Rautavaara, "Choirs, Myths and Finnishness": 6.

PART II:
ANALYSIS

Chapter 5:
Analysis of Rautavaara's Instrumental Works about Angels

As one of only very few contemporary composers who write works with angelic references, Rautavaara leaves many traces of this fascination. They can be found in his instrumental music by virtue of titles, but they are also detectable in his vocal music, particularly in the operas and choral works. Sivuoja-Gunaratnam notes that the figure of the angel has appeared in the guise of female characters in two of Rautavaara's operas, *Thomas* and *Vincent*.[1] The abstract and ethereal role of these characters makes them resemble angels, and their unexpected appearances are reminiscent of angelic visitations. The composer divided female operatic roles into good and evil (or constructive and destructive) characters. In the opera *Vincent*, Gaby is a kind of helper and muse to the main character Vincent van Gogh, in contrast to Maria Hoornik, the gloomy and fanatical figure who in some passages acts more like Vincent's opponent.[2] Following musical tradition, Rautavaara distinguished these two soprano roles by giving them different forms of musical expression: Gaby is a lyric, Maria a dramatic soprano.

While *Vincent* is Rautavaara's first opera demonstrating the two oppositional attitudes in female characters, a girl in the role of an angel—without a negative counterpart—appears already in the earlier opera *Thomas*. Here, the Girl, who symbolizes ethereal purity and hints at the Virgin Mary, performs only vocalises: ornamental arabesques without a verbal message. Hence the Girl's vocal part is reminiscent of birdsong; moreover, the utterances of this character are invariably announced by recordings of birdsong.[3] Thus the Girl in Rautavaara's *Thomas* can symbolize the angelic but also

---

[1] See Sivuoja-Gunaratnam, "Vincent–not a Portrait": 10-11.

[2] Maria from *Vincent* is reminiscent of Ira from Rautavaara's first opera *Kaivos*; there is an internal game on the word maRIA-IRA. Female characters in Rautavaara's operas are to a certain extent autobiographical: negative characters represent his first wife Mariaheidi, positive ones his second wife Sini. See Sivuoja-Gunaratnam, "Vincent – not a Portrait": 10-11.

[3] See Ivan Moody, "'The Bird Sang in the Darkness': Rautavaara and the Voice," *Tempo* 181 (1992): 20-21.

personify a bird. In the composer's opinion, both angels and birds are "citizens of two worlds."[4]

In addition to the operas, "angels" appear also in Rautavaara's choral music, in particular in *Vigilia* and *Die erste Elegie* dating from 1993. In the former composition, written to the text of Vespers and Matins of the Orthodox All-Night Vigil in Memory of Saint John the Baptist, angels are mentioned several times in the text but without specific musical corollaries. The latter work sets major passages from the text of the first of Rilke's *Duino Elegies* (for the excerpts Rautavaara chose, see Appendix). As the composer confided, he tried to limit the sense of the poem to the figure of the angel, who in his opinion has a fundamental role in the poetic cycle.[5] Later, Rautavaara integrated musical material from *Die erste Elegie* in *Angel of Light*. This corroborates that the correlation between Rilke's poetry and Rautavaara's music seems an important factor in the semantic context of his instrumental works.

Rautavaara's other vocal music also contains some references to the figure of the angel, albeit none as obvious as in the above-mentioned examples. Among them, probably the most spectacular representation of the celestial messenger can be found in the opera *The House of the Sun*. The postman, Hermesson, links the present-day world (outside the house) with the world of memories of the twins Noora and Riina (inside the house). The character's acts as well as his name point to Hermes as a god-messenger and his role of leading the souls of the dead to Hades. On several occasions Rautavaara uses the term *psychopompos* to describe the latter role.[6]

"Archangel Michael Fighting the Antichrist"

The earliest work referring to angels was composed as the last movement of the piano suite *Icons*. The cycle was written in New York, where Rautavaara studied with Vincent Persichetti at the Juilliard School of Music, and was dedicated to the memory of composer's parents. In his autobiography, Rautavaara discussed the process of composing *Icons*:[7]

---

[4] Sivuoja-Gunaratnam, "Vincent – not a Portrait": 11

[5] Personal communication, Helsinki, 19 June 2007.

[6] See Vikke and Rekku's ironic sentences in Act II : "Psychopom-pom-pompom! Psychopom-pom-pompom?" As the composer explains (personal communication, 6 December 2006): "He is scolding the boys and, being a lover of antiquity, threatens them with the 'psychopompos'."

[7] The extensive commentaries are quoted from the composer's autobiography *Omakuva*, in the English translation by Eila Tarasti. See Eila Tarasti, "Icons," 553-555.

Also *Icons* were launched in Vienna. I did not yet know that they were "Icons," since they were only ideas, [from] searching at the keyboard. Some ideas for this suite had been coming in their proto-form as early as my last days in the army, when the piano at the soldier's home was at my disposal. The polyharmonic, quarter-note texture was looking for its shape in my mind always when I sat at the piano. It still had not found its form when I was in Vienna, and only revealed itself to me a year later in Manhattan.

The lions of the Public Library sulk when I walk through them. They could as well be in Europe, as in Schönbrunn, Vienna. So one of course has to find behind them, in the big library, something European. I am not longing for Helsinki, for home. Not even necessarily for Finland. But the only thing that could comfort and take away this nostalgia, soften this glittering hard surface, must be something European. Some smell, for instance, or sound or color which is familiar and originates from the East, something which would represent that crazy, noble and sick hybrid, Hellenic —or rather Hellenistic—culture blended with Christianity, smelling of old Jewish religion.... And suddenly it is there amidst the art books: *Ikonen* published by Insel Verlag. Open it and there you are with all of Valamo bursting out! The bells and the black beards and the choirs and golden onions. So I took *Icons* along to West 110th Street. *Muttergottes* is already singing in the subway, it is radiating music. It comes out almost immediately at the piano. The next day it is ready and one turns the page: *Zwei Heilige*. Quite clearly from the wall of a tiny countryside church, green background—rustic saints. It comes as if it had been waiting. The third day: the *Black Mother of God of Blakernaja* and so on, the whole suite in almost two weeks. Of course then there remain weeks for finishing touches, specifications, changes and corrections.

In 2005, Rautavaara revised *Icons*, orchestrating the piano score, inserting short interludes entitled "Prayers," and adding a new finale, "Amen." Under its new title, *Before the Icons*, Leif Segerstam and the Helsinki Philharmonic Orchestra premiered the work in Finlandia Hall on 11 October 2006. In both the original and the revised version of the score, Rautavaara prefaces each movement with a commentary. Of "Archangel Michael Fighting the Antichrist" he writes:

> Imperturbably calm for all his speed, Michael rides his winged horse over the ugly, hairy body of the eternal enemy. He seems at first sight to have rather too many tasks to perform simultaneously: with his right hand he threatens the Antichrist with a spear and at the same time swings a censer, in his left he holds aloft the Book of Books; with his lips he blows the last Trumpet, and his

> scarlet wings rise proudly from his shoulders. But his youthful features bear so peaceful an expression that even the violent movement of the scene is constrained into a powerful, dynamic stillness.[8]
>
> When I showed Persichetti the last work of the suite, the "Archangel Michael Fighting the Antichrist," he sat for a while in deep thought, and then asked me to play it again. At the end he said that he had first believed that this was a virtuoso composition of the kind that the composer used to play "at the art clubs of elderly ladies." Upon hearing it a second time, however, he was convinced that real substance "was looming behind the show of virtuosity."[9]

"Archangel Michael Fighting the Antichrist" consists of two layers, which in the original piano version are distributed to the right and left hands respectively. The rhythmic structure is simple: the upper layer contains sixteenth-notes in regular and irregular groupings in a manner similar to a *perpetuum mobile*, whereas the lower layer is characterized by slower values (eighth-, quarter- and half-notes) and carries the main melodic line. The whole composition consists of 76 measures. Owing to the similarity of the musical material, its four main sections will be labeled A, A1, A2, and A'. Each section is divided further into smaller subsections that are based on different modes, a notion Rautavaara derived from Persichetti's harmony lectures, which he attended during his stay in New York.

> Technically speaking, in the *Icons* one can follow things that Persichetti lectured about. The quartal harmonies, polyharmonies, alternating meters, triads in thirds and tritone relations, all that which I had already tried in the *Pelimannit, Symmetrical Preludes*, and *String Quartet* were now suddenly coming into use, as if they were legitimate techniques. It was becoming my second nature, therefore a stylistic device.[10]

The two layers are distinguished from each other by motivic structure, modes, and rhythm. The modes used are predominantly church modes, and their role is essential to the whole cycle (Table 1). Section A presents a melodic and harmonic pattern that is repeated three times in variation.

---

[8] Einojuhani Rautavaara, commentary in the score of the piano suite *Icons* (Helsinki: Fazer, 1963).

[9] Rautavaara quoted in Eila Tarasti, "Icons," 561.

[10] Rautavaara quoted in Eila Tarasti, "Icons," 558.

Analysis of Rautavaara's Instrumental Works about Angels

TABLE 1: "Archangel Michael Fighting the Antichrist," sections, subsections, and modes

Sections	A			A1		
Subsections	a	b	c	a'	b'	d (c1)
Measures	1-4	5-15	16-20	21-24	25-33	34-40
Modes in layers - r.h.	C Lydian	D Dorian	E,A Aeolian F# Ionian	C Lydian	D Dorian	C Ionian
- l.h.	B Aeolian	D Phrygian	Wholetone C Ionian	B Aeolian	D Phrygian	F# Ionian

Sections	A2			A'		
Subsections	a"	b1	d1 (c2)	b"'	c'	a'''
Measures	41-44	45-49	50-57	58-68	69-73	74-76
Modes in layers - r.h.	C Lydian	C Lydian	C Ionian	D Dorian	E,A Aeolian F# Ionian	C Ionian
- l.h.	B Aeolian	Wholetone	F# Ionian	D Phrygian	Wholetone C Ionian	B Aeolian

Although in section A there are many different modes built on various tones (B, C, D, E, A, F-sharp), it is possible to view these as transpositions of various modes onto a tonic A. In accordance with Persichetti's lectures, in the first twenty measures Rautavaara used a variety of modes with a stationary tonic center of A (Example 13).

Persichetti taught his pupils that there exists a tension between modes that produce a dark or bright effect, according to the number of flats or sharps they contain; he even classified modes in order of brightness from dark to light (Fig. 4), as can be gleaned from the records included in his lectures notes.[11] All of Persichetti's pupils probably had to compose an exercise in which the melody shifted from bright to dark and the harmony from dark to light.

---
[11] See Eila Tarasti, "Icons," 270 and 272.

EXAMPLE 13a: Modulation of brightness in "Archangel Michael Fighting the Antichrist," mm. 1-19

1. A Aeolian   A Dorian

2. A Lydian

1. A Mixolydian

2. A Mixolydian

1. A Mixolydian

2. A Mixolydian

1. A Mixolydian

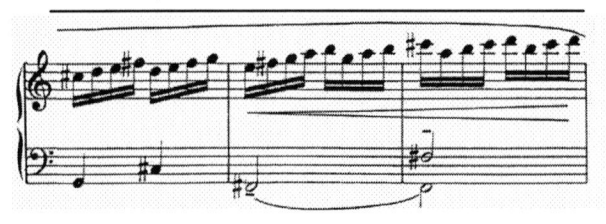

2. A Mixolydian

Analysis of Rautavaara's Instrumental Works about Angels 99

EXAMPLE 13b: Modulation of brightness (cont.)

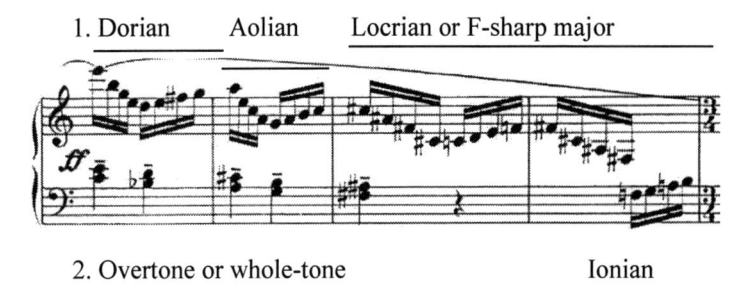

1. Dorian   Aolian   Locrian or F-sharp major

2. Overtone or whole-tone   Ionian

FIGURE 4: Persichetti's characterization of modes, ranging from dark to bright

dark———————————— neutral ————————————bright
Locrian Phrygian Aeolian   Dorian   Mixolydian Ionian Lydian

The greatest number of flats that can be applied to a model scale on a particular tone will produce the "darkest" mode, the Locrian. Subtracting flats (and then adding sharps) from a diatonic key signature order will produce an arrangement of modes from "darkest" to "brightness." The Dorian mode is the middle point and sets the norm.[12]

Surprisingly, in "Archangel Michael Fighting the Antichrist" most sections are based on a similar succession of modes. In [a], [a'], [a''], and [a'''], the two layers start from two different levels of brightness: the right hand based on the Aeolian mode (a dark mode) and the left hand using the Lydian mode (the brightest mode). In [b], [b'], [b''], and [b1], the first layer shifts from the dark Aeolian through the neutral Dorian to the brighter Mixolydian, while the contrasting second layer progresses from the very bright Lydian to the darker Mixolydian mode. Finally, in the first two measures of [c] and [c'], the first layer returns to the previous darker modes of Dorian and Aeolian. A passage through the darkest mode, the Locrian, alternates with the bright Ionian in [c], [c'], [d], and [d1] and creates a strong contrast between dark and bright. (Regarding them as modes is more helpful than analyzing them as major scales a tritone apart, on F sharp and C). This contrast is crucial to the composition. Rautavaara intensified the effect by ordering the four sections by register, moving from a low register in section A, through the middle registers of section A1, to a higher *tessitura* in section A2, and returning to a low register in section A'. The movement unexpectedly ends with divergent registers: high in the first layer, low in the second. The

---

[12] Vincent Persichetti, *Twentieth-Century Harmony* (London: Faber and Faber, 1962), 35.

dynamic level grows from *mezzoforte* in sections A and A1 to *forte* in A2 and finally *fortissimo* in A'. The gradations of modes and registers from dark to light, together with the increasing dynamic level, emphasize the coloristic features of the work and its iconic character.

The motivic and rhythmic content of the two melodic lines appears at first glance completely different. The basic motif of the upper melodic line is a tetrachord in an upward or downward direction; sometimes Rautavaara combines two tetrachords to create an entire mode. Before the backdrop of constant sixteenth-notes, the prevalence of half and whole steps gives the line a figurative and ornamental character. The typical durations of the lower layer—eighth- and quarter-notes—are essential because they are very often placed on the strong beat, emphasizing the line's importance. Moreover, the composer indicates that the line should be played *marcato*. To discover the hidden relationship between the melodic lines in the two different layers, the notes in the first melodic line that fall on a downbeat (every quarter) were marked in the example below, while the other notes were eliminated:

EXAMPLE 14: Mirror writing in
"Archangel Michael Fighting the Antichrist," mm. 1-15

If the intervals larger than a tritone are treated as intervallic inversions, then it seems that the two lines are written to some extent as mirror images of one another, in accordance with Persichetti's lecture. In this sense, the upper melodic line, with its constant sixteenth-note motion, is an ornamentation of the basic line in the left hand. According to Eila Tarasti, these two lines may also be regarded as "[...] two places from different times, [...] viewed as simultaneous, as when all the phases of a saint's life and the places where he dwelt are pictured side by side at the same time."[13]

In view of the fact that the two lines in the composition represent different aspects of the icon that inspired Rautavaara, it is revealing to look at the instrumentation the composer fashioned exactly fifty years later. Here, various instruments are used to emphasize certain elements of the original. Although Rautavaara increased twofold the rhythmic values and time signature, the tempo is a little slower than in the original piano version. The upper melodic line is scored for woodwinds and strings, while the main line in the lower register is given to brass. The scoring of the lower line is given in the following table:

TABLE 2: Disposition of brass instruments in
"Archangel Michael Fighting the Antichrist"

Sections	A	A1	A2	A'
Disposition of brass instruments in measures	Tb (5-11) Fg, Cfg, Tb (12-15) Cor (16-18)	Cor (25-28) Tr (29-31), Cor (32-33)	Tr (45-46) Cor (47-48) Cor, Tbn (49-57)	Cor, Tr, Tbn, Tb (58-69) Tbn, Tb (69-70)

The main melodic line, representing the archangel, passes through all brass instruments, from the lowest, the tuba in section A) through the middle register (horns in [A1]) to the highest (trumpets) in section A2. In the final section, the composer joins all these instruments together, adding trombones in imitations of the main melodic line, to give the effect of a textural crescendo. This can be regarded as an instrumentation *summa* of the three previous sections or a summation of the principal idea of passing from dark to light on three levels—modal, registral, and instrumental—together with gradations of dynamics. Beside this leading role of the brass ensemble, the other instruments act as secondary players, doubling the melodic line in unisons or octaves:

---

[13] Eila Tarasti, "Icons," 555.

EXAMPLE 15: Imitation of brass theme
in "Archangel Michael Fighting the Antichrist," mm. 58-65

In its use of modality and chorale textures, the passage is reminiscent of "The Great Gate of Kiev" from Mussorgsky's *Pictures at an Exhibition* (1874) in Ravel's orchestration (1922). Mussorgsky's cycle and Rautavaara's *Icons* share the same source of inspiration—the Orthodox Church—along with similar ideas of musical painting and formal structure. In the orchestral version of the suite, Rautavaara magnifies these similarities through the insertion of newly-composed prayers between movements, which appear as counterparts of the "Promenades" Mussorgsky uses to bind together the individual movements in his *Pictures*.

Angels and Visitations (Angel Trilogy, Part I)

The most significant of Rautavaara's compositions referring to angels are those constituting the Angel Trilogy—a series of three works commissioned by the Finnish Radio Symphony Orchestra in the 1970s. The commissioners wanted three works that together would form a conventional concert program of overture, concerto, and symphony.[14] In 1978 Rautavaara completed the overture, *Angels and Visitations*; in 1980 followed *Angel of Dusk*. Having composed a first candidate for the intended third component, the Fifth Symphony, in 1985, he replaced it nine years later with *Angel of Light* (1994).

Just as *Angels and Visitations*, the first component of the Angel Trilogy, was intended as an overture of the kind that often opens orchestral concerts, the analysis offered below fulfils the function of an opening analysis, in the sense that it shows the majority of the musical aspects used in a similar way in his subsequent instrumental works about angels. In his first commentary on *Angels and Visitations*, Rautavaara explains the meaning of the angelic title and the essential role of angels in his artistic outlook with reference to Rilke's *Duino Elegies* and his childhood dreams. This first commentary is not only replete with references to works about angels from the other arts, it is also the longest commentary on an instrumental composition Rautavaara ever wrote. As with all of his commentaries,[15] it is divided into a longer programmatic and a shorter analytic section.

> *Angels and Visitations* (1978) is the first of the works in the "angels" series that was later to include *Angel of Dusk, Playgrounds for Angels* and the Seventh Symphony *Angel of Light*. These angels are not figures out of a children's fairytale, and nor are they religious kitsch; they spring from a conviction that other realities, quite different modes of consciousness exist outside

---

[14] Kimmo Korhonen, *Finnish Concertos* (Jyväskylä: Finnish Music Information Centre, 1995), 40.

[15] The interpretation of commentaries is somewhat problematic since Rautavaara almost invariably writes multiple versions for CD booklets, scores, and concert programs. These are sometimes completely different and create something akin to a set of (verbal) variations.

our everyday awareness. Arising out of this alien consciousness are beings that could be denoted as angels. They are possibly reminiscent of the visions of William Blake, and they are almost certainly akin to the horrifying figures of Rainer Maria Rilke bursting with saintly fury: "... ein jeder Engel ist schrecklich..."

The idea for *Angels and Visitations* occurred to me on reading the lines by Rilke "And even if one were suddenly take me to its heart, I would vanish into its stronger existence." I was reminded of a figure that repeatedly entered my dreams to frighten me when, as a child of seven or eight, I dreamt again and again of a big, grey, mighty, silent being that drew near, enveloped me in its embrace till I was afraid it would suffocate me in its great and powerful existence. I fought for my life-just as one is supposed to fight for one's life with an angel- until I woke up. The figure returned again night after night, and by day I feared its imminent return. Finally, after seeking to resist it dozens of times, I learnt to surrender, to cast myself at its mercy, to become a part of it, and its visits thus gradually ceased.-It was a "visitation," a presence and a scourge, a trial. And the words "angel" and "visitation" stuck in my mind like a mantra, until in 1978 I composed *Angels and Visitations*.

This music seems to be clearly epic in tone; it is a "narrative continuum." But if the narrative could be transformed into words, it would tell about this reality, and that is not the case; these works do not have a "program." They are absolute music by a composer whose mindscape has been crossed by strong, archetypical associations, and inherently contrasting ones. For *Angels and Visitations* is set in a world of sharp contrasts in which the hymn rising from the depths may follow along like a flock of rampant devils-only to give way to Palestrinian texture of the violins on high or the clear tinkling of the harp or celesta. The work is a set of variations in which the theme is contrast, polarity, the logic of opposition. Kundera likened the symphony to a journey through the outer world, but variations to the equally endless world "inside," the boundless world of inner transformation and difference that exists in everything.[16]

Angels and Visitations is a one-movement composition for large symphony orchestra and extended percussion group, with a performance time of approximately twenty minutes. Although its musical form is complex, consisting of many different and often overlapping elements and thus creating

---

[16] Einojuhani Rautavaara, commentary on *Angels and Visitations,* in the booklet accompanying the recording Ondine 881-2 (1997).

Analysis of Rautavaara's Instrumental Works about Angels

Rautavaara's popular "domino form,"[17] its structure is easy to comprehend. It presents the most typical example of the composer's use of the arch form in which the musical material from the beginning recurs at the end. The arch form plays an important role in the composer's philosophical outlook according to the theory of organic music as a birth and its oppositional reflection, death. Both the beginning and ending start slowly, with thin textures and low dynamic levels (*pianissimo* or *piano*) that gradually increase. Rautavaara originally used this idea in compositions from his first serial period[18] and developed it in his Neo-romantic period in such compositions as the *Soldier's Mass* (1968), the Cello Concerto (1968), and the Flute Concerto (1973).[19]

TABLE 3: Formal scheme of *Angels and Visitations*

Sections	A	B	C	D	E
Measures	1-28	29-72	73-85	86-128	129-184
Themes	1	2	1	3	4
Tempos	♩=52	Meno mosso ♩=46	Andante assai ♩=56	Più mosso ma tranquillo ♩=92, ♩=60 from m.113 Furioso ♩=132, Allegro ♩=120	Poco meno mosso ♩=112

Sections	F	G	H	I	J	K
Measures	185-224	225-250	251-268	269-295	296-310	311-336
Themes	------	3,5	3,6	7,1	2,1	8
Tempos	Furioso ♪=144	Come andantino ♪=126, Furioso ♪=144	Come andantino ♪=126 ♪=92 ♩=72	♪=92 ♩=52 ♪=80	Meno mosso ♩=40	Solenne ♩=48

---

[17] See the analysis of the Organ Concerto *Annunciations* based on the composer's suggestions written by Lovejoy, 87-116.

[18] Such retrogrades can be found as early as in the Second String Quartet (1958). See Sivuoja-Gunaratnam, *Narrating with Twelve Tones*, 234-235.

[19] See Sivuoja-Gunaratnam, *Narrating with Twelve Tones*, 234-235 and Aho, *Einojuhani Rautavaara as Symphonist*, 88.

As with the structure of the macroform, the microform also encompasses retrogrades in which homogeneous sections based on the same harmonic backgrounds are often linked and overlap through the use of aleatoric techniques. Some sections or themes are variations of his original version, although at first glance this is not immediately clear (Table 3).Some sections are repeated or correspond to each other: as a result, there is a noticeable symmetry of form in both the composition as a whole and in individual musical elements. The separate homogeneous sections are based on Messiaen's mode 2^1 (Fig. 5) and mode 6^4 (Fig. 6), which also show a symmetric arrangement.

FIGURE 5: Intervallic structure of Messiaen's mode 2^1

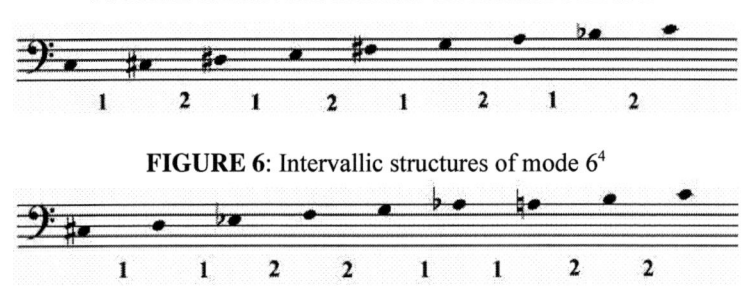

FIGURE 6: Intervallic structures of mode 6^4

As a harmonic background, Rautavaara uses mediant combinations of triads[20] and "mirror" harmonies together with symmetric instrumentation (where the melodic line of the high instruments is transposed to or reflected in the low instruments according to the rules of mirror writing). The composition thus contains certain "mirror image" elements in all of its constituent parts.[21]

Section A consists of short melodic lines based on Messiaen's modes 2^1 and 6^4, given first to the strings and then to the woodwinds. These two modes form not only the basis of the opening melodic material but also all of the harmonic background, scored for several strands in the divided first

---

[20] Such mediant relations of chords are common in Rautavaara's style, particularly from the late 1960s. Samuli Tiikkaja tried to explain the rules of these relations, comparing Rautavaara's system to the most famous historical systems of harmonic circles provided in the eighteenth century by David Heinichen, David Kellner and in the nineteenth century by Gottfried Weber and Hugo Riemann. See Tiikkaja, "The Harmonic Circle as a Tool for Analyzing the music of Einojuhani Rautavaara," unpublished materials from 11th International Doctoral and Postdoctoral Seminar in Musical Semiotics, Helsinki 2005.

[21] "Symmetrical scales, inversions of melodies and mirror harmonies have in fact always been typical of my music." Einojuhani Rautavaara, "Some Reflections on a Symmetrical Year," *Highlights* 12 (2002).

and second violins and the divided violas. This creates a coloristic, rustling effect. Contributing to the climax, the dry percussion and cymbals add material that counterbalances the delicacy of harp and metallophones. The material of section A appears in the work several times and always introduces upward movement, chromaticism, lack of a tonal center, changeable rhythms, lack of meter, anxiety, dynamics, emotions, and sudden contrasts in color between instruments: dark-light, smooth-sharp.

The introduction of the first theme reaches a climax with the brass instruments playing mediant combinations of chords. The techniques used to build this climax—upward motion, chorale construction, and a Brucknerian use of the brass ensemble—resemble those found in Rautavaara's Third Symphony. At the same time, the first theme's diatonicism and the fact that tonal centers as well as cadences fall on downbeats provides sharp contrast with the unstable, coloristic section A .

EXAMPLE 16: First chorale theme, *Angels and Visitations*, mm. 73-79, 4 horns and 4 tubas

In the course of the work, several other chorale themes emerge that are similarly given to brass and characterized by diatonicism, cadences on strong beats, and stabile tonal centers while being based on mediant combinations. They all seem to be distant echoes of passages from the Third Symphony with its neoromantic Brucknerian instrumentation and atmosphere.

EXAMPLE 17: Chorale construction of the fifth theme, *Angels and Visitations*, mm. 247-251

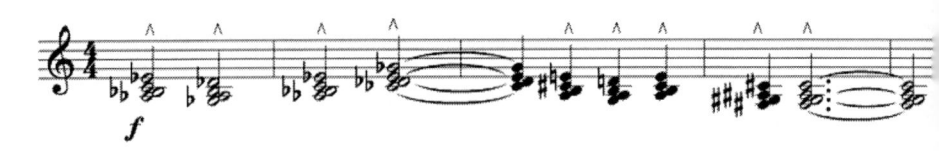

The seventh theme (mm. 282-285), which is used cadentially, is derived from the Third Symphony and is thus one of the auto-citations that forms such a recognizable part of Rautavaara's style.

It may seem odd that Rautavaara used this thematic material to build a short fragment, thus interrupting the previous musical narration. For although it is a citation, its musical application appears at first unsuitable. To understand this, it helps to know that the passage was used prior to *Angels and Visitations* in the composer's cantata *True and False Unicorn* (1971). In the text of the first part of this satirical composition, entitled "The Unicorn," the mythical animal speaks about himself: "I am the unicorn, but is that I?" As in *Angels and Visitations*, the musical setting derives from harmonic and melodic material used in the Third Symphony (compare Ex. 18 with Ex. 19).

If one interprets the unicorn as the composer himself does, the ironic utterance "I am the unicorn, but is that I?" becomes transparent to a question the composer asks of his own act of creation: "Did I make this. No it is impossible. I only helped this musical idea as a midwife." The composer's metaphysical aesthetics prompts him to consider himself an artistic medium. Section B does not contrast with the previous section. Instead, it comes across as a kind of musical eruption that bursts forth from section A. A sudden *fortissimo* in the woodwinds (using Bartolozzi's techniques[22]), four different trumpet strands creating a cluster chord, and sharp arpeggios of minor seconds in the first and second violins together with aggressive attacks by the four kettledrums generate an atmosphere of horror and chaos (m. 29). Subsequent entries from metallophones such as the vibraphone, glockenspiel, and celesta emphasize the free twelve-tone structure of the passage and accentuate the important role of sonority in the work. At the same time that

---

[22] This technique is named after Bruno Bartolozzi, who, in 1967, wrote a book describing unusual sounds produced with wind instruments. By using unorthodox fingerings and ways of blowing, it is possible to produce, and control, all kinds of striking sounds, even including chords, harmonics, and microtones. These sounds, once considered taboo, are now part of the musical language of composers like Luciano Berio and Stockhausen, and of performers like the oboist Heinz Holliger and the trombonist Vinco Globokar.

Analysis of Rautavaara's Instrumental Works about Angels 109

EXAMPLE 18: Seventh theme, *Angels and Visitations*, mm. 282-285, 4 horns and 4 tubas

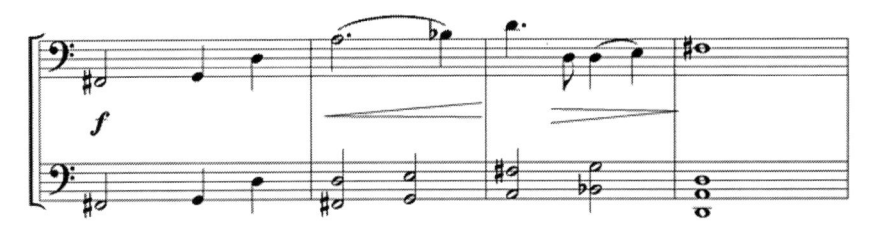

EXAMPLE 19: "The Unicorn," *True and False Unicorn* no. 4, mm. 1-5

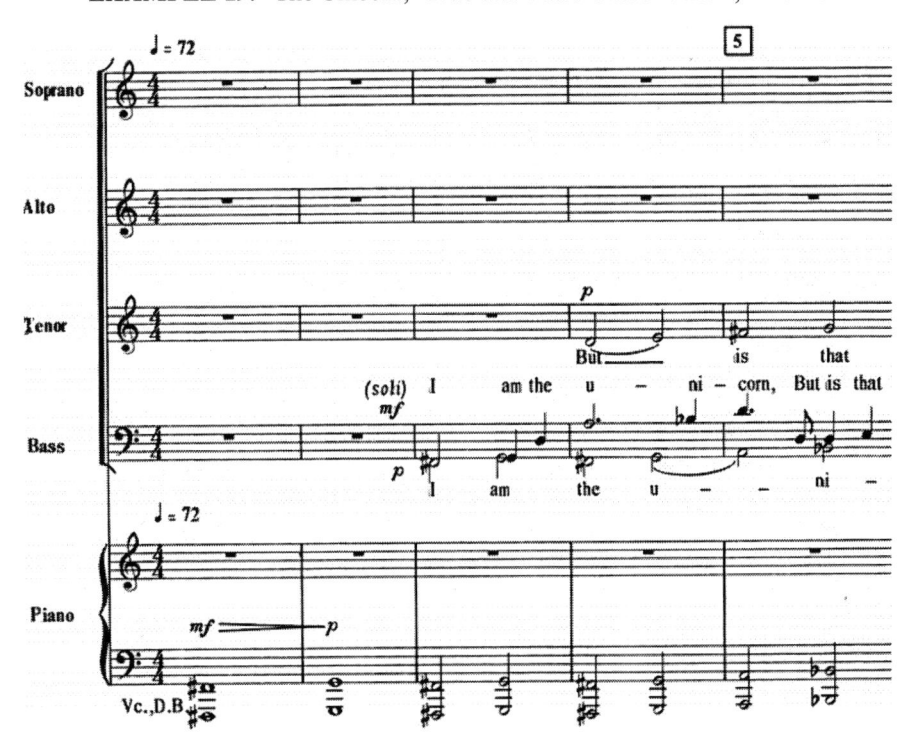

this jumble of noises occurs, there is also a very stable C-major chord played by violas, cellos, and basses. The aggressive noises swiftly descend into silence and the lingering C-major chord grows in strength to become the harmonic foundation of the second thematic group. A few measures before the change of tempo an interesting effect is used in the brass: breathing into the instrument without tone, a technique repeated by the composer at the end of the work (mm. 325-327, 330, 332). The second violins join the violas'

C-major chord, and after A-flat-major and E-flat-major chords, short motifs occur in the woodwind, reflected symmetrically in the horns and tubas (from m. 40). The woodwinds begin to provide ornaments, arabesques, and birdsong-like motifs (from m. 61). Hence there are three layers: the stable C-major chord, the short motifs in various instruments related by mirror reflection, and the woodwind arabesques. These layers provide the background for the development of the lyrical second theme. Like this theme, the layers are based on a hexatonic scale created from the overlay of three major chords (A-flat, E-flat, and C).

FIGURE 7: The hexatonic scale

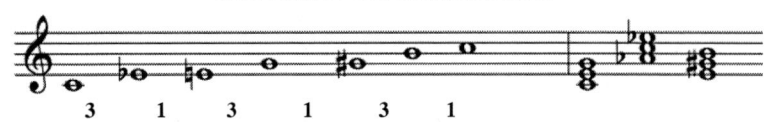

In contrast to the first theme, the second is melodic rather than chordal and given to the first and second violins rather than the brass. It presents itself as an elaborate and undulating melodic line, like a wavy picture, and is loaded with a strong, emotional charge. Its contour is reminiscent of the arch-like melodic structures of medieval Gregorian chants with several climatic points:

EXAMPLE 20: Excerpt of second theme, *Angels and Visitations*, mm. 48-59, violins

Analysis of Rautavaara's Instrumental Works about Angels 111

Immediately after the second theme, the first theme in its full version returns in the brass and then in the strings. As it fades out, the third theme is launched in the first and second violins and initiates section D. This third theme is another auto-citation, taken from the choral work *Lehdet lehtiä* (Leaves are leaves) on which the composer was working in the year in which he also wrote *Angels and Visitations*. The theme has a polyphonic three-voiced texture based on modal scales, mainly the Phrygian, played *pianissimo* without *crescendo* and *diminuendo*. Its non-emotional character is underlined with the expression marking *senza sentimento* and the circular shape of the melodic lines. The homorhythms and polyphonic textures resemble the beginning of Sibelius's Sixth Symphony.[23]

In *Angels and Visitations* Rautavaara uses the third theme three times, each time orchestrated differently: the first time for three violins, simultaneously imitated in the brass; the second time for two oboes with English horn; and the third time for glockenspiel, celesta, and harp. These successive re-orchestrations of the same passage create a strong effect of illumination, which will be discussed further. (Ex. 21) Each time the theme appears, strongly contrasting material from the brass ensemble, low woodwinds, strings, and percussion seemingly tries to interrupt its continuation. The noisy, sonoristic sounds and aggressive outbursts of these instruments do not carry any new melodic or harmonic qualities; most of them can be regarded as coloristic effects. Rautavaara applied many new types of sounds to achieve the "disturbance," such as Bartolozzi sounds, flutter-tonguing, and tremolo with glissando. No rule controls form in the "disturbance" passages; the massive, tremendous attacks from the brass ensemble are supported exclusively by dynamics, chaotic rhythms, and free twelve-tone writing. The "disturbance" technique thus presupposes two planes in sharp contrast: one smooth, lyric, non-emotional, diatonic, and stable, here represented by the third theme; the other restless, aggressive, emotional, chromatic, and unstable, as provided here by the "motifs of disturbance."

Sections E and F bring completely new musical material. The role of section E is to create a strong climax on the basis of monotonous sixteenth-notes in a *nota-contra-notam* texture. This is done through the development of short melodic phrases and textural extensions, achieved by means of the addition of one instrument after the other, starting from the low basses and contrabassoon and rising through the entire symphony orchestra. Short melodic phrases are also worked up from the low register to the high register in a manner reminiscent of the beginning of the composition. The rhythms

---

[23] See Kimmo Korhonen, *Finnish Orchestral Music 2* (Jyväskylä: Finnish Music Information Centre, 1995), 40.

112 Chapter 5

EXAMPLE 21: The polyphonic third theme, *Angels and Visitations*, mm. 96-106, divided violins

of the percussion group are different from those of the rest of the orchestra, consisting repeated triplets. The climax is crowned by a simple, naive trumpet theme based on diatonic clusters (Ex. 22). Both the percussion's triplet rhythms and the trumpet's theme evoke military music and the composer's *Soldier's Mass*, written a few years earlier. The section is tonally based on

Analysis of Rautavaara's Instrumental Works about Angels 113

Messiaen's mode 2^1 and free twelve-tone writing; its powerful character is emphasized through the prominent use of seconds and sevenths in a loud dynamic.

EXAMPLE 22: Fourth theme, *Angels and Visitations*, mm. 175-181, four trumpets

Like section E, section F is also based on short motifs in triplets. Its source, however, is the final movement of the Second Symphony. Rautavaara uses this passage by retaining its structure in its entirety while changing only minor elements of orchestration.[24] The motifs in this section are conceived as contrasting opposites. The first motif is a chord constructed from an augmented fourth and a perfect fifth, which is repeated in triplet 32nd notes; the second motif is characterized by chromatic writing and sonoristic elements such as flutter-tonguing, tremolos, trills, and clusters in rapid irregular rhythms. The composer initially separates the two components, then joins them before separating them again. Both motifs are based on dissonant intervals drawn from the previous sections (seconds, tritones, sevenths, and ninths), thereby making the section harmonically and motivically homogenous and ascetic. The second motif functions as a kind of "disturbance" motif which interrupts the development of the first, but its effect is not as clear-cut as in previous sections.

The section is shaped by a distinct symmetricality. The first three measures present the first motif in high register, played by woodwinds, metallophones, and first violins. One measure later, this is reflected in the second sonoristic motif, which arises in the low register, scored for bassoons, trombones, cellos, and basses together with tom-toms. The same strategy of mirror-harmonies (or mirror writing) is noticeable in the level of harmonic structure. The most spectacular example is a short fragment in which two layers are inverted: the woodwinds with xylophone in the trumpets with first violins and marimba, and irregular rhythmic motifs scored for second violins and violas. At the same time, the cellos, basses, and tubas are moving at half this speed, as a free reflection of harmonic structures from previous measures

---

[24] Surprisingly, this is a double auto-citation because the final passage of the symphony uses material from the seventh of Rautavaara's very early piano work *Seven Preludes*, composed in 1956 during his stay in New York. See Aho, *Einojuhani Rautavaara as Symphonist*, 80.

that can be regarded as an augmentation of them. Rautavaara has used this fascinating conception of symmetricality on several occasions.[25]

Most important for the discussion of angels in Rautavaara's music is the combination of symmetrical writing with the "disturbance technique," which can be found in the brass as a conjunction of the section's two main motifs. The resulting "motif of disturbance" occupies only one or two measures in the form of a brief interpolation from trumpets and trombones, but even in this minimal space Rautavaara uses symmetrical writing between and within these instrumental groups.

The "disturbance technique" does not end at the close of section F; it is prolonged to fulfill its function and to become oppositional material that contrasts with the calm entrance of the third theme in section G. The violent *furioso* of section F is now juxtaposed with the moderate *Come andantino* of the diatonic third theme. The strong climax that results from the development of the "motif of disturbance" is crowned by the diatonic chorale theme.

The sections following section G do not introduce any important new musical materials; rather they develop previous ideas. Section H is a kind of transition to section I in which the central E-major is stabilized and the second theme appears as a symmetrical reflection of the beginning of the work. The tempo *Come andantino* reintroduces the third theme in the metallophones and harp with delicate attempts of "disturbance" from the strings and kettledrums in allusion to section A. The sixth theme seems to be a continuation of the variation of the fifth theme. It is hard to separate this section and the subsequent section I because they overlap and some material appears in both of them. The signal of the return of the material from section B is an E- major chord, which moves to a C-major chord in the violas. The sixth theme then appears along with rustling sounds in divided strings based on short chromatic motifs derived from Messiaen's mode 6, in a manner reminiscent of the beginning of the work. The section is crowned by the last appearance of the first chorale theme in the brass ensemble.

Section J is launched by a change of tempo (*meno mosso*) and an abridged version of the second theme is introduced in parallel thirds in the first and second violins. At the same time, the woodwinds also start to play various arabesque-like motifs that create a dense and constantly-changing web of sound, reminiscent of the opalescent effect. On this rich sonorous foundation, the short version of the first theme is given to the brass ensemble, and the music fades out, leading into section K.

---

[25] There are other examples of it in section F in measures 207-210, 212-215, 220-224.

The large, extensive passage from the beginning of section K (marked as the eighth theme) is another citation from the Third Symphony. Its duration is the same as in the source of the citation (10-11 measures), and there are only small changes to the instrumentation; the only significant changes are to the rhythm (compare Ex. 23 with Ex. 24).

More surprising is the fact that Rautavaara placed this polyphonic passage in the same position as in the Third Symphony, just before the ending. Aho describes this as the last cathartic point in the Symphony;[26] correspondingly we could speak of the last clear harmonic section of *Angels and Visitations*. Its harmonic foundation both in the Symphony and the work referring to angels is based on mediant relationships between major and minor chords, played in the symphony by bass tubas, trombones, cellos, and basses, in *Angels and Visitations* by five tubas, three bassoons, and double basses.

After the citation from the Third Symphony, the music returns to the beginning of the composition: a harmonic background containing several strands in divided strings based on mode 6 and short motifs on glockenspiel, celesta, and harp. Although these motifs are reminiscent of effects from the very beginning, their construction is different because they are based on the chorale motifs from the woodwinds in section B. The change of instrumentation from woodwind to metallophones creates the same illumination effect as that found in the three appearances of the third theme.

Angels and Visitations ends with metallophones, rising glissandi in the harp (played with keys on the strings), and the sonorous effects of breathing into brass instruments without tone, all accompanied by rolls of the kettledrum. It seems as though the composer wanted to say that "the vision slowly dissipates." The harmonic background, coloristic elements, instrumentation, and level of dynamic are thus the same at the beginning and ending of the work, which creates a kind of magical aura.

To summarize, although the composition is constructed symmetrically, the themes contrast with the fragments in various regards such as chromatic/diatonic, lack/presence of a harmonic center, changing/constant rhythms, calm/anxiety, dynamism/stasis, darkness/light, harshness/gentleness, and emotional involvement/unemotional distance. Most of the fragments show a similarity of construction, as they are based on short homogeneous motifs derived from Messiaen's modes 2 and 6 or organized in free twelve-tone technique; they lack definable harmonic centers and are dynamic as well as emotionally anxious. In contrast to the fragments, the thematic material

---

[26] See Aho, *Einojuhani Rautavaara as Symphonist*, 88.

EXAMPLE 23:
Third Symphony,
mvt. IV,
mm. 154-155

EXAMPLE 24:
Angels and Visitations,
mm. 311-312,
brass ensemble

forms fairly self-contained phrases. They are based on diatonicism or hexatonic, constant rhythms, clear harmonic centers, and generally remain calm. The fragments demonstrate movement, whereas the thematic ideas present states of being. Sonoristic passages with modern performance techniques that create noisy, brutal sounds are contrasted with traditional thematic ideas that focus on the beauty of the sound.

TABLE 4: Musical oppositions in *Angels and Visitations*

THEMES	FRAGMENTS
DIATONIC	CHROMATIC
PRESENCE OF	LACK OF
A HARMONIC CENTER	A HARMONIC CENTER
CONSTANT RHYTHMS	CHANGING RHYTHMS
CALM	ANXIETY
STASIS	DYNAMISM
LIGHT	DARKNESS
GENTLENESS	HARSHNESS
UNEMOTIONAL	EMOTIONAL
DISTANCE	INVOLVEMENT

As the composer describes it in his commentary, the duality expressed in the title *Angels and Visitations* is represented within the work in musical dichotomies in terms of contrast, polarities, and the logic of opposition. The question that remains is how the words "angels" and "visitations" can be understood in connection with the oppositional musical material. This will be addressed in Chapters 6 and 7.

The Double Bass Concerto *Angel of Dusk* (Angel Trilogy, Part II)

Two years after *Angels and Visitations* Rautavaara wrote his Concerto for Double Bass *Angel of Dusk*.[27] In 1955 the Koussevitzky Foundation had awarded Jean Sibelius a scholarship in honor of his ninetieth birthday, stipulating that the money be used to enable a young Finnish composer of his choice to study in the United States. Sibelius chose Rautavaara, who subsequently spent two years, 1955-1956, studying composition with Persichetti

---

[27] Rautavaara describes the process of composing the concerto in great detail, from his first non-musical thoughts to the first performance, in a chapter of his autobiography. See *Omakuva*, 296-300.

at the Juilliard School of Music in New York. Rautavaara also participated in the summer courses at Tanglewood taught by Roger Sessions and Aaron Copland. It was Olga Koussevitzky's idea to dedicate Rautavaara's Concerto for Double Bass to her dead husband Serge, who was both a conductor and a great double-bass player.[28] But after Olga's death, the composer decided to dedicate it to her memory, as described in his commentary to the work:

> This concerto was initially requested by Olga Koussevitzky, who had been my patron while I was a student, when I met her in New York in 1977, two decades after my studies in New York. While returning to Helsinki I was reflecting upon this new challenge when, looking out of the window of the plane, I saw a strikingly shaped cloud, gray but pierced with color, rising above the Atlantic horizon, Suddenly the words "Angel of Dusk" came to mind. Those words remained with me and turned to me like a mantra, when I heard the news of Olga Koussevitzky's death the following year and the project had to be postponed. A couple of years later the idea of such a concerto resurfaced when the Finnish Broadcasting Corporation commissioned the work. The help of the double bass virtuoso Olli Kosonen was quite indispensable during my work on the piece and, by borrowing a double bass and experimenting at home, I also worked out new types of playing technique for this unusual but captivating solo instrument.[29]

The concerto, written for double bass is and symphony orchestra (with numerous divisi strings and an extensive percussion group), was completed in 1980 and premiered on 6 May the following year in Helsinki by the soloist Olli Kosonen and the Finnish Radio Symphony Orchestra conducted by Segerstam. After the first rehearsals in February 1981 Rautavaara changed a number of elements and added some new material at the suggestion of Kosonen.[30] In 1993 he further arranged it for a chamber group of double bass, two pianos and percussion (1 player); in this form it was performed in 1994 in Kuhmo with the double bassist Sampo Lassila. In both versions, the work lasts approximately 27 minutes and consists of three movements which the composer subtitles "His First Appearance," "His Monologue" and "His Last Appearance."

---

[28] See Einojuhani Rautavaara, *Omakuva* [Autobiography] (Juva: WSO, 1989), 296-297.

[29] Rautavaara's commentary on the Double Bass Concerto *Angel of Dusk*, published in the booklet accompanying the recording Finlandia Records 4509-99969-2 (1981).

[30] See Rautavaara, *Omakuva*, 299-300, also Korhonen, *Finnish Concertos*, 49.

"His first appearance"

The formal structure of movement I can be described in terms of three sections: an introduction (int) is followed by two larger sections (A and B); these may be further divided into short subsections [a], [a1], [b], [b'], [b1], [c], [d], [e]:

TABLE 5: Formal and harmonic structure of movement I of *Angel of Dusk*

Sections	int	A							
Subsections	a	b	b'	b	b'	b	b'	b1	c
Measures	1-11	11-15	16-21	22-26	27-33	34-36	37-43	44-53	54-75

Sections	B					
Subsections	d	a1	b	e	b	e
Measures	76-82	83-94	94-101	102-103	104-107	108-111

FIGURE 8: Harmonic structure of the introductory section [a]

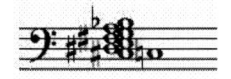

The introductory section [int] is based on the harmonic structure shown in Figure 8, which ultimately plays a less important role in distinguishing this particular composition than the subsequent harmonic structures of [b] and [b'] since it opens the musical action in many of Rautavaara's compositions from the 1970s and '80s. This structure, based on a symmetrically alternating succession of semitones and whole tones, is identical with Messiaen's mode 2^1 or the octatonic scale used by Scriabin and other composers (see Fig. 5). The entire introduction is based on this mode, which first appears in the divided violas and violoncellos, developing into short phrases split into eight lines of divided parts in a perpetual motion of sixteenth-note septuplets, thereby creating a dense sound cushion. Violins enter in the third measure, and the texture gradually thickens to sixteen lines. These are then transposed to a higher register where they are interwoven with short, symmetrical melodic lines for woodwinds.

The opening harmonic structure creates a harmonic background for the introduction's chorale theme. This theme, which consists of three half-notes that move in opposite directions and are based on the triadic harmony

Analysis of Rautavaara's Instrumental Works about Angels 121

derived from the background layer, is first heard in m. 3, where it is played by trumpets and horns, along with its inverted version in trombones, tuba, and double basses. The harmonic backdrop in the strings is like a mirror that reflects the chorale theme: the composer's typical device, found in many of his compositions. The chorale character is reminiscent of analogous brass themes, particularly the fourth and fifths scenes in *Angels and Visitations*, and belongs to the category of themes in Rautavaara's output that may be considered "Brucknerian":

EXAMPLE 25: Opening chorale theme in brass, *Angel of Dusk*, mvt. I, mm. 2-3

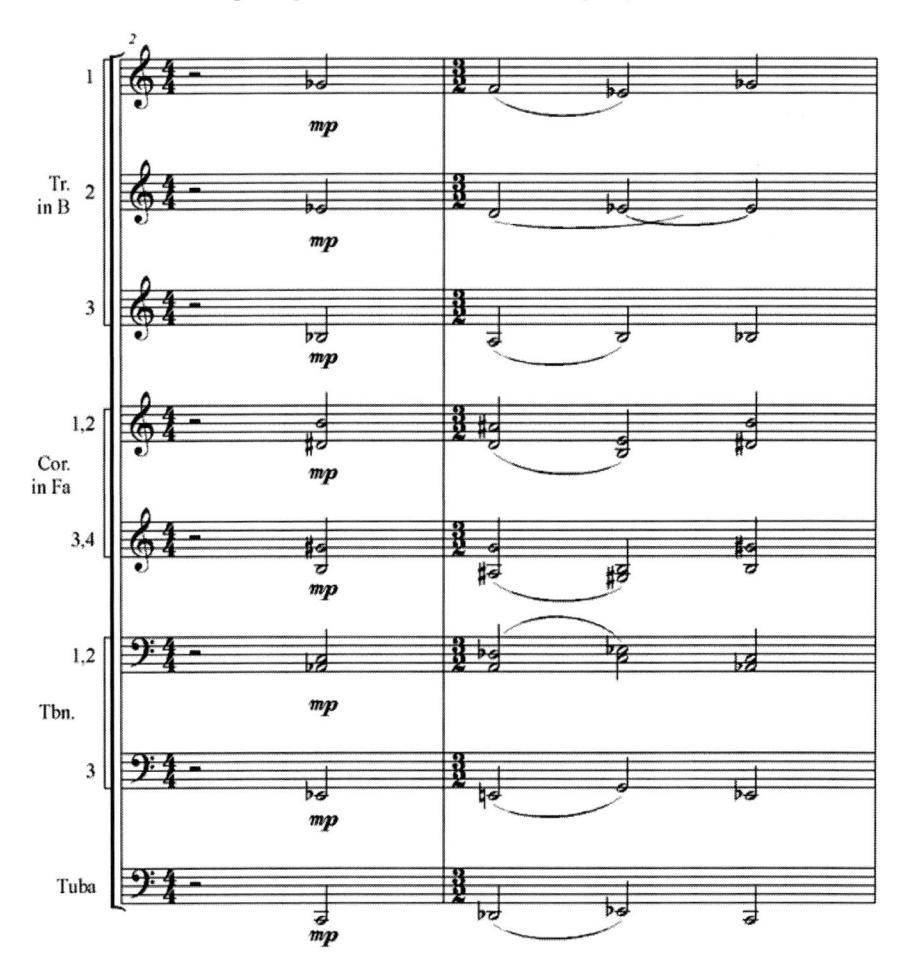

Section A introduces the solo double-bass part with a cantilena supported by two harmonic structures: one for [b], another for [b']. Both are played as arpeggios by marimba, celesta, harp, and glockenspiel and share the same intervallic construction: [b'] is a transposition of [b] one semitone higher. Together, they create a neutral background suitable for the *impassibilité* technique, as in *Angels and Visitations*:

FIGURE 9: Two harmonic structures in [b] and [b']

Against the neutral accompaniment, the double bass plays an unbroken melodic line that rises to a high register in various figurations and reaches a climax on a suspended note G1 (m. 52). A number of sudden and dissonant outbursts from the brass punctuate this line, which is suspended on long notes during such interruptions: it is as if the brass wanted to interrupt and disturb the natural melodic process of the soloist. The solo line gradually decreases in energy and comes to a halt with a strong climax in the brass. This is a perfect example of the "disturbance" technique already used in *Angels and Visitations* (Ex. 26).

The brass interruptions share similar rhythmic structures and intervallic patterns based on minor and major seconds. Here Rautavaara once again uses the technique of mirror writing: the motif in the tuba is an inversion of that in the first and second trumpets. Inversions can also be found between third trumpet and trombone and between the first and second trombones (Ex. 27). These short chromatic motifs in the brass contrast the soloist's part in terms of melody, harmony, rhythm, dynamics, and texture.

Subsection [c] is similar to [b] and [b']: once again the brass ensemble interrupts the solo part. But there is one key difference: the harmonic background is no longer supplied by metallophones and harp. Furthermore, the "disturbances" provided by the brass not only interrupt and suspend the musical action of the soloist, as before, but also cut and stop its narration.

This leads to the third section B, which opens the long series of "disturbance" subsections (labeled [d], [a1], and [b]), in which the "disturbance motif" is developed. After this, the harmonic structure appears as a reminiscence of that from the introductory section, and the chorale theme also returns. Simultaneously, "motifs of disturbance" arise in the brass, making use of the symmetrical constructions introduced in section A. The remainder of the movement encompasses two components ([b] and [e]). In the foreground is the melodic line of the solo bass with material from the main theme played glissando in constant half-notes and in intervals of seconds; the

Analysis of Rautavaara's Instrumental Works about Angels 123

EXAMPLE 26: *Angel of Dusk*, mvt. I, mm. 12-49, solo part[31]

background consists of several short melodic strands in the strings, harp and celesta, based on the diatonic harmonic structure from [b], [b'], [b1] and on chromatic clusters. The strands in the strings are extinguished and finally cease near the end of the movement, leaving behind only a double stop in the solo part that leads into the middle movement.

---

[31] Vertical arrows mark moments of brass "disturbances."

EXAMPLE 27: The "disturbance motif," *Angel of Dusk*, m. 20[32]

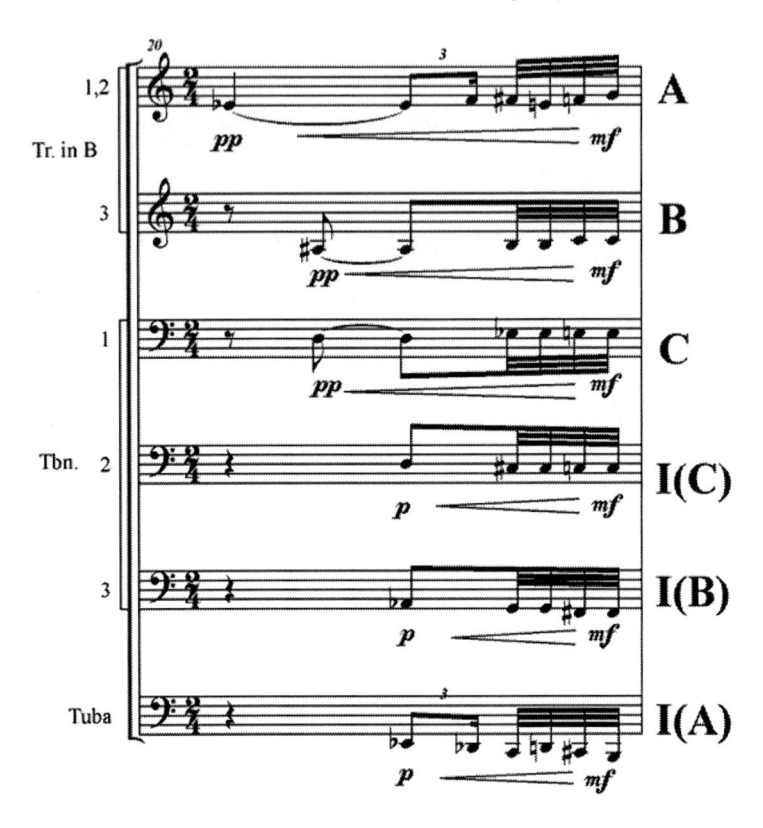

"His monologue"

The movement title "His Monologue" defines the nature of the music: it consists of a long cadenza for the soloist, which is only occasionally interrupted by the orchestra. Rautavaara acknowledges that the final shape of the central movement was influenced by Kosonen's remarks. The combination of Kosonen's suggestions and Rautavaara's experiments on the double bass gave rise to a range of new types of performance technique. Before analyzing the movement, it is necessary to explain these, given the frequent changes of articulation used in the cadenza.

---

[32] I(A), I(B), I(C) = inversion of motifs A, B, C.

Analysis of Rautavaara's Instrumental Works about Angels 125

EXAMPLE 28a: Extended double bass techniques in *Angel of Dusk* with the composer's explanations[33]

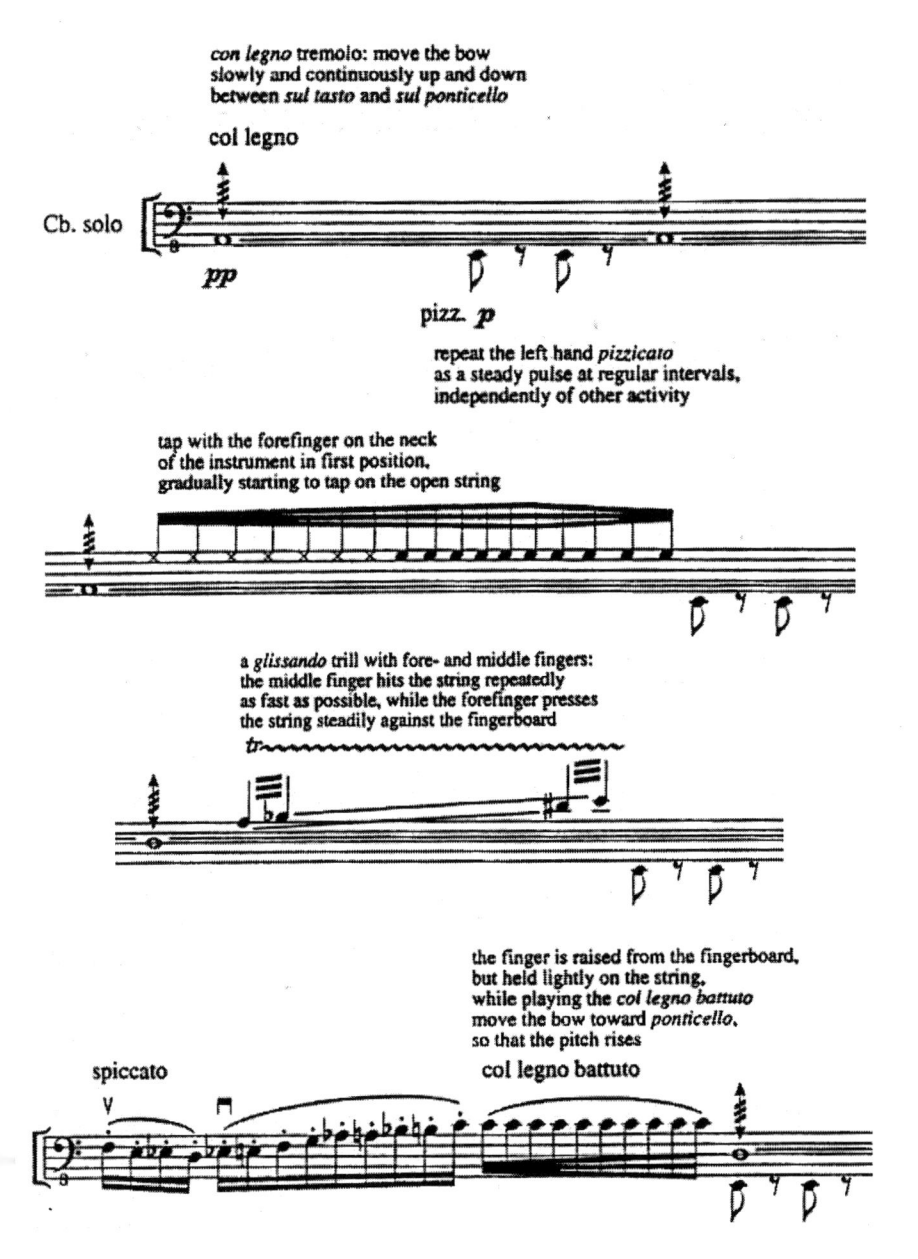

---

[33] The explanations are taken from the score (Helsinki: Warner/Chappell Music Finland Oy, 1980).

126 *Chapter 5*

EXAMPLE 28b: Extended double bass techniques in *Angel of Dusk* (cont.)

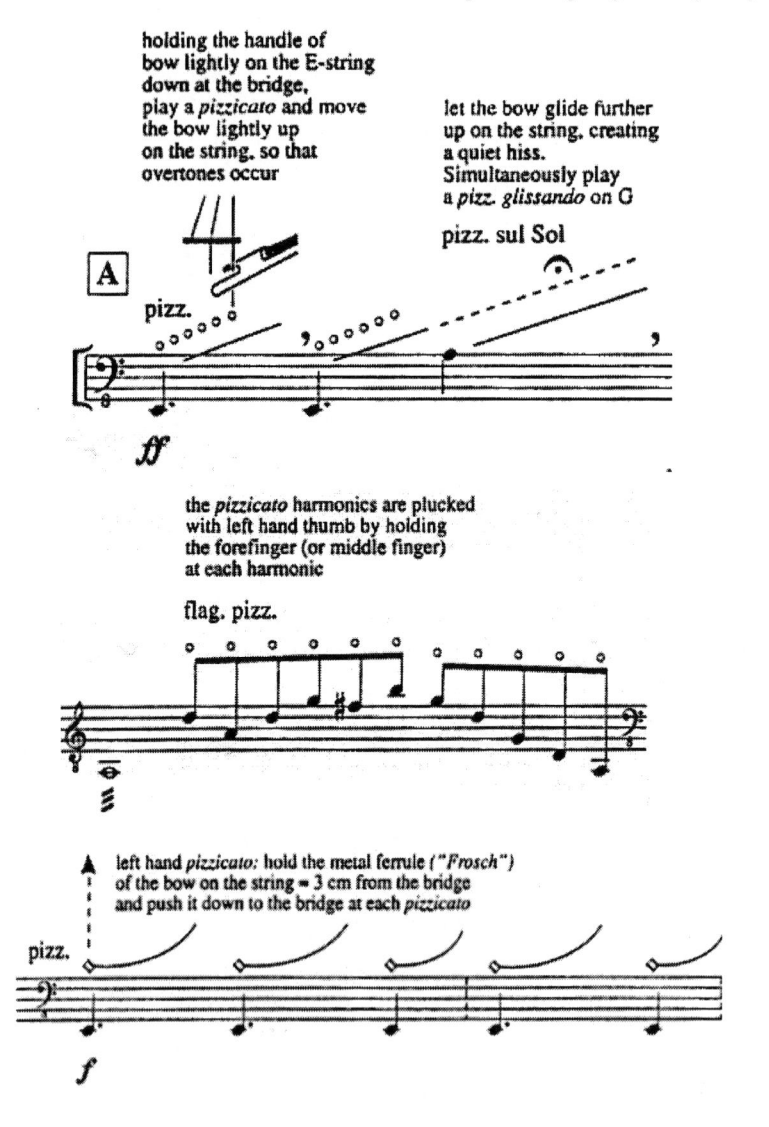

The many varied forms of articulation give the movement a wide range of color and expression, despite the fact that the orchestra barely participates.[34]

---

[34] Rautavaara describes the strong effect of the solo cadenza on listeners during the first performance: "All the listeners seemed to be immobilized, imprisoned by the tension." See Rautavaara, *Omakuva*, 300.

The cadenza is written entirely without bar lines; Rautavaara merely divides it with six rehearsal figures, marking sections as A, B, C, D, E, and F. (The section preceding A will be referred to as 0 here.) The first and last two sections are for soloist alone; in the three middle sections he adds some orchestral instruments (see the rectangle in Figure 10). There is symmetry also in the distribution of the motivic material (indicated by horizontal brackets).

FIGURE 10: Correspondences of motivic material and articulation techniques

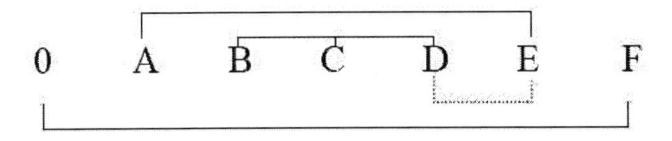

```
            ┌─────────────────┐
    0    A    B    C    D    E    F
                  └..............┘
    └─────────────────────────────┘
```

Section 0, which introduces many of the new techniques, focuses on single notes on three of the four open strings: E, A, and D. The dynamic level increases gradually from an opening *pianissimo* through to a closing *fortissimo* (with a Bartok *pizzicato*). This section is the most colorful and sonoristic of the movement, since it contains most of Rautavaara's new types of articulation. It is thus a good way to exhibit the timbral range of the double bass (and the performer's skill in realizing these).

Section A moves from the exploration of new sounds to dyads and a melodic line with figurations (developed later, at the beginning of movement III). Within this section, there are strongly contrasting rhythmic patterns and dynamic levels, coexisting with passages of slow and fast tempo. If section 0 focuses on raising the dynamic level from soft to loud, section A centers on bringing various registers into play: from low through mid-range back to low, then a leap to the highest register. This gives the performer the opportunity to display the melodic potential of his instrument.

In section B, the first and second violins create harmonic clusters that move by glissando. After the free tempi of sections 0 and A, sections B, C, and D introduce a constant pace (eighth-note = c. 80). The solo part is based on a three-measure structure, with shifting metric groups (8/8, 5/8, 6/8) and motoric rhythms.

As this description shows, the structure Rautavaara creates in this movement is determined beyond scoring and harmonic features by changing expressive emphasis. The result is a cadenza that progresses from a sonoristic section (0) to one that is melodically defined (A) and on to a string of rhythmically determined sections (from B onward.)

Section E can be considered a continuation of the last passage of section D as it shares the same rhythmic structures. Its closing theme (Ex. 29) is cast in the Phrygian mode and uses artificial harmonics. Its modal flavor and melodic structure suggest that it may be based on Finnish folk melodies or traditional Finnish Lutheran songs, although actual sources are unclear.[35] The use of harmonics makes the theme somehow unreal, mystic and eternal.

EXAMPLE 29: Soloist's theme, *Angel of Dusk*, mvt. II, section E

Section E brings together three different elements: irregular meters, motoric rhythmic structures, and a cantilena. This sequence of rhythmic and lyrical aspect seems intended to retrograde through the last two expressive elements mentioned above. It is followed by a passage that is similar to Section 0, which leads *attacca* into the concerto's third movement.

"His last appearance"

The musical form of the last movement in *Angel of Dusk* seems "compressed," due to the reshuffling of musical material from the previous movements. As in movement I, the third can be divided into five main sections, which the composer emphasizes with double barlines.

TABLE 6: Formal scheme, *Angel of Dusk*, mvt. III

Sections	A	B	C	D	E
Subsections	a a1 a2	b b1 b2	c c1 c2 c3 c4 c5 c6	d	e
Measures	1-30	31-48	49-169	170-199	200-233
Tempos	♪=100	♪=92	♪♪♪=138	♪♪♪=69	♩=60

Sections A and B are divided into three similar subsections: [a], [a1], and [a2]. In section A, the melodic line of the solo bass ascends from a low to a high register, as in the middle movement; the texture also thickens through the introduction of the higher string instruments in [a1] and [a2]. The solo part contains eleven pitches, lacking only the note B-flat; this note is given to the orchestral basses in [a], to the first violins in [a1], and the violas and cellos in [a2].

---

[35] The use of the theme thus corresponds to the main theme in Berg's Violin Concerto, in which he cites a Carinthian folk song and a Bach chorale. See Pople, 30-34.

FIGURE 11: Incomplete row from the double bass melody, *Angel of Dusk*, mvt. III, mm. 1-10

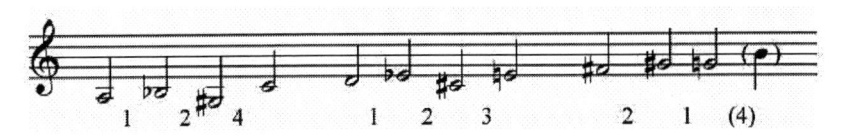

This incomplete twelve-tone row is divided into two groups of four notes and one group of three; the prevailing intervals are seconds and thirds. The first two groups each contain a minor and a major second as well as one of the thirds. These intervallic formulations can be found everywhere in the melodic lines and also in the harmonies. Sivuoja-Gunaratnam describes Rautavaara's use of the "row" in a non-serial way as a paradigm for motivic relationships.[36]

The soloist is accompanied in [a] by two tutti basses in *pizzicato* and a timpani roll, while brass players blow into their instruments without tone. Subsection [a1] introduces fourteen strands of short phrases played by divided strings; as in movement I, these are always in motion while the underlying harmony remains constant. The cellos "try" ineffectively to imitate the melodic lines of the soloist.

The stabilization of the tonal center on E initiates section B. It is also designed in three parts, but here the contrast between subsections is almost imperceptible due to their similar harmonic content. In each subsection there are three independent layers: the soloist's melodic line, arabesques in the clarinets, and chords played by the strings. The soloist's melodic line, which is repeated three times with little modification, is a combination of passages from movement I with the harmonic theme of the second. The clarinet arabesques move in parallel thirds and seconds, based on a pitch collection that can be regarded as Messiaen's mode 2^1 without the third and seventh steps.

---

[36] Sivuoja-Gunaratnam cites Rautavaara: "In certain cases the function of the series was to act as a motivic automaton that creates coherence at the grass-roots level, at the lowest fractal level, because everything is derived from the series and the intervallic formations are everywhere in the piece, in the melodies and harmonies, in the vertical and horizontal dimensions. They create a network of intervallic figures; this is a kind of motivic technique on the small scale. Why would I call it an automaton? It is because you do not need to pay any attention to it; you are free to consider other things, viz. larger formal entities and the global form." Sivuoja-Gunaratnam, *Narrating with Twelve Tones*, 37.

FIGURE 12: Messiaen's mode 2^1 without its third and seventh steps

Section B forms a sort of interlude before C, which is the movement principal section. Its main characteristic is the constant meter: an eighth-note pulse in three-measure phrases. The result is a juxtaposition of irregular and regular meters, emphasizing the overriding role of rhythm in this section:

FIGURE 13: Juxtaposition of irregular and regular meters in section C

8 (3+3+2)   5 (3+2)   6 (3+3)
8   8   8

The metric groups are arranged symmetrically, creating a palindrome:

FIGURE 14: A palindrome of metric groups in section C

→   3 + 3 + 2 + 3 + 2 + 3 + 3   ←

The consequences of such symmetrical rhythms are profound, since Rautavaara also reverses melodic lines and treats them in a similar manner. The best example of such symmetry is the solo bass part in [c] and [c1]. Every group of three or two notes from [c] (read from beginning to end) corresponds with groups from [c1] (read from end to beginning). In Examples 30 and 31, I have labeled the different groups with Greek letters [α], [β], [γ], [δ], [ε], and [ζ] to demonstrate how the solo bass line in section [c1] is a retrograde of groups from [c].

The symmetry is also visible in [c2], in which the orchestra joins the soloist. Outbursts from the brass once again use symmetrical harmony, joined by sonoristic effects from the strings in [c3]. The next passage reintroduces the lyrical theme from section E into the solo part. From m. 114

EXAMPLE 30: Part of [c], *Angel of Dusk*, mvt. III, mm. 55-60

[α   β   γ   δ   ε   ζ   β

  α   β   ε   δ   ε   ζ   ]

Analysis of Rautavaara's Instrumental Works about Angels   131

EXAMPLE 31: Part of [c1], *Angel of Dusk*, mvt. III, mm. 67-72

[ζ ε δ ε β α

β ζ ε δ γ β α]

to the end of section C, Rautavaara builds up a strong climax, making use once more of the "disturbance" technique in [c4], [c5], and [c6]. The perpetual motion of eighth-notes in the solo bass part continues here through the brass interruptions and sustains the musical action of the soloist. (The similarity of [c6] with movement I is quite obvious, if one compares Ex. 32 with Ex. 26.)

EXAMPLE 32: *Angel of Dusk*, mvt. III, mm.137-159, soloist's line[37]

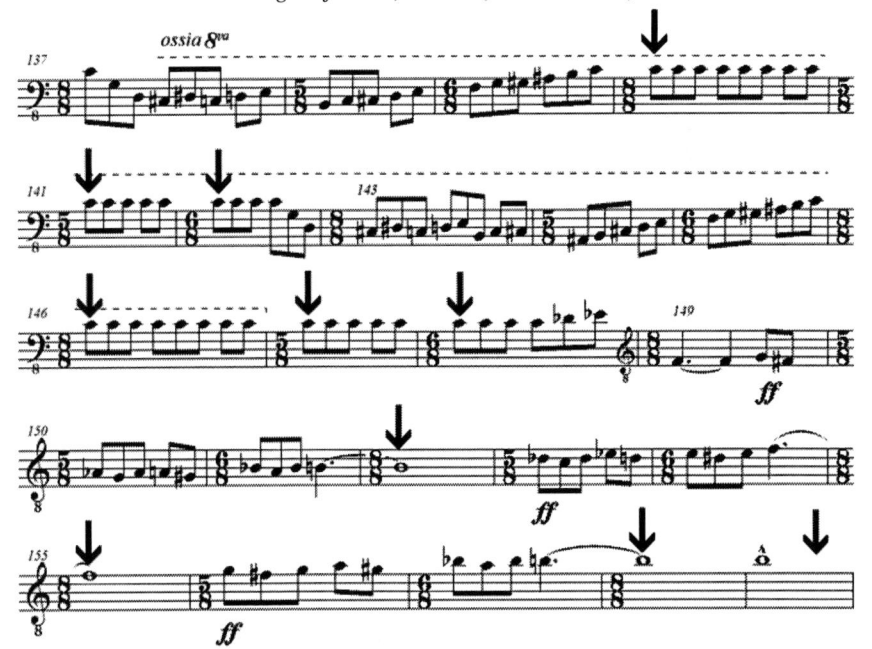

---

[37] Vertical arrows mark "disturbance" motifs.

The differences between these two examples are due to the additional instruments in the second one, where Rautavaara thickens the texture with woodwind and strings. The other elements are comparable, particularly in the use of mirror harmony in moments of "disturbance." This time, the whole orchestra participates in the presentation of the "disturbance" motifs and becomes an opponent to the soloist, trying to interrupt its appearance and to deny it the chance to participate in the musical action.

Section D is a reminiscence of the first subsection of movement II. The soloist plays *pizzicato*; strings join in with several strands. The symmetrical structure, built from twenty short phrases, is texturally as dense as at the beginning of concerto. It flows in waves from the low to the high registers; the pitch material is based on Messiaen's mode 6^4.

Near the end of the movement, the string lines ascend, and after a short crescendo with interruptions from the brass, the action ceases. At the same time, the soloist plays a *glissando* in a high register that culminates on high G. The tempo suddenly changes to a moderate pace of one quarter-note = 60 (that is, walking pace). The harmonic structure of section E is the sum of three layers of chords: C major and C-sharp minor in the first layer, E major and F minor in the second, and A-flat major and A minor in the third. Altogether, these create another symmetrical scale: Messiaen's mode 3^2 (Fig. 15 and Ex. 33).

FIGURE 15: Intervallic structure of mode 3^2

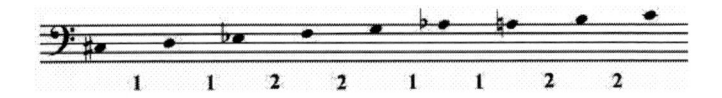

Celesta, vibraphone, harp, and subsequently the strings, woodwinds, and brass play ascending chords. The constant quarter-note pulse of these superimposed chords creates an effect of "musical illumination." This "musical landscape" serves as a background for the lyrical cantilena of the double bass, which moves in the opposite direction. In the second part of his commentary on the work, Rautavaara described this surprising coda as a *catharsis*. It is a purification of the musical material, which leads to a return of the opening G-major chord of the concerto. The musical action is "born with this chord" and is finally "dead on it." The soloist's final note dissolves into a G-major chord with celesta and double basses, perhaps an illustration of Rautavaara's famous metaphor, the "oceanic feeling."

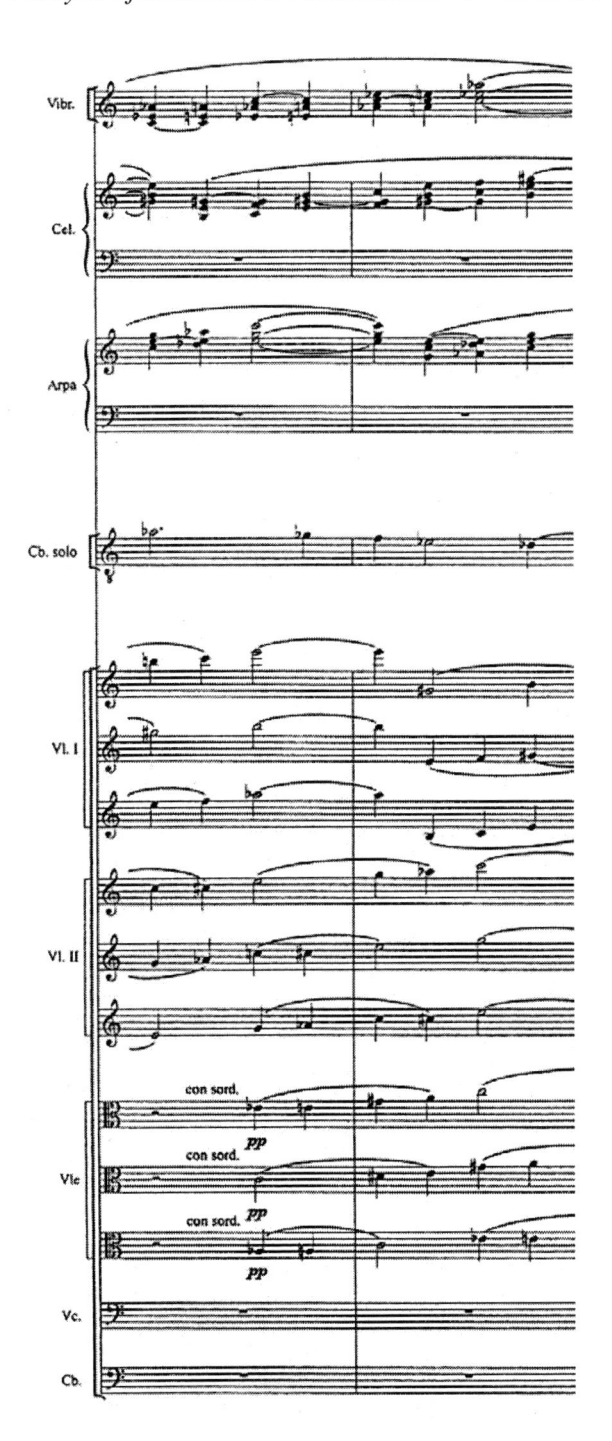

EXAMPLE 33:
Angel of Dusk,
mvt. III,
mm. 208-209,
metallophones, harp,
soloist, strings

Conclusion

In *Angel of Dusk,* Rautavaara realizes his idea of a "dramatic" concerto, a conflict between soloist and orchestra. Although the form of the composition is that of a traditional three-movement concerto, it nevertheless has nothing in common with the classical and romantic idea of a concerto: firstly, because movement II is a long and extremely complex solo cadenza; and secondly, because after the short orchestral introduction, the soloist plays continually in all of the movements and there is thus no "concertizing" alternation. The subsections share similar motivic materials and are closely connected. The macro-form is symmetrical: the introduction corresponds to the coda, and the subsections of the middle movement are symmetrical. There is also symmetry on the micro-scale, in the technique of mirror writing in both melodies and harmonies, and in palindromic melodies and rhythms. (In Table 7, "2^1" etc. refers to Messiaen's modes while "diat." and "free" indicate other scales).

FIGURE 16: Messiaen's modes in Rautavaara's *Angel of Dusk*

Messiaen's mode 2^1, used in the introduction to movement I

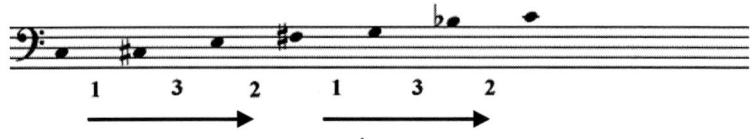

Excerpt from Messiaen's mode 2^1, used in movement III, section B

Messiaen's mode 6^4, used in movement III, section D

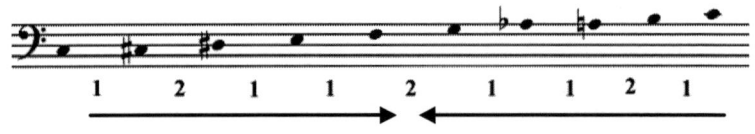

Messiaen's mode 3^2, from third movement, section E

Analysis of Rautavaara's Instrumental Works about Angels 135

TABLE 7: Structural overview in the three-movement *Angel of Dusk*

Movements	I			II						III				
Sections	int.	A	B	0	A	B	C	D	E	F	A	B	C	D	E
Mode/scale	2^1	diat.	2^1 diat.				free				free	2^1	free	6^4	3^2

As the table shows, Rautavaara chooses only three of Messiaen's seven modes. All of them are exclusively built from semitones and whole tones. (A larger interval results only when he creates an excerpt of one of the modes and uses it as something like his own addition to Messiaen's list.) The altogether four modes create a structure spanning the entire work (see Fig. 16 above).

Berg's Violin Concerto undoubtedly influenced Rautavaara's Double Bass Concerto. *Angel of Dusk* is thus a kind of requiem with a double dedication to Olga and Serge Koussevitzky, just as Berg's is a dedication to two Mutzis. In fact, the title *Angel of Dusk* and the three subtitles of its movements, "His First Appearance," "His Monologue," and "His Last Appearance," refer to Serge Koussevitzky and his double bass. Just as the solo violin in Berg's concerto can be said to portray Mutzi as an angel, the title *Angel of Dusk* depicts Serge Koussevitzky through the solo bass. Unlike Berg, Rautavaara did not use musical quotations, but rather composed a melodic line that evokes diatonic and modal folk or religious songs in the second and third movements. Although *Angel of Dusk* consists of three movements rather than the two of Berg's composition, its serene and calm conclusion, with the soloist in the upper register, is reminiscent of the close of Berg's Violin Concerto. In the second movement, a solo cadenza, there is also a musical symbol corresponding to the soul of the double bass by virtue of notes on open strings, as at the beginning of Berg's work.

Monologue with Angels

In the early 1980s Rautavaara was planning his next work referring to angels: a symphonic composition that would complete his Angel Trilogy. He had a working title—*Monologue with Angels*—but he had no idea how to transform this inspiring title into music. He discusses this question in his autobiography:

> I might here as well confess that the Fifth symphony was supposed to be named after Angels too, before it spoke to me its intentions —which were that it wanted to remain only a symphony. I was planning a work to be titled "Monologue with Angels"—just like one can have, for example, a painting about dogs that is called "Portrait WITH a Dog." Then, one could ask the question, is at all possible to have a monologue "WITH" someone? Would that still be a monologue in any meaningful sense of the word? Perhaps an angel would be, to a sufficient degree, an internal being, so as to constitute an exception? Etc, etc. (Perhaps, too, the tendency towards angelography had its origins in the grammar lessons of my school days, where one spoke about this mysterious "inside being." The composition project was never, in any case, taken up. Maybe Playgrounds was similar enough; perhaps I had outgrown the world of William Blake.[38]

Aho has treated this working title as a pre-title of the Fifth Symphony (1985-86)—a title that the composer subsequently withdrew[39]– although the musical language and style of this symphony, which initiated his synthetic serial period, is completely different from that of his previous compositions concerning angels. At the same time, its character is not dramatic but rather epic, a point Rautavaara emphasizes in his program note to the symphony. In fact there are no real connections between *Monologue with Angels* and the Fifth Symphony. The title *Monologue with Angels* is essential with regard to the interplay between angelic titles and music, which will be discussed in Chapter 7. Its case is similar to that of Sibelius's Eighth Symphony, where the name remains "[...] as the only trace of the work of art that has materially disappeared,"[40] or the work that was never actually written but existed only in the composer's mind.

---

[38] "Tunnustettakoon tässä, että myös viidennen sinfonian piti olla 'enkeliniminen,' ennen kuin se kertoi haluavansa pysyä vain ja juuri sinfoniana. Suunnittelin teosta, joka olisi 'Monologue with Angels,' siis niin kuin taulu saattaa olla 'Portrait with a dog – muotokuva jossa on koira.' Samalla kun voisi pohtia, onko mahdollista harrastaa yksinpuhelua jonkun 'kanssa'; olisiko se enää yksin-puhelu, vai näyttäisikö Enkeli kyllin sisäiseltä oliolta muodostaakseen poikkeuksen, jossa se kuitenkin olisi, ja niin edespäin. (Kenties taipumus angelografiaan alkoikin noilla kansakoulun kielioppitunneilla, joilla esiintyi salaperäinen 'sisäolento'). Puheenaolevaa sävellystä ei siis koskaan tehty. Ehkä *Playgrounds* oli kylliksi sitä lajia, ehkä olin kasvanut William Blaken maailmasta ulos." See Rautavaara, *Omakuva*, 327. I am deeply indebted to Otto Lehto, who kindly translated this passage from Finnish into English.

[39] See Aho, *Einojuhani Rautavaara as Symphonist*, 98.

[40] Sivuoja-Gunaratnam, *Narrating with Twelve Tones*, 205.

The Seventh Symphony *Angel of Light* (Angel Trilogy, Part III)

The most famous of Rautavaara's compositions was commissioned by the Bloomington Symphony Orchestra for its 25th anniversary, and premiered by that ensemble in 1995. Together with *Cantus arcticus* (1978), the symphony became Rautavaara's most successful work. Ondine's recording of it received two international awards, the Cannes Classical Award (1996) and the ABC Classica FM Award (1997). As a result of this success, Rautavaara became the most prominent Finnish composer after Sibelius.

When the American conductor David Pickett commissioned a composition for the Bloomington Orchestra, he expected a short work, but Rautavaara claimed that he was not in a mood for that, preferring instead to write a symphony.[41] The orchestra accepted his suggestion, and the composer wrote a first version that was revised after its initial performance. The first version was called the "Bloomington" Symphony in honor of the work's commissioners, and was premiered under this title in Bloomington on April 23, 1995. Ultimately Rautavaara changed the title to *Angel of Light*, and it replaced the Fifth Symphony in the Angel Trilogy. When it was announced that the symphony was going to be recorded, the composer and Kiilunen, the managing director and founder of Ondine, discussed the title.[42]

> Originally composing my seventh symphony I had in mind an angelic title, but I dropped it because of the growing popularity of angels—appearing in every second shop window. So in the first performance in Bloomington and then in Helsinki the work was called *Bloomington Symphony*. However, when Ondine was going to record it, I discussed the title with Reijo Kiilunen and he said he absolutely wanted the title *Angel of Light*.[43]

Kiilunen felt that the title *Angel of Light* was suitable for promoting Rautavaara and his music abroad and would therefore be used as the record title. To find an attractive cover, he announced a competition asking for a painting of an angel. This was won by Pekka Hepoluta, whose painting was also printed on the posters and postcards that accompanied the promotion of the recording.[44]

Angel of Light differs from Rautavaara's others compositions about angels in that it has fewer musical elements and shares few techniques with the other works in the series. The work reflects the dialectic synthesis of his

---

[41] See Anderson: 71.

[42] Personal communication, 11 July 2007.

[43] Personal communication, 11 July 2007.

[44] See Finch: 24.

cycle of symphonies. "*Angel of Light* is a brighter work than its precursors; calm, assured, even serene."[45] The twelve-tone technique in particular sets the musical material apart.[46] In the approach adopted here, where the symphony is regarded not only as a coherent, independent work, but also as the final component in the Angel Trilogy and the pinnacle of Rautavaara's angelic series, pitch-class theory is only one aspect of an analysis, and not the most important, as it does not help to link all the compositions in the series together. Seeing the trilogy as a whole allows us to stress the intertextuality of the work, that is, the use of musical materials from previous compositions and techniques from other works depicting angelic beings.

Like Classical and Romantic symphonies, *Angel of Light* is in four movements, the second of which is a *scherzo* and the third a slow movement. Rautavaara's traditional approach to the symphony as a genre can be observed also in his earlier Third Symphony and in his late Eighth Symphony. None of these symphonies is written according to strict dodecaphonic principles. The composer's dodecaphonic style is based on the notion that the twelve-tone structures of a composition should be hidden.[47] Rautavaara demonstrates this approach in his second serial period, when he composes by drawing on Berg's experiences and without observing the limitations set by Schoenberg regarding the use of repetitions, thirds, and chords in rows.[48] Remaining free of such bans allowed the composer to continue writing in a kind of Romantic style even in the 1990s; *Angel of Light* is the most compelling example of these tendencies and musical interests. The work is full of intertextual references: every movement is based on musical materials that were written around the time of the Symphony's composition but in other contexts. Hence *Angel of Light* can be understood as the culmination of a group of minor works such as the choral works *Die erste Elegie* and "Fragmentos de Agonía" from *Canción de nuestro tiempo* (1993) as well as the instrumental works Canto IV (1992) and *Notturno* (1993) for violin and piano (1993).[49] Rautavaara chose these compositions because they share motivic relations and were written in his version of the twelve-tone

---

[45] Einojuhani Rautavaara, commentary on the Seventh Symphony *Angel of Light,* in the booklet accompanying the recording Ondine 869-2 (1996).

[46] Tiikkaja has examined the symphony and the relationship between its rows in the light of pitch-class theory. See Tiikkaja, "Einojuhani Rautavaaran."

[47] The idea is reminiscent of the mystical technique of writing isorhythmic motets during the Ars Nova.

[48] In Schoenberg's music, the dodecaphonic structure is far more apparent in the scores than in comparable works by Rautavaara.

[49] See Tiikkaja, "Einojuhani Rautavaara – Postmodern Intertextualist": 45; Sivuoja-Gunaratnam, "Narcissus Musicus": 12-13.

Analysis of Rautavaara's Instrumental Works about Angels 139

technique. As mentioned earlier, the main row of the symphony derives from the *Die erste Elegie*. In his commentary on the choral work, Rautavaara links for the first time his various compositions referring to angels and emphasizes the role of angels on an "extramusical level."[50] Beyond the row, *Die erste Elegie* and "Fragmentos de Agonía" provide also the harmonic foundation of the symphony's first movement. The popular third movement is a transcription of the *Notturno* for violin and piano, and the finale, an orchestration of the second half of Canto IV for strings.

Rautavaara used five twelve-tone rows as the basic musical material of the symphony, some of them only in one movement, some across the whole work.[51]

FIGURE 17: Row I in *Angel of Light*

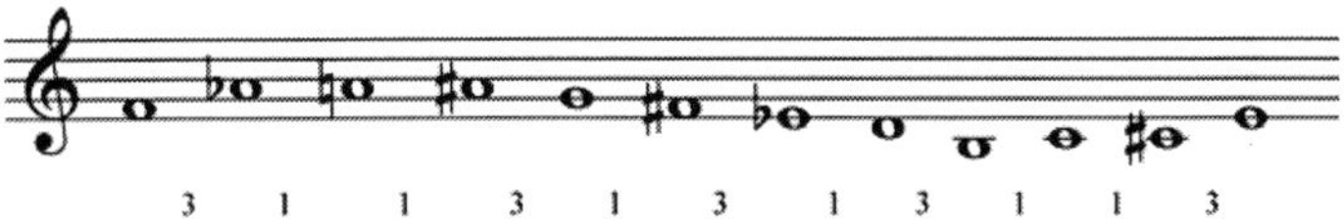

FIGURE 18: Row II

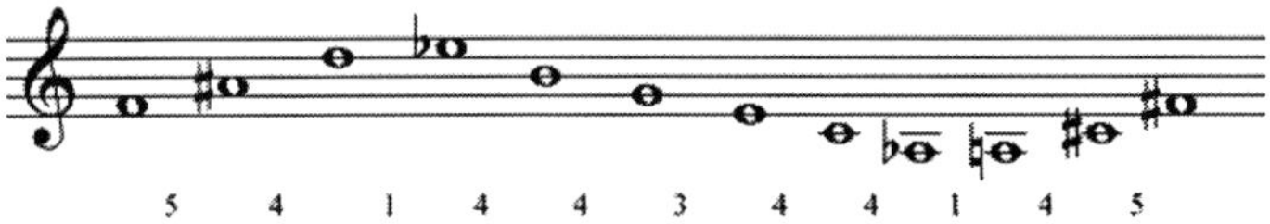

FIGURE 19: Row III

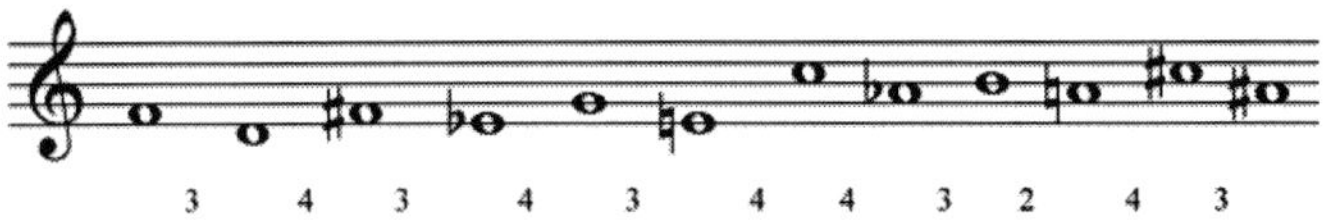

FIGURE 20: Row IV

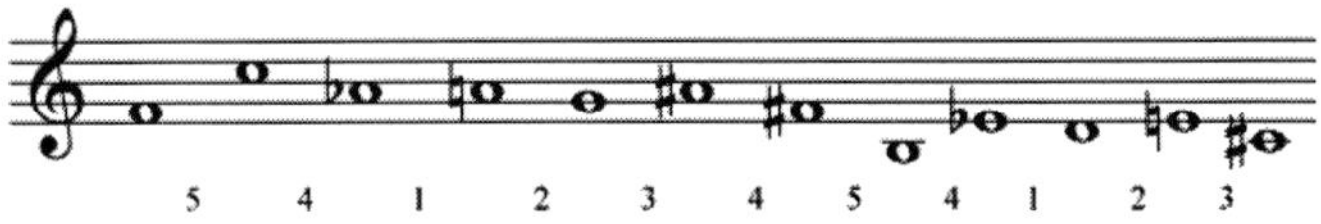

FIGURE 21: Row V

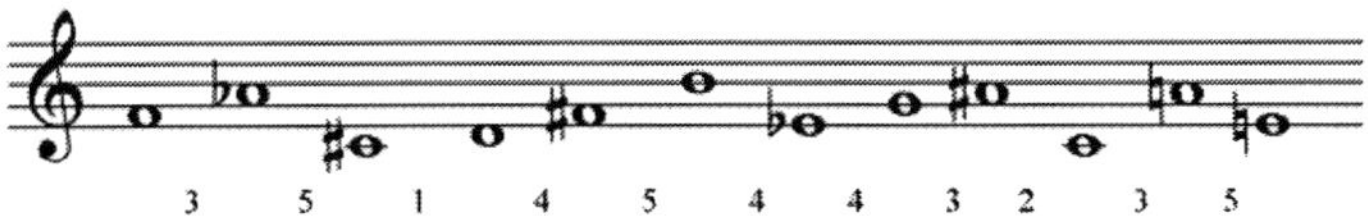

---

[50] Tiikkaja, " Einojuhani Rautavaara – Postmodern Intertextualist": 54.

[51] The five rows were first discussed in Tiikkaja, "Einojuhani Rautavaaran," 16-28.

140 Chapter 5

On the advice from Vladimir Vogel, his teacher in Ascona, Rautavaara ultimately created an additional row, in which he combines row I, the chromatic scale, and the circle of fifths.[52]

FIGURE 22: Row I

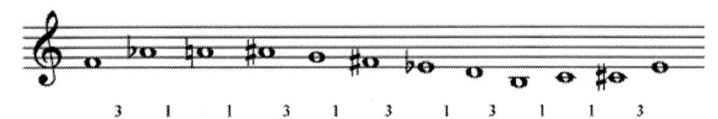

FIGURE 23: The chromatic scale combined with the circle of fifths used as an auxiliary row

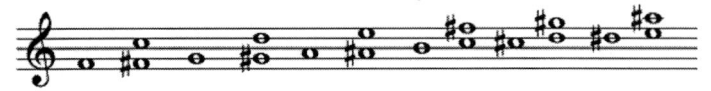

FIGURE 24: Row VI

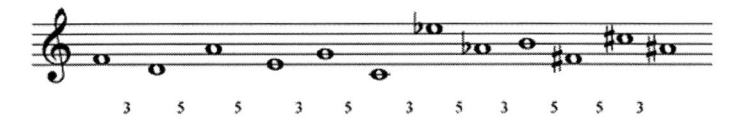

The construction of row VI is the same as that of the main row from *Die erste Elegie*: it arises from four triads and can be divided into two halves, in which the second is a retrograde inversion of the first at the interval of a tritone (Fig. 25). The descending minor and major chords influence the melodic and harmonic structure and give *Angel of Light* its special flavor.[53] The chords, generated from the transformation of one chord into another within the row, play an essential role in each movement and support modulations from one transposition of row VI to the next.

FIGURE 25: The row from *Die erste Elegie* as used in *Angel of Light*

d   C   g#   F#

d   C   c G# g# B   F#

---

[52] For Figures 22-24, see Sivuoja-Gunaratnam, *Narrating with Twelve Tones*, 35-36.

[53] Rautavaara, personal communication, 26 November 2008.

Analysis of Rautavaara's Instrumental Works about Angels 141

Row VI is in some ways the musical backbone of the symphony, since the other rows are used more sparingly and only in opposition to it. Of course, Rautavaara did not use only the prime form of a row [$P_{VI}0$], but very often linked it with its transpositions and also used it vertically as four chords. Other rows are also used in a variety of transpositions; besides row V, row II in particular is important. Its construction is similar to the theme of the symphony; Rautavaara called this the "Bloomington" theme. It is built on nine notes in an overall descent. In Germanic letter-naming, these notes spell B-G-Es-H-C-H-E-Es-A; Rautavaara derived them from (B)LOOMIN(G)TON (S)YMP(H)ONY OR(C)(H)(E)(S)TR(A). According to Tiikkaja, the first five thematic notes in particular have an intervallic structure that is reminiscent of row II.[54]

FIGURE 26: The "Bloomington" theme and its motivic correspondence to row II

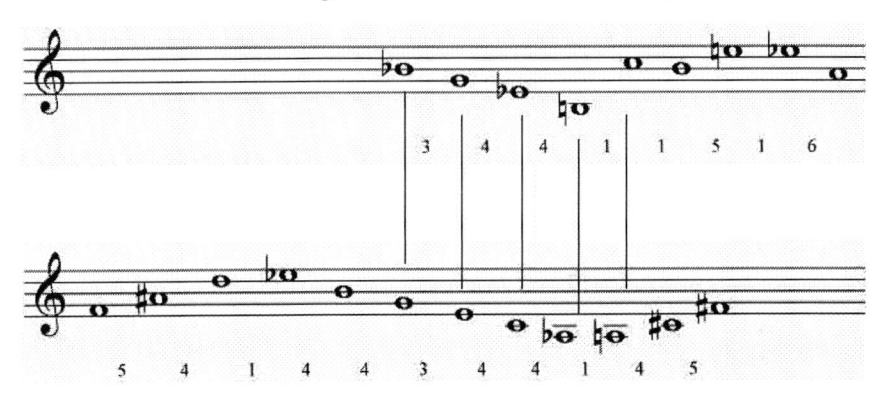

Like row VI, the "Bloomington" theme serves to establish coherence between the four movements of the symphony, although it fulfills different roles in each. Apart from its thematic role, it helps in the development of motifs (particularly in movement II), creates climaxes, and builds both the beginning of the symphony and its finale. In addition to six different rows and one theme, Rautavaara frequently used motifs built on Messiaen's modes. In *Angel of Light* the modes are needed to create opalescent, dense, and movable harmonic fields that become the harmonic foundation for the development of the "Bloomington" theme. At the same time, they function in transitional passages to support modulations between different rows. The most frequently used modes are mode 3^2 and mode 6^4, described above in the analysis of *Angel of Dusk*. As with the rows, the modes are used at a variety of different transposition levels.

---

[54] Tiikkaja, "Einojuhani Rautavaaran," 55.

TABLE 8: Formal scheme of *Angel of Light*

Movements	I						
Sections	A			A1			B
Subsections	a	x	b	a1	x1	b1	
Measures	1-92	93-98	99-144	145-157	158-163	164-186	187-200
Rows (I-VI) and modes	VI	3	I, VI	VI	3	VI	6

Movements	II				
Sections	A	B	C	D	E
Subsections					
Measures	1-31	32-59	60-109	110-130	131-157
Rows (I-VI) and modes	VI, II	VI	VI, III	II	6

Movements	III				
Sections	A		B	A1	
Subsections	a	a1		a2	a3
Measures	1-19	20-50	51-64	65-84	85-91
Rows (I-VI) and modes	VI		VI, II, 6	VI	

Movements	IV					
Sections	int.	A	B	C	B1	coda
Subsections						
Measures	1-9	9-54	55-74	75-95	96-108	109-121
Rows (I-VI) and modes	II	V, 6	V	V	V, 6	6

Movement I

Movement I can be divided into three sections: A, A1, and B. Sections A and A1 each encompass two substantial subsections, here labeled [a] and [b], which are connected a short linking passage presenting the "Bloomington" theme [c]. Subsections [a], [a1], [b1] are based on row VI, while subsection [b] uses row I in various transpositions. The linking passages ([x] and [x1]) are built from Messiaen's mode 3^2 rather than from rows.

Analysis of Rautavaara's Instrumental Works about Angels 143

The beginning of the work reveals the essential role played by row VI and the "Bloomington" theme. Up until the end of [a], the harmonic material is based on four different transpositions of row VI, beginning from the prime form of the row: $P_{VI}0$, $P_{VI}9$, $P_{VI}4$, $P_{VI}11$, $P_{VI}2$.[55] Descending chords that emerge from the transitions between the chords of row VI create harmonic material over which the melodic lines can flow (Fig. 27). The analogous subsection [a1] and [b1] from section A1, though shorter, are based on the same harmonic structures.

FIGURE 27: *Angel of Light*, harmonic and melodic foundation of mvt. I, mm. 1-92

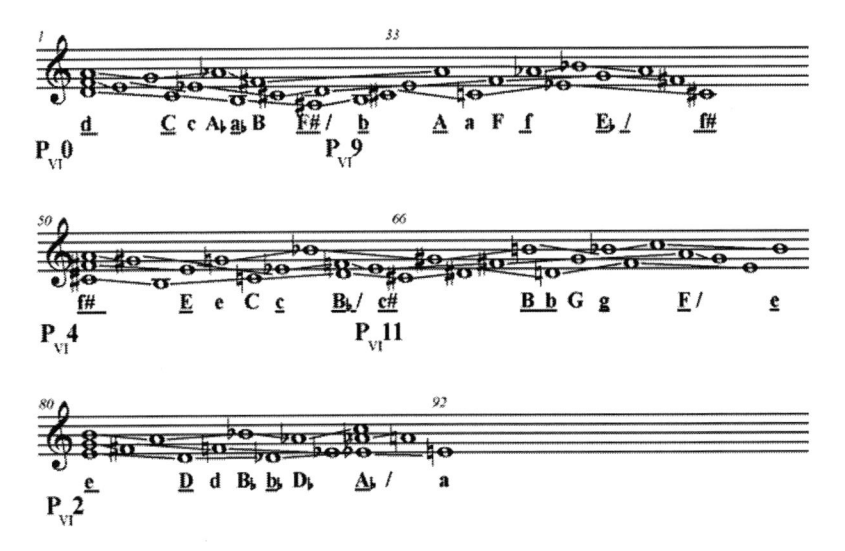

The "Bloomington" theme appears first in thirds in the glockenspiel and vibraphone. It is intentionally hidden by the composer, for it is divided into four motifs that are separated by breaks and tinged by dissonant minor seconds or major sevenths.[56] This treatment of the theme is not limited to this movement; it occurs again over the course of the symphony, always in conjunction with metallophones and harp.[57] Over chords in the strings that are derived from the motion between the chords of row VI and its transpositions, the short phrases of the main theme in the metallophones (marked by

---

[55] The subscript Roman numeral identifies the row employed here, the Arabic number specifies the transposition.

[56] See mm. 4-6, 8-9, 21-22, 23; shown below in Ex. 34.

[57] See, [a] (mm. 27-28, 30-32, 37-38, 42-43, 52-54, 62-63), [a1] (mm. 155-156), and coda (mm. 190-191, 193-194).

bold barlines in the following example) are like sudden flashes of meteors against the background of a night sky.

EXAMPLE 34: "Bloomington" theme, *Angel of Light*, mvt. I, mm. 4-6, 8-9

The "Bloomington" theme finally resounds in all its splendor, in parallel thirds, in the link [x], where it is first played by four horns, then by woodwinds with the third trumpet, and finally by four trumpets with the first trombone. The harmonic background consists of two layers: the first with rapid motifs in sextuplets based on mode 3^2 in the violins and violas, the second with an ascending progression of major chords in the lower strings.

In [b], which is based on different transpositions of rows I and VI,[58] the composer focuses on dialogues between single instruments, in particular between a horn, two flutes in thirds, and an oboe. As an instrumental background, a string quintet also participates in dialogues, playing motifs in a thick polyphonic texture.

Section A1 is shorter than section A and draws on different variations of motifs derived from the "Bloomington" theme. The similarities of these motifs to the theme are due to the use of augmented triads (Ex. 35). The link [x1] is built in a similar way to the previous one and is also based on mode 3^2. Finally, [b1] is polyphonic, with dialogues between single instruments as in subsection [b].

Section B provides important musical material that will be used again in movement IV. It consists of a progression of minor and major chords starting from C-sharp minor and ending with G minor. It is reminiscent of the quasi-religious chorale topic so typical of the composer's style. The opening motif of the "Bloomington" theme in the metallophones and harp is twice interpolated into the chord progression, thus referring back to the beginning of the symphony. The theme also returns in the last five measures, in divided first violins over a stable G minor chord. This chord gradually rises in the harp and the cellos, and then in the violas and second violins, eventually reaching a high register that gives the effect of brightness and anticipates the ending of the symphony (Ex. 36).

---

[58] Row I appears as P_I0, P_I6, P_I2, P_I1, P_I4, and P_I5; row VI as $P_{VI}2$, $P_{VI}9$, $P_{VI}6$, $P_{VI}3$, $P_{VI}10$, and $P_{VI}5$.

Analysis of Rautavaara's Instrumental Works about Angels   145

EXAMPLE 35: *Angel of Light*, mvt. I, m. 150

EXAMPLE 36: *Angel of Light*, mvt. I, mm. 198-200, harp and strings

Movement II

If movement I can be interpreted in traditional terms as a sonata form without a development section, then movement II with its fast tempo (*Molto allegro*), perpetual motion, and short ironic motifs is reminiscent of a scherzo written in Dmitri Shostakovich's style.[59] While traditional scherzos tend to be composed in ternary form (ABA), Rautavaara opted for a structure based on five non-recurring sections (A, B, C, D, and E)[60] that are not further subdivided. The most characteristic feature of the movement is a perpetual change of texture and use of variation technique.[61]

At a first glance, section A seems to have a harmonic structure that is completely different from movement I. But closer examination reveals that it is equally based on $P_{VI}9$ and uses the same descending chords emerging from the transition between row chords (Fig. 28). There is also a similar linking passage (mm. 20-32) with the "Bloomington" theme and a harmonic background based on mode 6^4, providing further correspondences with movement I.

FIGURE 28: Descending chords derived from $P_{VI}9$, *Angel of Light*, mvt. II, mm. 1-11

The most distinctive element of movement II is the use of short motifs played by various instruments in pairs, a minor second apart. At the same time, the use of two trumpets in minor seconds on every quarter-note of these motifs gives them an ironic character and thus creates the scherzo atmosphere. This mood is further enhanced by the woodwind instruments, whose pairing—two clarinets against two oboes—is reminiscent of the parodistic orchestration in Stravinsky's ballet *Petrouchka* (1911).

The woodwind presentation of the theme is joined first by the cellos, then by both violins. This leads to the movement's first climax with motifs based on mode 6^4. Rautavaara employs here a wide range of sonoristic

---

[59] Similar scherzi can be found in Rautavaara's Third and Eighth Symphonies.

[60] Tiikkaja provides a different analysis of this movement, dividing it into six sections and placing the sectional divisions in different measures. See Tiikkaja, "Einojuhani Rautavaaran," 65.

[61] Rautavaara himself discusses these; see his commentary on the Seventh Symphony, in the booklet accompanying the recording Ondine 869-2 (1996).

effects, such as flutter-tonguing in the woodwinds and brass, *glissandi* on the xylophone, and *con sordini* for the trombones. This brings about a drastic change: from the *legato* articulation of the strings and the long, resonant metallophone sounds in movement I to the dry, short *staccato* emphasized by wooden sounds of the xylophone, sharp beats of the snare drum, and *pizzicato* of violas, cellos and basses in movement II. The four measures before the linking passage are based on a harmonic ground that consists of two chords, E major and B-flat major, which play a fundamental role in the movement's final section.

The following passage can be treated both as a closure of section A and as a kind of transition from section A to section B. Here, the composer once again uses the "Bloomington" theme, although not all of this transitional passage is based on mode 6^4. Most of its material derives from row II and its various transpositions, as can be seen in the opening melodic line in the flutes.

EXAMPLE 37: Using different transpositions of row II (II^3), *Angel of Light*, mvt. II, mm. 20-23

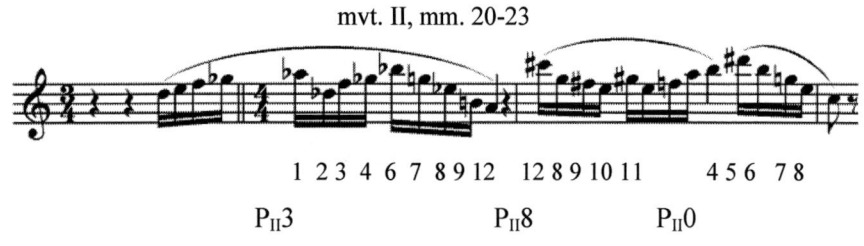

1 2 3 4 6 7 8 9 12   12 8 9 10 11   4 5 6 7 8

$P_{II}3$ $P_{II}8$ $P_{II}0$

Before the theme is heard in its majestic version played by brass, Rautavaara gives a short version to the xylophone. The theme then appears in the solo horn over a string accompaniment based on mode 6^4; the texture becomes much smoother, leading to section B.

Section B is based on row VI and its transpositions, in the same form as it appeared in at the beginning of the symphony and with similar arpeggio motifs in the violas (see movement I, mm. 38-92). This section can be considered as a theme that is subjected to variation in the two sections that follow. The variations provide the first important synthesis of materials in the symphony: row VI is simultaneously linked with both row II and the "Bloomington" theme. At times it is difficult to distinguish the additional rows that are used at different transposition levels in various parts; at times these overlap. Generally, the harmonic material is based on row VI, while the melodic lines are based on material deriving from row II and mode 6.

Section C spawns two variations, C1 and C2, which the composer separates by a double bar line in the score, an increase in tempo, and a change of time signature from 4/4 to 4/8). Another important distinction between the variations is the transformation of the sixteenth-note motifs from binary to ternary rhythms, apparent in the replacement of a musical cell of four sixteenth-notes with triplet sixteenth-notes. Every motif is based on diatonic material derived from tetrachords or on chords drawn from major or minor scales. Sometimes motifs are combined to create diatonic passages based on mode 6 (an example can be found in mm. 60-64 in the bassoon, clarinet, oboe and strings). Woodwinds, violins, violas, and cellos play these motifs in alternation so as to create several musical dialogues, while the brass and basses provide supporting harmonies. This corresponds closely with similar melodic passages from previous sections, as can be seen in the following example:

EXAMPLE 38: Analogous motifs and motivic transformations, *Angel of Light*, mvt. II

The slower passage linking both variations (mm. 88-91) is based on mode 6; here, the rhythmic structure of the motifs is broken down by the division of quarters into quintuplet sixteenth-notes. The material of the second variation is derived from the first and retains the dialogue between the first and second violins.

Section D, the third variation, continues from the previous section with the use of triple rhythms, motivic dialogues that are thickened texturally through the addition of brass and percussion instruments, and an increase of the dynamic level to *forte* and *fortissimo*. Rautavaara masterfully transforms the motifs into variations of the "Bloomington" theme by using row II and changes of rhythm (particularly by presenting the theme in diminution). Moreover, the entire harmonic structure of this section is reminiscent of the corresponding fragment from the first variation.[62] The third variation can thus be described as synthetic since it links all the musical materials together and simultaneously transforms them:

EXAMPLE 39: Variant of the "Bloomington" theme, *Angel of Light*, mvt. II, mm. 110-111, oboes

The gradual thickening of texture and a more pronounced appearance of the theme in the brass serve to announce the emphatic climax at the beginning of section E. The "Bloomington" theme in metallophones links the section back to movement I, and the use of the "disturbance" technique relates it to the other compositions referring to angels. The climax is divided into three similar passages in which the theme appears and is then disturbed by violent motifs in the trumpets and a subsequent outburst in the orchestra. The motifs of "disturbance" have their roots in the ironic motifs from the beginning of movement:

EXAMPLE 40:
Similarities between "disturbance" motif and main motif,
Angel of Light, mvt. II

The final emergence of the "disturbance" motif is not followed by an orchestral eruption; instead, the music gradually fades out over a long-sustained E in the cellos and basses. This leads *attacca* into the slow movement.[63] The ending of section E, with alternating tonal centers on E and B-flat, demonstrates the integral construction of the symphony, for these anchors will be used once more in the final movement.

---

[62] Compare mm. 60-76 and 110-130.

[63] The *attacca* transition between the second and third movement was used also in Rautavaara's Eighth Symphony. As in the Seventh Symphony, the second, scherzo-like movement with disruptive moments leads to a strong climax, the energy of which is dispersed in the calm, peaceful third movement dominated by the long cantilena of the single horn.

Analysis of Rautavaara's Instrumental Works about Angels 151

Movement III

The slow movement is marked *Come un sogno* (Like a dream); it has all the features of a neoromantic symphonic movement. It is written in ABA form in which the return of A is ornamented. The melodic lines are long and smooth, using characteristically romantic instruments: violins, solos woodwind, and horn. The listeners' sense of time is as if suspended, and their attention is shifted from action to timeless being.[64] The material of all three sections is derived from row VI employed in different transpositions, sometimes simultaneously.

The initial section can be divided into two subsections, [a] and [a1]. It consists of two musical layers, the first a long cantilena in the violins, the second an accompaniment played by divided violas. While the violins play chorale-style material in four-part setting, the accompaniment, entrusted to the divided violas, is based on a succession of chords in *ostinato* rhythm. Both layers derive from three different transpositions of row VI.

EXAMPLE 41: The chorale construction of the cantilena, *Angel of Light*, mvt. III, mm. 2-18

[64] See Leland, 349-351.

152　　　　　　　　　　　　　　　　　　　　　　　　　　*Chapter 5*

Subsection [a] contains three different transpositions of row VI; [a1] repeats these, adds some new passages and then returns to the untransposed from of row VI (Fig. 29).[65] Subsection [a1] thickens the texture through the introduction of ornamental motifs in the woodwinds, together with short motivic references to the violin's cantilena (see mm. 20-21); the material of the fourth, fifth, and sixth divided violas is transferred to the divided cellos. In the middle of the subsection, a single horn is introduced, which together with two bassoons plays an important role in the short linking passage to section B.

FIGURE 29: *Angel of Light*, the harmonic structure of mvt. III, mm. 20-47

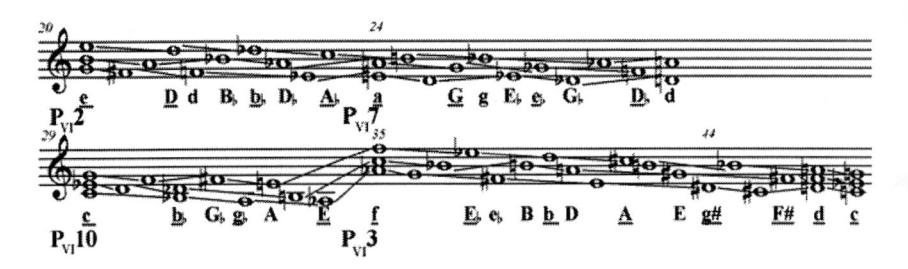

Although the composer always uses passing chords in the violins or violas, he never articulates these chords with the same accompaniment pattern. Chords derived from the transition between the chords of row VI in movement I use a motif similar to arpeggios in nocturnes; in movement II they are performed with tremolos; and in movement III they are presented in chorale texture. By virtue of these settings, the internal harmonic structure remains the same from one version to the next, but their characters are different (Exx. 42, 43, 44).

EXAMPLE 42: Arpeggiated "nocturne" motifs, *Angel of Light*, mvt. I, mm. 34-37

---

[65] [a] = $P_{VI}2$ (mm.2-8), $P_{VI}7$ (mm. 8-12), $P_{VI}10$ (mm. 13-19); [a1] = $P_{VI}2$ (mm. 20-24), $P_{VI}7$ (mm. 25-28), $P_{VI}10$ (mm. 29-35), $P_{VI}3$ (mm. 36-42) $P_{VI}6$ (mm. 42-47), $P_{VI}0$ (mm. 48-50).

Analysis of Rautavaara's Instrumental Works about Angels 153

EXAMPLE 43: Tremolo passages, *Angel of Light,* mvt. II, mm. 3-6

EXAMPLE 44: Chorale texture, *Angel of Light,* mvt. III, mm. 1-5

Section B is in a faster tempo and links to the final section by returning to the previous musical material. It is based on the transposition of the second variation from movement II. Here, the violins' melodic lines are replaced by the first oboe and clarinet, then by horns, strings and the rest of the woodwinds. The most noticeable connection between these two fragments is the repetition of a cello line from movement II in movement III.[66] Short motifs, based on seconds with trills in the strings, serve to decorate the main melodic line in the woodwinds; they imitate the sensation of motion. To make the section brighter, the composer gives the "Bloomington" theme to a solo violin in harmonics, supported by the vibraphone.

After a short climax, the music returns to the material of [a]: the violas play the chorale-style accompaniment while two clarinets add ornamentation with the trill motifs from section B. Following the brief [a3], based again on a fragment of row VI, the five notes of the cantilena are repeated in the first and second violins, and a sustained E appears in the basses, a gesture reminiscent of the beginning of the movement. More important than the famous cantilena, however, is the concluding horn line derived from the "Bloomington" theme, which leads to the finale:

EXAMPLE 45: Horn melody based on the "Bloomington" theme, *Angel of Light*, mvt. III, mm. 85-90

Movement IV

The final movement builds on material from previous movements, including the "Bloomington" theme (cast in row II) and various transpositions of row V. Its characteristic feature is the chorale texture alternating short phrases in various instrumental groups, especially brass and strings. The movement's second half (from mm. 55) reworks the final section of Rautavaara's Canto IV for string orchestra.

The finale begins with a nine-measure introduction in which the "Bloomington" theme is passed through various instruments, first as a fanfare in the brass, then transformed into a cantilena for the violins (using row $P_{II}3$). The introduction anticipates later climaxes in section C and in the

---

[66] Compare mvt. II, mm. 94-103 with mvt. III, mm. 57-62.

Analysis of Rautavaara's Instrumental Works about Angels 155

cathartic coda. After the enigmatic second movement and the passacaglia-like structure of the slow movement, the form of the finale—introduction, four sections A, B, C, and B1, and coda—seems very simple.

The simplicity is apparent in section A, which is built on transpositions of short passages of chords in the strings that alternate with arabesques in the woodwinds based on mode 6, forming a kind of melodic supplement to the string chorale. The entire section is based on related chords; this is reminiscent of the four-chord structure of row VI and the chorale passages from *Die erste Elegie*. Thus in contrast to the previous movements, the row is not used horizontally here, but rather vertically, in the form of harmonic successions of minor and major chords.

When the prime form of the row is reached, the texture is thickened through the addition of arabesques in the woodwinds and harmonic support from the horns and vibraphone. This is the turning point of the whole symphony, for Rautavaara changes row V into row VI and starts to build the finale. (As Tiikkaja has noted, these rows have many elements in common, as shown in Fig. 30).[67]

FIGURE 30: Comparison of row V (above) with an inversion of row VI (below)

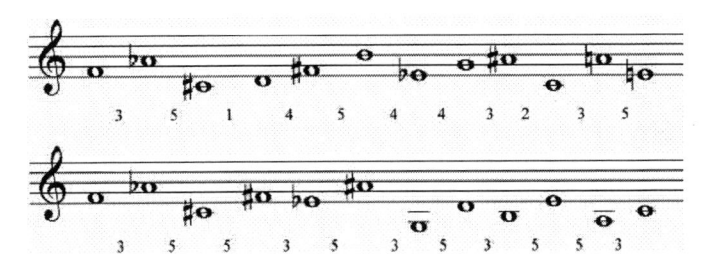

By replacing some of row VI with different notes, Rautavaara creates new but related material with which he built sections B, C, B1, and the coda. He then orchestrates his earlier string composition Canto IV. Apart from the introduction of the "Bloomington" theme in the final coda, the auto-citation remains unchanged.[68]

---

[67] See Tiikaja, "Einojuhani Rautavaaran," 28.

[68] In private communication the composer remarked that he had treated Canto IV as a sketch for the Seventh Symphony.

156 *Chapter 5*

EXAMPLE 46: Canto IV, m. 215

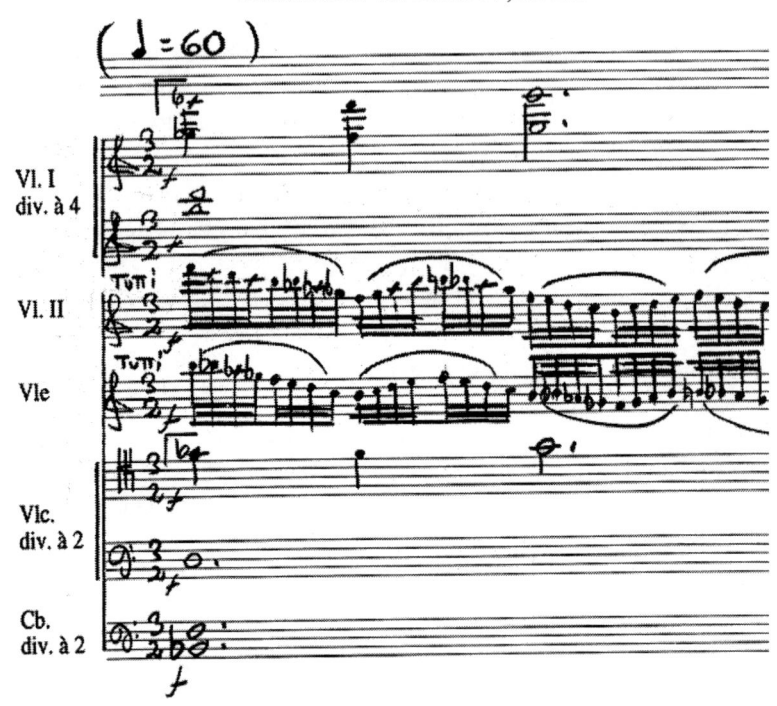

The second half of the final movement consists of two related sections: B and B1; these correspond to one another through the use of chorale texture and of material based on mode 6. The chorale, based on four chords that are derived from verticalizations of row V, is given to four horns and three trombones plus tuba in unison with cellos and double basses. Like row VI, row V can also be read as four chords: a major chord, a minor chord (a major second lower), another major chord (a major third above the latter), and another minor chord (a tritone apart from the third chord) (Fig. 31). Rautavaara does not always use the four chords in this order, but sometimes permutes them or treats them freely.

FIGURE 31: Row V presented horizontally and vertically

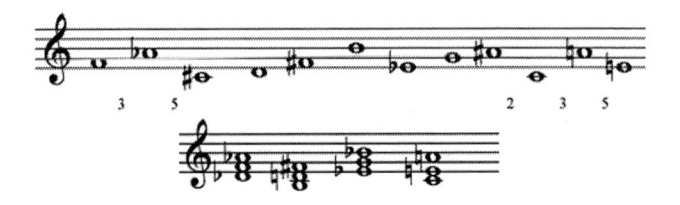

Analysis of Rautavaara's Instrumental Works about Angels 157

Section C, wedged between sections B and B1, contains two important layers: the first is the "Bloomington" theme in four-part chords given to the divided violins and thus corresponding to the long cantilena in movement III; the second is the viola's Alberti-bass accompaniment, fashioned from transpositions of row V and thereby reminiscent of the use of row VI in corresponding passages from movement I. Hence section C seems to be a synthetic section, as it brings together different materials from the previous movements. The remaining instruments supplement this harmonic and melodic material with arabesque motifs (three trumpets *con sordino*, then three trombones) and sustained bass notes (cellos and double basses).[69]

The laconic finale of *Angel of Light* is based on two chords: B-flat major and E major. These provide the harmonic background against which the "Bloomington" theme is heard, played by first violins, flutes, oboes, and four horns. Other instruments, such as the clarinets, second violins, violas, and harp, play rapid arabesques that give this passage lightness and brightness but also a splendidly solemn character. The entire coda seems like a prolongation of these two chords, which first arose in movement II (mm. 133-144) together with the "Bloomington" theme. While the coda establishes a solemn and majestic mood, the symphony does not ultimately conclude with this rather ecstatic character. In the last five measures, Rautavaara thins the texture to divided strings playing a succession of ascending seconds in a protracted *decrescendo*. Together with a similar passage that moves from the low to the high register at the end of movement I, this presents a spectacular example of Rautavaara's use of "light" in music, providing interpreters with a key to discerning the "light" in the work's title.[70]

This analysis of *Angel of Light* has provided evidence that despite the use of twelve-tone technique, the work has many features in common with other works in the angelic series: the "disturbance" technique, instrumentation (with the important role played by trumpets), the use of symmetrical modes, and illumination effects. Moreover, the composer uses row VI, which first appeared in his choral work *Die erste Elegie*.

---

[69] Rautavaara uses here many different transpositions of row V ($P_V 6$, $P_V 11$, $P_V 0$, $P_V 9$) and also a retrograde of its third transposition ($R_V 3$, mm. 90-92).

[70] In this context, Eero Tarasti has also emphasized the lightening effect in the third movement as juxtaposed "with an equally impressive darkening effect." See Eero Tarasti, "A Theory of Light in Music," M.Janicka-Słysz, T. Malecka, K.Szwajgier, eds., *Muzyka w kontekście kultury* [Music in the context of culture] (Cracow: PWM, 2000): 685.

Playgrounds for Angels

One year after completing *Angel of Dusk*, Rautavaara decided to write another composition with a reference to "angels" in the title. The inspiration was a commission from the British Philip Jones Brass Ensemble. At the time the ensemble was probably the best brass ensemble in Europe; friends and experts from the Sibelius Academy told the composer that he could write absolutely anything for them. As he writes in his autobiography, "It was a challenge. Certainly the question is not to write anything, but to compose for them something idiomatic, real music for brass."[71] In fact he began to compose music for ten musicians (four trumpets, four trombones, horn, and tuba), striving as in his double-bass writing in *Angel of Dusk* to explore every possible and impossible effect on the instruments. He had several long meetings with friends who played the trumpet and trombone in order to test out effects such as aliquot notes, fast arpeggios and glissandos, passages in which the trombonist sings and plays simultaneously, etc. "The whole composition was born from the internal nature of these instruments. It was something in the style of a spectacle written for real actors."[72] In other words: during the compositional process Rautavaara was thinking of real people—virtuosos—and thus applied a kind of concerto technique. The work was first performed by the Philip Jones Brass Ensemble at the Helsinki Festival in 1981.

> *Playgrounds for Angels* is a work both poetic and structuralist. Its title provided the first germ and impulse for the music. As with my other "angel" compositions, there is no narrative involved—although the listener is free to invent one if so desired. Nevertheless, the three words of the title seemed to conjure up an inspiring poetic atmosphere that gradually translated itself into music. The structure of the composition derives from the technical features of the trumpet, trombone, horn and tuba. Those features guide the process, variations, details and overall form of the music. Each group of instruments has its own musical playground.[73]

In *Playgrounds for Angels*,[74] a one-movement composition lasting about twenty minutes, *concertante* techniques can be found not only between

---

[71] Rautavaara, *Omakuva*, 325. I am indebted to Filip Sikorski who translated these passages from Rautavaara's autobiography into English.

[72] *Omakuva*, 325 (Sikorski's translation from Finnish).

[73] Rautavaara, commentary on *Playgrounds for Angels*, in the booklet accompanying the recording Ondine 957-2 (2000).

[74] "I remember inventing the title *Playgrounds for Angels* during composition of movement I." Personal communication, 11 July 2007.

Analysis of Rautavaara's Instrumental Works about Angels 159

groups of instruments but also within the groups. The four trumpets and four trombones form two corresponding groups because of the numbers of instruments in them; the horn and tuba are alone and their role is different.

Three Timbral Groups in Asynchronous Sections

The first group consists of four trumpets, two in C and two in B-flat. The form of their music can be divided into sections characterized by different intervallic schemes. The four sections are individually homogenous by virtue of the correlation between tempo and intervallic patterns. In each section patterns are repeated, varied, or developed; the main structuring feature are the breaks between them.

TABLE 9: Sections and musical material in the trumpet parts, *Playgrounds for Angels*

Measures	1-111	116-193	194-231	236-296
Characteristic features	motif [a] and its variations (Ex. 47, 48, 49)	motif [b] with minor and major seconds (Ex. 50, 51, 52)	minor thirds in combination with seconds (Ex. 53)	motifs with minor and major seconds
Tempos	♩=96	♩=96, ♩=72, ♩=66	♩=46	♩=104

In all four sections the trumpet parts share material. The opening of the first section is introductory, based on motif [a], a major chord (Exx. 47, 48, 49). Next, the composer changes the constituent intervals into seconds, creating motif [b] and a chromatic field (Exx. 50, 51, 52). In the third section, motifs [a] and [b] are brought together (Ex. 53), and the final section features chromatic motifs reminiscent of motif [b]. For the most part, the trumpets play motifs simultaneously and are treated as a homogenous group.

EXAMPLE 47: Motif [a], *Playgrounds for Angels*, m.1

EXAMPLE 48: Motifs [a] + [a'], *Playgrounds for Angels*, m.3

160   *Chapter 5*

EXAMPLE 49: Motifs [a1']+[a1], *Playgrounds for Angels,* m.73

EXAMPLE 50: Motif [b], *Playgrounds for Angels,* m.124

EXAMPLE 51: Motif [b1], *Playgrounds for Angels,* m.143

EXAMPLE 52: Motif [b2], *Playgrounds for Angels,* mm.149-153

EXAMPLE 53: Motifs [a] and [b], *Playgrounds for Angels,* mm.194-195

Analysis of Rautavaara's Instrumental Works about Angels 161

The first two sections are mostly in the same tempo; the tempo of the third section is half this speed and the last section much faster than in the first two. All through this strand, the rhythmic element is very important: sections are mostly homorhythmic and there are several rhythmic *ostinati*. The tempo is steady, without *accelerandi* or *ritenuti*, and motifs are to be performed in a mechanical and automatic manner. In the light of the composer's commentary about real actors, the group of trumpets can be compared to marionettes controlled by someone or by instinctive animal behavior.

The second group contains the trombones. They play five sections rather than the four of the group of trumpets.

TABLE 10: Trombone sections and their musical material, *Playgrounds for Angels*

Measures	68-74, 91-97	112-148	149-178	179-233	260-287
Characteristic features	long low suspended notes, combination tones, singing tones (Ex. 54)	passages up and down in group for two trombones, glissando, tremolo, harmonics (Ex. 55)	long notes in seconds, motif with minor seconds and thirds, blowing into instruments (Ex.56)	glissando *con sordino*, tremolo (Ex. 57)	motifs with seconds and thirds (Ex. 58)
Tempos	♩=96	♩=96, ♩=66	♩=72,♩=96,♩=66	♩=46	♩=104

The material given to the trombones is much more rhythmically varied than that of the trumpets. Although the motifs are still mechanical, as in the trumpet parts, the composer gives the trombones a coloristic role, achieved through varied techniques of articulation, such as players asked to sing while playing, to blow into their instruments, to perform harmonics or combination tones (Ex. 54), or to play passages in *piano* and *pianissimo*—a dynamic that is atypical for trombones and creates a special atmosphere (Ex. 57). For these reasons the group of four trombones can be considered to be a supplement to the trumpets.

EXAMPLE 54: Combination and singing tones, *Playgrounds for Angels*, mm. 68-72, trombones

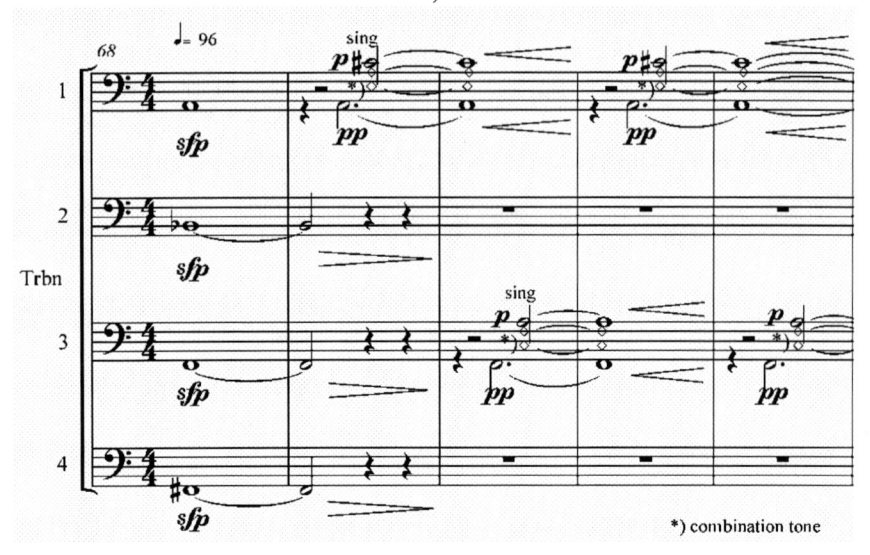

*) combination tone

EXAMPLE 55: Passages up and down, *Playgrounds for Angels*, mm. 112-113, trombones

Analysis of Rautavaara's Instrumental Works about Angels 163

EXAMPLE 56: Mirror harmony, *Playgrounds for Angels*, mm. 149-153, trumpets and trombones

EXAMPLE 57: Glissando *con sordino, Playgrounds for Angels,*
mm. 199-201, trombones

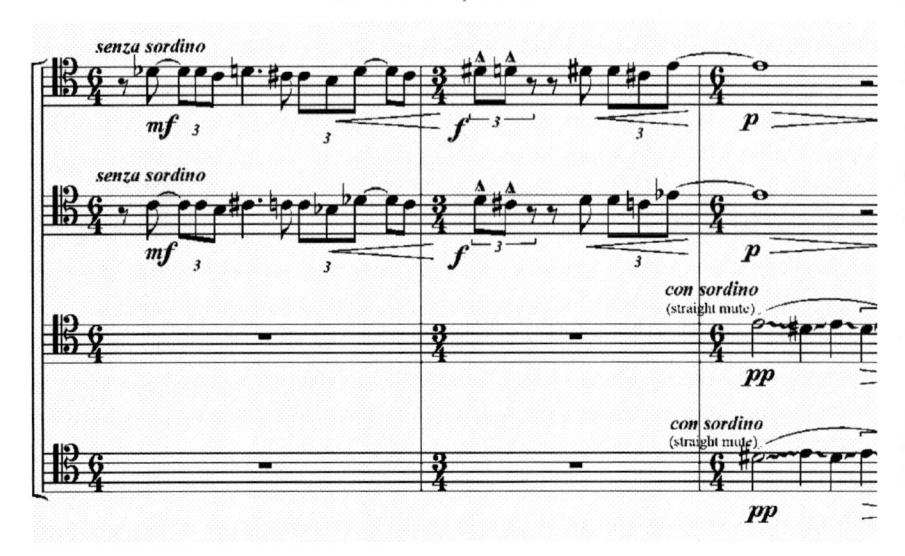

EXAMPLE 58: Motifs with seconds and thirds, *Playgrounds for Angels,*
mm. 260-264, trombones

Whereas Rautavaara treats the trumpets and trombones as homogeneous groups (both in that they play together and in that they share the same musical material and rhythmic patterns), the remaining two instruments, a French horn in F and a tuba, are given parts that are so heterogeneous that they must be regarded as separate. That they are joined in a combined table results exclusively from the fact that the two instruments interact in the fourth and fifth sections.

TABLE 11: Horn and tuba sections, *Playgrounds for Angels*

Measures	1-109	110-148	149-178	179-222	234-297
Horn	single suspended notes	free line predominantly in sixths and sevenths	continuation of free melodic line from previous section (Ex. 59)	alternating seconds and thirds, melodic motif (Ex. 60)	single notes, motifs with seconds, thirds – *ostinato*, free melodic line – seconds, thirds
Tuba	———	*ostinato* of minor seconds	seconds and thirds motif in alternation	alternating seconds and thirds, melodic motif (Ex. 60)	single notes, motifs with seconds, thirds – *ostinato*,
Tempos	♩=96	♩=96, ♩=66	♩=72, ♩=96	♩=66, ♩=46	♩=104

Instrumental Interactions and Relations

The three groups of instruments are independently divided into sections: the trumpets into four, the trombones, tuba and horn into five. The section boundaries do not necessarily align; particularly at the beginning of the work the groups seem almost oblivious of one another. Their interaction increases as the composition unfolds.

The first section (mm. 1-112) is dominated by the trumpets; the trombones only interrupt the trumpets' mechanical motifs with static coloristic chords in a different meter, while the sustained notes in the horn sound like *bourdons*. There is no interaction between the groups.

In contrast, the next section is full of interrelationships between timbral groups. The main focus is shifted from the trumpets to the horn's long cantilena. *Ostinato* passages in the trombones and a tuba motif in seconds provide an accompaniment: the trombones embellish the horn's line and the tuba establishes the harmonic center. The trumpets do not contribute to the accompaniment as such; rather, they interrupt the horn's cantilena (Ex. 59) with chromatic and mechanical motifs, thus suspending the horn's progress for a short while.

The frequency of the trumpet interruptions increases, as does their dynamic level. Finally, the horn plays its cantilena twice in a slower tempo (mm. 135-136, 141-143), before losing its position of prominence within the texture in the third section. The trumpets' second section coincides with the third section of trombones, horn, and tuba (from m. 149). Here, the trumpets develop a motif based on a second whereas the other instruments introduce completely new material (Ex. 56). Prominent for listeners is the alternation of the rapid versions of the trumpet motif and the slow chorale-motifs initiated by the trombones but later also taken over by the trumpets. Like an uninvited guest, the horn appears with a laconic cantilena that is interrupted

EXAMPLE 59: Horn cantilena, *Playgrounds for Angels*, mm. 116-135[75]

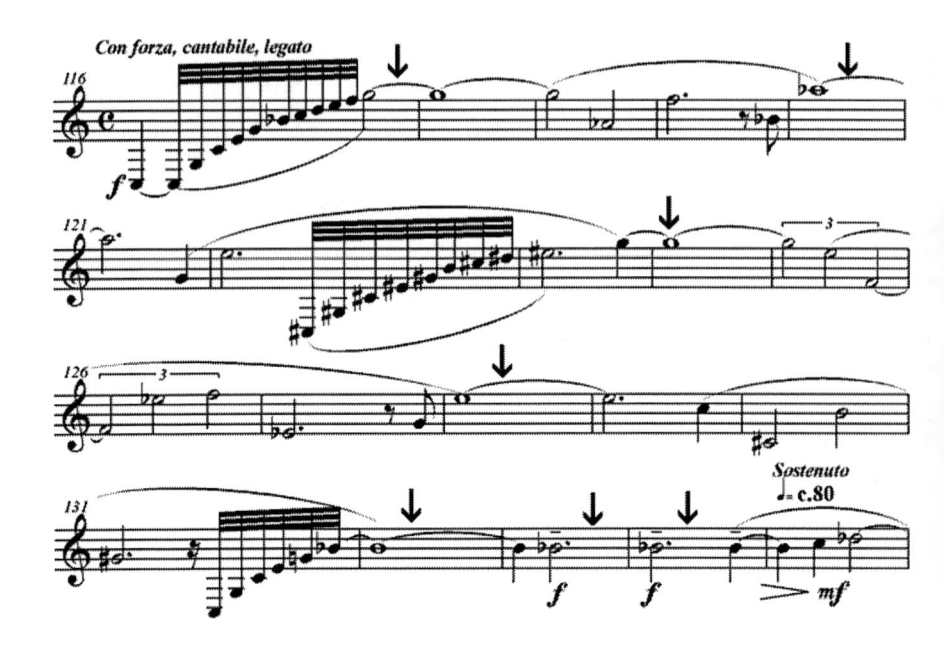

by "disturbance" motifs from the trumpets. Measures 175 to 234 demonstrate how the sections in the different groups overlap and should be examined as three independent layers. The "disturbance" technique in the trumpets is continued, interfering by means of short motivic interjections with the melodic lines of horn and tuba.

EXAMPLE 60: *Playgrounds for Angels*, mm. 179-182, horn and tuba

---

[75] Trumpet "disturbances" marked by vertical arrows.

The fourth section begins with the tempo change to *Largo*; here, all three instrumental groups have new roles. The trumpets, dominant in the two previous sections, recedes into the background to provide harmonic support for the trombone. Horn and tuba join the trumpets with material based primarily on minor seconds, which acts as a kind of padding between the trumpet and trombone passages. The tuba, having initially played an inversion of a motif heard in the first trombone, then joins this timbral group.

The final section is divided. In the first of these subsections (mm. 234-269), the three timbral groups independent layers: the trumpets play very fast chromatic motifs in an imitative texture (Ex. 61), the trombones juggle short, accented two- or three-note motifs (Ex. 58), while horn and tuba merely add one or two notes in a low register. Although melodically independent, the groups are rhythmically related: when the trombones pause, the horn and tuba play, and vice versa in what may be described as mutual supplementation. This launches the process of instrumental unification, which is further intensified in the second subsection (mm. 275-297). Here, the tuba doubles the fourth trombone a perfect fifth below, and the horn doubles the third trombone a perfect fifth above. A little later, the horn detaches itself from the trombones and joins the group of trumpets so that the three groups become two. Finally, the motifs in the trumpets gradually decrease in length while the pauses separating them increase. This deceptive vanishing act prepares the final surprise: the tuba emerges with two last notes that the composer desires to sound reminiscent of a loud "lion's roar."

Conclusion

Playgrounds for Angels contains all of the features found in Rautavaara's earlier compositions referring to angels, as well as mechanical and repetitive elements that appeared previously only in "Archangel Michael Fighting the Antichrist." Although *Playgrounds for Angels* is not the last of the composer's works about angels (*Angel of Light* postdated it), by virtue of its mechanical and repetitive elements it acts as a corner stone of that formal arch over the angelic series which is held up at the other end by the movement from the piano suite. Within this arch, *Angel of Dusk* occupies the central place, while *Angels and Visitations* corresponds with *Angel of Light*. Whereas "Archangel Michael Fighting the Antichrist" shares with *Playgrounds for Angels* elements of mechanicalness and repetitiveness, *Angels and Visitations* and *Angel of Light* both feature passages in "disturbance" technique, many chorale textures reminiscent of Bruckner, and passages that give the effect of "brightness" through the use of metallophones. The central work, *Angel of Dusk*, contains all of these features and for that reason among others seems to be the most significant of the series.

EXAMPLE 61: Fast chromatic motifs, *Playgrounds for Angels*, mm. 236-247, trumpets

Analysis of Rautavaara's Instrumental Works about Angels 169

TABLE 12: Rautavaara's compositions referring to angels as a cycle

Archangel Michael Fighting the Antichrist	Angel Trilogy			Playgrounds for Angels
	Angels and Visitations	Double Bass Concerto *Angel of Dusk*	Seventh Symphony *Angel of Light*	
1955/2006	1978	1980	1994	1981

An alternative overview is one in which the angelic compositions are listed in chronological order:

TABLE 13: Chronological order of Rautavaara's compositions referring to angels

Archangel Michael Fighting the Antichrist (from *Icons*)	*Angels and Visitations*	*Angel of Dusk*	*Playgrounds for Angels*	*Angel of Light*	Archangel Michael Fighting the Antichrist (*Before the Icons*)
1955	1978	1980	1981	1994	2006

It appears that the orchestration of "Archangel Michael Fighting the Antichrist" signaled the composer's desire to bring his series of compositions referring to angels to a close by returning to the earliest work.[76] It is interesting to observe that the time that elapsed between the movement from the piano suite and *Angel of Dusk* is identical with that between *Playgrounds for Angels* and the final movement in *Before the Icons*: 25 years. With the benefit of hindsight, analysts may detect two symmetrical groups of three compositions. It is tempting to ask whether this is entirely coincidental or a case of rational planning, since there is a visible symmetry in both the cycle and the chronological tables. If asked, Rautavaara would probably not give an answer, but rather repeat Pablo Picasso's declaration: "Je n'invente pas, je trouve."[77]

---

[76] Grieg did something similar when he arranged his *Arietta*, the opening miniature in his piano cycle *Lyric Pieces*, op. 12 (1867), to become the conclusion in his *Remembrances*, op. 71 (1901). The time between those two compositions is 34 years; in Rautavaara's case, it is almost 51 years.

[77] Rautavaara, "Thomas – Analysis of the Tone Material": 48.

PART III:
INTERPRETATIONS AND ASSOCIATIONS

Chapter 6: "Angelic" Features in Rautavaara's Instrumental Works

Angels and Visitations contains internal dichotomies that are based on binary oppositions. The subsequent compositions concerning angels extend this idea through conflict between two instrumental planes (disturbance technique), expressionless musical passages (*musica automata*), contrasted instrumental color, the manipulation of musical "brightness," and the use of symmetry. The distinctive characteristics of Rautavaara's instrumental works referring to angels thus account for three of the five musical mythologems listed by Adamenko (binary opposition, repetitiveness, variability, symmetry, numerical organization).

The "Disturbance" Technique

The "disturbance" technique occurs in all but the first of the compositions referring to angels, "Archangel Michael Fighting the Antichrist." Sometimes this technique is applied throughout a whole work, as in *Angels and Visitations* and *Angel of Dusk*; elsewhere it is limited to certain movements or sections, as in the second movement of *Angel of Light*[1] and in *Playgrounds for Angels*. As various examples analyzed in the preceding chapter have shown, the technique is based on the notion of conflict between two instrumental planes: one plane interrupts or disturbs the musical processes of the second. In such instances, the melodic line of the second plane is suspended and its ability to narrate is thwarted until it disappears altogether. In *Angels and Visitations*, the dissonant outbursts of the brass disturb the passage of the main diatonic theme. In *Angel of Dusk*, whenever the soloist's line is interrupted, it "freezes" on a long sustained note. Once the outbursts cease, the solo line continues or, ultimately, stops entirely (see Ex. 26). In *Playgrounds for Angels*, trumpet, trombone, and tuba attempt to disrupt the free, open melody of the horn (see Ex. 59).

---

[1] The use of the "disturbance" technique at the end of the second movement of *Angel of Light* is the exception: there the trumpets' "motif of disturbance" exists for dramatic and rhetorical purposes.

The "disturbance" technique contrasts two groups of instruments in *Angels and Visitations*, but one group with a solo instrument in *Angel of Dusk* and in *Playgrounds for Angels*; the latter case is remotely reminiscent of concerto passages. Anna Nowak distinguishes a variety of such conflicts, noting that dramaturgical tensions resulting from the interactions between the soloist and the group are much more intense here and very often are produced as a consequence of collision, i.e., the violent interruption of the leading narration by a musical adversary.[2] Nowak uses a passage from Witold Lutosławski's Cello Concerto (1968-70) as an example, in which the action of the solo cellist is interrupted mostly by the brass. Mstislav Rostropovich, the dedicatee and first performer of the work, has suggested that he feels impersonated by the cello while the brass outbursts represent the communist system with which he was in conflict.[3] Lutosławski did not care for extra-musical allusions of this nature, but admitted that during the process of composition he wanted to create a process of musical conflict similar to that of theatrical drama: "My aim was to find some justification for employing these two contradictory forces: the solo instrument and the orchestra."[4] Rautavaara also treats the concerto as a kind of drama—a conflict between the individual and the community[5]—although he claims that he did not know Lutosławski's Cello Concerto when composing *Angel of Dusk*.[6]

The idea of conflict and contrasting material between a single instrument and a group is also comparable to the opposition between subject and opponent in Greimas's mythical model: "Actoriality in music is represented by all those features that render abstract musical structure as anthropomorphic."[7] According to Tarasti, musical actants or actors (in the Greimassian sense) are themes in musical works that function like dramatic roles in prose or theater. Similarly, in Rautavaara's operas *Thomas, Vincent, Aleksis Kivi*, and *Rasputin*, the hero is always in conflict with his environment, and this relationship is fundamental to the plot. Sivuoja-Gunaratnam discovered that the musical

---

[2] Anna Nowak, *Współczesny koncert polski: przemiany gatunku* [The contemporary Polish concerto: transformation of genre] (Bydgoszcz: Akademia Muzyczna im. F. Nowowiejskiego, 1997), 69.

[3] Charles B. Rae, *The Music of Lutosławski* (London, UK: Faber&Faber, 1994), 123-124.

[4] Tadeusz Kaczyński, *Conversations with Witold Lutosławski,* Yolanta May, trans. (London, UK: Chester, 1984), 60-61.

[5] Korhonen, *Finnish Concertos*, 48.

[6] A comparison of the beginning of Lutosławski's Cello Concerto with the first movement of Rautavaara's work highlights the similar use of conflict in these works; what is also noteworthy is that the solo cello and bass in the respective works are "disturbed" by interjections from the brass.

[7] Tarasti, *A Theory of Musical Semiotics*, 106.

subject in these operas is invariably enunciated by the cellos in a register that lies within the baritone range.[8] There is a relationship between the composer's operas and his instrumental works, in that Rautavaara often treats instruments as vocalists, giving them specific roles. On numerous occasions in his operas, an instrumental "voice" is given to the part of the main character so that it can be regarded as its musical representation, as suggested in Cone's theory of *musical persona*.[9] Apart from *Angel of Dusk,* Rautavaara's instrumental compositions referring to angels are not real concertos; the relationship between a soloist or instrumental group and the brass ensemble in these works is informed rather by the notion of *concertante* music and *concerto grosso*. Such features heighten the sense that the personification of instruments is an important facet in compositions about angels.

To explore further connotations with angels in the light of the idea of conflict between two instrumental planes, it is necessary to look at vocal scores featuring spirits or deceased people. The metaphysical appearance of spirits takes place in those fantastic and dramatic stories in which a person who was killed appears unexpectedly as a spirit, or in which a spirit appears as an intervention from God or from a demon. In Mozart's *Don Giovanni*, the Commendatore murdered by Don Giovanni in Act I appears again as a spirit in Act II. His appearance as a moving statue during Don Giovanni's supper breaks linear time and cadences after scene XIV, whereas the listener would expect a continuation of the previous light melodic line. Surprisingly, Mozart concludes the scene with a second inversion of the tonic F major, which is later transformed into a diminished chord that initiates a modulation to D minor. There is opposition on all musical levels: tonal (F major versus D minor), dynamic (*piano* versus *forte* and *fortissimo*), instrumental (strings with woodwinds versus *tutti*), rhythmic (simple quarter- and half-notes versus dotted eighths) and tempo (*Molto Allegro* versus *Andante*). This opposition is used to highlight the contrast between two planes, one earthly (represented by Don Giovanni and his servant Leporello), the other spiritual (represented by the spirit of the Commendatore).

This musical contrast (or "disturbance") is a representation of the religious phenomenon of visitations, which includes both the appearance of deceased persons to the living and the materialization of angels or other spirits. In Mozart's opera the Commendatore urges Don Giovanni to repent his sins and change his life; insofar as this can be treated as a message from the beyond, it casts the Commendatore in the role of a typical angelic messenger. When comparing this passage to "disturbances" in Rautavaara's

---

[8] Sivuoja-Gunaratnam, *Narrating with Twelve Tones*, 191.

[9] See Cone, 81-114.

compositions, it is evident that trumpets and trombones are in *Don Giovanni* the musical symbol of the terrifying angel (the spirit of the Commendatore) challenging the mythical hero (Don Giovanni), who exemplifies "terrified man."

Nowak argues that there are numerous types of relationship between instruments in contemporary concertos, including rivalry, conflict, dialogue and complementation.[10] The idea of rivalry is based on aspiring to dominate various oppositional tonal corpuses in different variants. The notion of dialogue is based on a relationship without conflict between the music of the soloist and orchestra, in which the voices are mutually cooperative. Complementation avoids rivalry, replacing it with "togetherness."

An analysis of the relationship between instruments in Rautavaara's *Angel of Dusk* provides many remarkable insights. Some instruments are permanently in conflict with each other, such as the soloist with the trumpets and trombones. Others engage in dialogue, in that the musical material is divided between two instruments that play in alternation without rivalry, or in that two instruments share the same musical material or harmonic structure, such as the soloist and the string section. In yet other cases, instruments complement one another, as when they play in unison or in octaves, or when one provides a counterpoint to the other. Given that instruments have specific musico-dramatic roles in the concerto, it is possible to reformulate the relationships between them in Greimassian terms.

FIGURE 32: Greimas's mythical actants in *Angel of Dusk*[11]

helper	subject	opponent
(strings, basses)	*(soloist)*	*(brass)*

object
(chord come un flageolet)

Tracing of the process of transition from one relationship between instruments in *Angel of Dusk* to another reveals the narrative structure of the concerto. As a consequence, these relationships create a musico-mythical narrative structure comparable to the structure that, according to Lévi-Strauss, underlies every myth. Rautavaara gives subtitles to every movement of the concerto—"His first appearance," "His monologue," and "His last appearance"—demonstrating that he treats the soloist as the main subject or actor.

---

[10] See Nowak, 66-72.

[11] Passages played "come un flageolet" by the double basses are treated like a different instrument, even though it is a particular feature of double bass playing. The strange timbre of the basses' flageolet tones is reminiscent of that of the *flageolet*—a little recorder with a muffled timbre.

The use of the "disturbance" technique" in the brass to interrupt the soloist in the first and third movements may represent the mythical fights of the hero and his final battle with his opponents. Conversely, the second movement (in which the soloist is for the most part unaccompanied) focuses on the main character (the hero), and can thus be called his monologue; it functions as a representation of his mythical banishment and loneliness. The G-major chord marked *come un flageolet* in the *divisi* orchestral basses appears only at the beginning of the composition, in the first movement, and at the end of the work as the final chord. Its disappearance after the first movement allows it to be described as a representation of a special mythical implement (for example, a magic ring, sword, or Holy Grail), which in every mythical story is stolen or lost. The hero, represented by the solo double bass, searches for the absent implement, i.e., for the chord *come un flageolet*, during the whole composition, fights for it, and after the final battle with his opponent, gains it. The concerto's coda can be heard as a reconciliation of the hero with his environment, since there is no more conflict between the orchestral instruments and the soloist; the double bass solo plays a line based on pitches from the orchestra's harmonic background. (Table 14 is one of several possible attempts to relate Lévi-Strauss's mythical structure to the relationships between instruments in Rautavaara's concerto.)

Although the mythical structure of *Angel of Dusk* is not sufficient proof that listeners would interpret the concerto as a mythical story in which the soloist is a hero and the brass ensemble its opponent, there is nevertheless a noticeable similarity between the structure of the music and Lévi-Strauss's mythical structure. Of all the instrumental works referring to angels, the concerto is unique in its use of mythical structure; hence this composition, similar to the recurrent plots in Rautavaara's operas, can be considered an autobiographical work.[12]

Musica Automata / Senza Espressivo

In the compositions analyzed above, the "disturbance" technique opposes two symbolic levels, the earthly or human and its antithesis, the non-human or spiritual. If brass instruments, particularly trumpets and trombones, are symphonic works referring to angels, it may be assumed that their harmonic

---

[12] At the end of the 1970s Rautavaara wrote his (subsequently withdrawn) autobiographical opera *En dramatisk scen*. There is no proof that he used material from the opera in *Angel of Dusk*, but Kalevi Aho, who has seen the score of the opera, told me in private conversation that a relationship is possible. Provided this were true, the concerto would function not only as an instrumental requiem for Olga and Serge Koussevitzky but also as the composer's diary of his private struggles at that time.

TABLE 14: Lévi-Strauss's mythical structure juxtaposed with sections of *Angel of Dusk*

The structure of myth (Lévi-Strauss/Tarasti)	The relation between mythical actants in *Angel of Dusk*	Sections, measures
The appearance of a lack in the universe	the magic mythical object (G major chord come un flageolet) has disappeared	introduction (mvt. I, mm. 1-11)
Early on, the hero reveals his abilities	subject I (soloist) leads a cantilena, fights with the opponent (brass) to attain the mythical object (G major chord come un flageolet) at the end the object disappears	A, B, (mvt. I, mm. 12-107) (mm.108-111)
The hero's departure (the journey): banishment, gripe, loneliness, search for the object	soloist's monologue (cadenza)	the entire mvt. II
The hero's return	soloist (subject I) goes from low register to high register, strings (helper) counterpoint it	A, B (mvt. III, mm. 1-48)
The final battle	soloist (subject) against the brass (the opponent)	C (mvt. III, mm. 49-169)
The hero's fall or his victory	sustained notes in part of soloist, musical material comes back from II movement	D (mvt. III, mm. 170-199)
The reconciliation	soloist and brass, purification of material in the end the magic object appears	E (mvt. III, mm.200- 233)

and melodic structures are the same across these works. A comparison of the material written for brass in *Angels and Visitations*, *Angel of Dusk*, *Playgrounds for Angels* and *Angel of Light* demonstrates that they do, in fact, share similar material, characterized mainly by chromaticism, similarity of rhythmic patterns, and mirror constructs in the harmony. These features support the claim that these instruments should be regarded as representations of the "angelic." To provide a salient example, the ensuing paragraphs examine one of the most significant features of trumpet and trombone writing, that of "expressionless" passages or *musica automata*.

Musica automata is a term denoting music that tries to imitate, reflect, or mimic a mechanism or mechanical structure.[13] According to Abbate, mechanicalness can be detected in any pervasive rhythmic *ostinato* that imitates the mechanisms of *automata*: non-stop rhythmic repetitions, schematic melodic or sometimes harmonic patterns based on one pitch class, or the parroting of one short motif, phrase, or passage. Absence of expression occurs through the avoidance of *rubato* and results in the performance sounding mechanical rather than human; a so-called *inexpressive "espressivo."* The avoidance of *ritardando* and *accelerando* is paralleled by an avoidance of *crescendo* and *diminuendo*, those musical signs that "[...] betray the human presence in the performance machine," thereby making the performance soulless.[14]

Modern composer's deliberate use of expressionlessness must be understood against the backdrop of the history of automata. The most famous examples are music boxes that play popular melodies with the timbre of chimes or pipes. Somewhat more removed from actual music are small contraptions like some clocks: the cuckoo-clock, the trumpeter clock, and the mechanical singing bird. Whereas music boxes were treated as toys, small musical automata had the function of signaling events, such as hours or half and quarter hours through the imitation of animals. Some builders also invented automata in which the human voice was generated mechanically, resulting in monotonous intonation (for example, the Euphonia). The most popular automata in music were those that replaced human performance through machines that imitated real players, and for which music was written as an inscription on a cylinder, disk, or roll of paper or brass. Such instruments include the *flauteur automate* and the *pianola*, but there were a dozen with even stranger names, such as the symphonion and the orchestrion. They were built as normal instruments, but during the performance, keys were pressed by internal mechanisms, thus making it seem as if phantoms or ghosts were playing the instrument.

The important aspect in the context of this study is to trace how composers were inspired by the idea of automatism and mechanical elements. These sources of inspiration may be divided into five types:

1. imitation of mechanical singing birds;
2. imitation of clocks or chimes;
3. imitation of machines or vehicles;
4. imitation of mechanical instruments: music boxes, barrel organs, hurdy-gurdys;
5. mechanical elements.

---

[13] See Abbate, 185-246.

[14] See Abbate, 214-215.

There are also the well-known examples of *musica automata* in the *perpetuum mobile* genre, in which rapid movement was often used to create a striking finale (as in the last movement of Fryderyk Chopin's Sonata in B-flat minor and in Ravel's *Bolero*). Yet, it must be noted that composers often used rhythmic ostinatos, melodic patterns, and unchanging tempi while simultaneously altering dynamic levels. In cases such as Grieg's *In the Hall of the Mountain King*, it is debatable whether the *perpetuum mobile* serves the representation of mechanical music.

Mechanical Elements

Rautavaara seems not to have noticed that his early work "Jacob Könni" from the piano suite *The Fiddlers*, subsequently rearranged for brass as "Credo et dubito" in *A Requiem in Our Time*, is a perfect imitation of a clock mechanism, and is thus his first work to contain *musica automata*.[15] Its fast figurations imitate the ticking of Könni's clocks. As the composer comments in the score: "Surrounded by his big clocks and mechanical wonders lives Jacob Könni."

EXAMPLE 62: *Fiddlers*, "Jacob Könni," mm. 1-4

In his youth, Rautavaara was inspired by a number of composers for whom the idea of music boxes was important. Stravinsky's ballet *The Rite of Spring* was a major influence on Rautavaara's *Requiem in Our Time*, the last movement of his Second Symphony (1957/1984), as well as on the middle section of *Angels and Visitations*.[16] As a result of this influence, rhythm became an ongoing concern for Rautavaara, and his rhythmic language developed until his serial period and the Fourth Symphony *Arabescata*. The neoclassical example of Stravinsky, together with that of other neoclassical composers such as Sergei Prokofiev, had a strong impact on Rautavaara's

---

[15] Sivuoja-Gunaratnam claims that in "Credo and dubito" "the ticking texture refers to the poignant voice of suspicion ('dubito'), and the chorale texture with its ecclesiastical connotations alludes to faith ('credo') within the semantic context provided by the title." See Sivuoja-Gunaratnam, "Narcissus Musicus": 12.

[16] See Aho, *Einojuhani Rautavaara as Symphonist*, 82.

own neoclassical phase.[17] His "Archangel Michael Fighting the Antichrist," a typical example of a *perpetuum mobile*, belongs to this phase. Despite the use of *crescendo*, this work is probably the best example of automatism in his music. The perpetual movement without human expression presents a musical analog to the notion of an icon as static art, timeless, lifeless, alien, and originating from another, invisible world. The use of mechanical elements in this work suggests a connection between *automata* and the understanding of the angel figure in Rautavaara's music (see Ex. 13); the orchestration of the work in *Before the Icons* retains the original structure with emphasis on the brass.

Angels and Visitations contains many mechanical elements both in the musical material and in the way components from previous compositions are re-used. The two most obvious auto-citations are from the choral work *Lehdet lehtiä* (Leaves are leaves, 1979) and from the fourth movement of the Second Symphony. While the latter occurs in the middle section of *Angels and Visitations*, material from *Lehdet lehtiä* is important throughout the whole work. The composer has suggested that the auto-citation from the choral work was used to provide a neutral background independent from other layers, in an instance of what he calls the *"impassibilité"* technique. In *Lehdet lehtiä* the polyphonic construction of the theme becomes the background over which the solo tenor part develops; and in *Angels and Visitations* it provides material that contrasts with the noisy, aggressive outbursts from the brass ensemble.

> Anyway, in the opera *The House of the Sun*, of 1990 it was used as a neutral background for many dramatic but dreamlike scenes. This use of a background could be called an *"impassibilité"* technique: there the music does not follow exactly what happens on the scene (like movie music mostly does—whatever Tom and Jerry do is described by the music). Here I wanted to have a continuous background which does not care about whatever goes on. It was quite effective. The same kind of *"impassibilité"* is also used in *Visitations*. There is a certain kind of strength in the soft music which does not appear to mind the forceful attacks of brass etc., but just continues on its way, until drowned.[18]

The auto-citation from the choral work is crucial not only as a neutral background, but as an element in opposition to the brutal brass attacks. Rautavaara indicated that in some places it should be repeated until the brass enters; this reflects the structure of the original choral composition. *Lehdet lehtiä* is based on repetitions of a melodic pattern lasting for four or five

---

[17] See Korhonen, *Finnish Orchestral Music* 2, 10-11.

[18] Personal communication, 8 February 2007.

measures, but these repetitions are veiled owing to changing time signatures and their linkage without noticeable breaks (Ex. 63). The melodic pattern is transposed onto different steps of various modal scales and is deployed in a constant rhythm.

EXAMPLE 63: *Lehdet lehtiä*, mm. 1-10

For these reasons *Lehdet lehtiä* seems like another *perpetuum mobile*, a magical mantra that creates a peaceful atmosphere in accordance with the composer's intention to present a dream or a flashback. It has all characteristics to classify it as mechanical: non-stop rhythmical repetition of the melodic pattern; near-ceaseless repetition of a four-measure phrase; absence of *ritardandos* and *accelerandos* in all but the brief coda (which does not use the main melodic pattern), avoidance of *crescendos* or *decrescendos*; and a single, overall dynamic level (*piano* and *pianissimo*). Rautavaara retains these elements when he reuses material from *Lehdet lehtiä* in *Angels and Visitations*, but as in *Before the Icons*, he emphasizes the repetitions through homogeneous instrumentation. When the passage is first heard, it is played by strings; later it moves to woodwinds and harp, and is finally taken up by celesta, glockenspiel, and harp (Ex. 64). If the first and second times are reminiscent of Palestrinian texture and vocal music, the third appearance seems inhuman and soulless. Celesta, glockenspiel, and harp play the notes like a clock mechanism; their timbres evoke a barrel organ or music box heard from a distance.

EXAMPLE 64: *Angels and Visitations*, glockenspiel, celesta, harp, mm. 255-256

The process of the material passing from the strings through the woodwinds to the percussion can be interpreted not only in coloristic terms (as an effect of brightening), but also as a process of humanity being lost (strings and woodwind are similar to the human voice, whereas metallophones are inhuman). A similar process occurs in "Archangel Michael Fighting the Antichrist," in which the motion from dark to bright modes colors the main melodic line as it ascends from a low to a high register. This important aspect needs some further discussion.

The affinity between the central movement of *Angels and Visitations* the last movement of the Second Symphony, from which it derives, extends beyond the re-use of material. They also have comparable musical structures: mm. 62-115 of the symphonic movement correspond to mm. 185-232 in *Angels and Visitations*. Examples 65 and 66 document some of the most spectacular similarities, where modifications or transpositions of pre-existing passages are wedged between newly composed ones.

While this composition contains no music-box allusions, Rautavaara uses auto-citations from his Second Symphony for rhythmic purposes, highlighting them by means of mechanical repetitions of a three-note motif in contrasting registers, one high (woodwind with glockenspiels, xylophone,

184 Chapter 6

EXAMPLE 65: Second Symphony, final mvt, mm. 62-63

and first violins), the other low (low strings, trombones, bassoons, and tom-toms). Later, these two groups combine to oppose the short, loud melodic motifs in the trumpets. The dynamic level is steady *forte* or *fortissimo* with negligible dynamic inflections and a pulse that remains constant. Trichords, repeated in different rhythmic and instrumental combinations, retain the same internal structure.

"Angelic" Features in Rautavaara's Instrumental Works   185

EXAMPLE 66: *Angels and Visitations*, mm. 185-186, percussion and strings

Angels and Visitations also encompasses numerous short passages with mechanistic repetition. For example, the material for the divided strings in the introduction features short motifs that through overlapping create the dense texture so characteristic of Rautavaara's later style, and are used in the same manner in the introduction to *Angel of Dusk*. Despite a certain dynamic gradation, these dense textures can be considered mechanical, for they exhibit an obstinate rhythm and repetitive melodic structures without tempo fluctuation (compare Exx. 67 and 68).

The beginning of the middle section of *Angels and Visitations* provides another example. The music in the divided strings is based on a motif of four sixteenth-notes that is introduced gradually, ascending from the low basses to the high first violins. Eventually, the other orchestral instruments join the strings, building a strong climax as a backdrop before which a simple melodic line appears, played by four trumpets and four trombones (m. 167). The diatonic structure of this line is characterized by a constant and mechanical repetition of a five-note motif, a steady tempo and, with the exception of a slight *crescendo* at the end of the phrase, by an unchanging dynamic level (see Ex. 22). With its mechanical nature, the line corresponds to the passage from *Lehdet lehtiä*, which is also based on material that is both diatonic and repeated.

The mechanical elements in *Angel of Dusk* are less obvious than those in *Angels and Visitations*. In the Concerto, Rautavaara uses the dense texture in divided strings described above both as a frame to the first and occasionally in the third movement; yet it does not play the decisive role. More significant is a rhythmic *ostinato* which the soloist plays in the third movement. It begins as a classical *perpetuum mobile*, but as it progresses, the brass enters with repeated attempts to interrupt and break the soloist's line. Eventually the solo part disappears, leading to a homorhythmic coda without any inflections of tempo or dynamics, a prototypical *inespressivo* (see Ex. 33). As celesta and glockenspiel start playing this passage (from mm. 200 to 224), along with the harp, they tinge the timbre of the whole orchestra with their metal sound, creating a music-box effect reminiscent of a similar passage in *Angels and Visitations*. This example of the composer's *"impassibilité"* technique is not, however, the only music-box effect in the concerto. In the first movement, too, vibraphone, celesta, and harp join their forces for arpeggios that sound completely mechanical (Ex. 69).

EXAMPLE 67: *Angels and Visitations*, m. 1, strings

EXAMPLE 68: *Angel of Dusk*, m. 1, strings

EXAMPLE 69: *Angel of Dusk,* mvt. I, m. 11

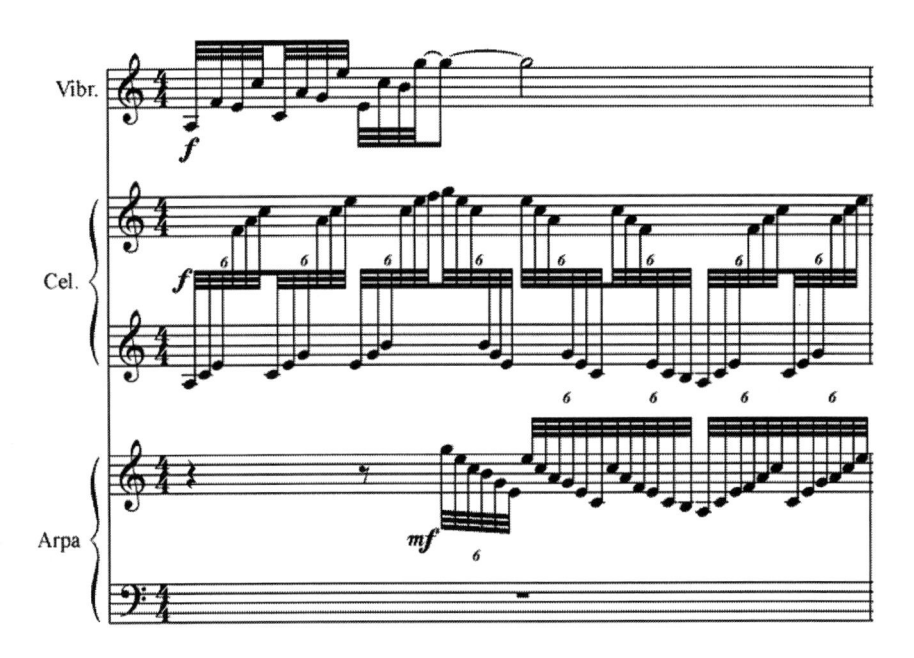

The use of such mechanical figures in *Angels and Visitations* and *Angel of Dusk* is an innocent beginning when compared with the later chamber composition in which practically every instrumental part is in some way mechanical. *Playgrounds for Angels* can be called the pinnacle of Rautavaara's *musica automata,* for it marks the extreme of mechanicalness in his music. In a commentary he describes the composition as structuralist, insofar as it grows out of only two motifs. The developmental process is completely mechanical: Rautavaara does not use the motifs to build new melodic cells but rather repeats them in inversion, transposition, combining or superimposing them. The element of repetition is omnipresent; it can be understood as part of a variation technique in which the structure of motifs remains invariant. While the dynamic level does not remain unchanged as in other inexpressive music but increases from *pp* to *ff,* the mechanical factors are so overpowering that *Playgrounds for Angels* emerges as the most spectacular example of Rautavaara's mechanical music; like some passages from *Angels and Visitations* and *Angel of Dusk* it gives the impression of imitating a mechanical organ.

EXAMPLE 70: Dialogues between trumpets, *Playgrounds for Angels*, mm. 1-18

Angel of Light differs from the preceding compositions referring to angels in that it barely employs the "disturbance" technique (which appears only in vestigial form in the second movement) and in that brass instruments are sparingly used. While this serene symphony contains no explicitly mechanical elements, and the mechanistic effect is limited to passages that are repeated several times. The third movement offers a perfect example of how Rautavaara builds a composition based on repeated melodic and harmonic patterns. Just as components of *Lehdet lehtiä* are re-used in *Angels and Visitations*, this movement is derived from Rautavaara's *Notturno e danza* for violin and piano. Two important sections grow from the melodic and harmonic material of the first eight measures, where a progression of descending minor seconds in the bass, used as a ground, creates a pattern similar to that of the baroque chaconne. This pattern, together with the main melodic line in the violins, is transposed and subjected to varied repetitions in order to create the long unending melody (Ex. 71). Although the whole movement is based on an accompaniment in quarter- and eighth-notes, Rautavaara often disrupts this rhythmic scheme with ligatures and changes of time signature.

The Signification of Musica Automata

Rautavaara used mechanical elements in conjunction with symmetry and mirror harmony in the brass for the first time in his Second Symphony; this will prove to be a significant characteristic of his "disturbance" technique. When auto-citing a passage from the symphony in *Angels and Visitations* he omitted the "disturbance" elements and placed them in a different section. Mirror harmony and symmetrical construction are the most recognizable elements of Rautavaara's style, but when given to the brass in the context of the "disturbance" technique, they become the most characteristic signs of the angelic aspects in Rautavaara's music; indeed, these elements play similar and important roles in *Angels and Visitations, Angel of Dusk*, and *Playgrounds for Angels*.

In passages featuring the "disturbance" technique, Rautavaara never employs a trumpet or trombone soloistically; they always from part of a three- to four-part homorhythmic setting. Significantly, the "disturbance" motifs in these three works about angels have the same intervallic structure: a succession of minor and major seconds that create a chromatic field in a harmonically symmetrical structure (compare Exx. 72, 73, and 74). This provides motivic coherence and allows the brass section to be treated as a single actor. In fact, mirror harmony in itself can be regarded as a kind of mechanical element; hence there is a connection between mechanicalness and the "disturbance" technique in the brass.

192   *Chapter 6*

EXAMPLE 71: *Angel of Light,* mvt. III, mm. 1-4

"Angelic" Features in Rautavaara's Instrumental Works

The "disturbance" technique can be interpreted in the light of Greimas's model of mythical actants again. The mechanical elements in the brass and the lack of such elements in the solo parts are also a kind of opposition between the mechanical and non-mechanical, representing the dichotomy non-human/human (Table 15).

EXAMPLE 72: *Angels and Visitations*, mm. 238-239, brass

194 Chapter 6

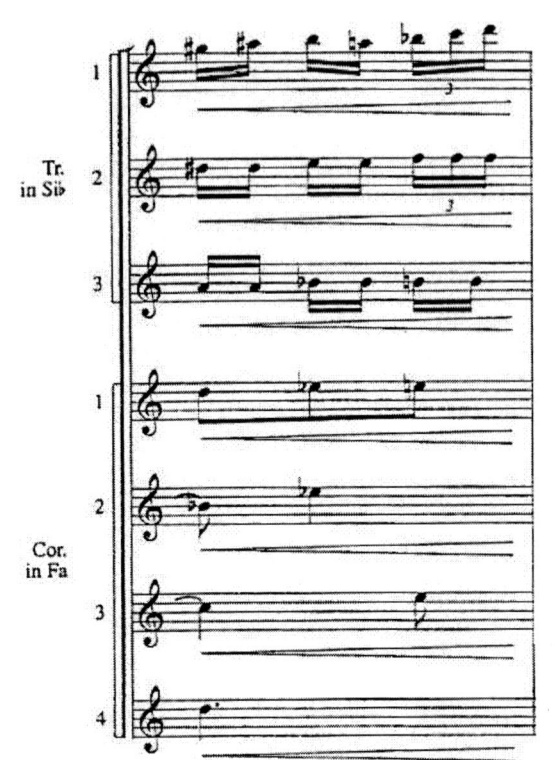

EXAMPLE 73:
Angel of Dusk,
mvt. I, m. 82

EXAMPLE 74:
Playgrounds for Angels,
m. 165

TABLE 15: Juxtaposition of mythical actants with instruments and *musica automata*

Mythical actants	subject	opponent
Instruments	soloist	trumpets, trombones
Musica automata	non-mechanical	mechanical
Signification	human	non-human

Trumpets and trombones not only act as an opponent but also as alien inhuman creatures, comparable to innocent children's toys or even Ernst Theodor Hoffmann's nightmares: ghosts, spirits, androids, or robots "both magical and terrible."[19] Rautavaara treats instruments symbolically, in the manner of vocalists, and gives them special roles according to their timbre and instrumental family.

Signification of Instruments

Rautavaara's inclination toward innovative orchestration is apparent throughout his career.[20] It is apparent not only in the orchestrations of larger solo and chamber works such as *Fiddlers, Fünf Sonette an Orpheus* (1955-56/1960), *Ballad for Harp and Strings* (1973/1980), and *Before the Icons*, but also in those smaller compositions that he later incorporates into larger instrumental and vocal scores, as when *Lehdet lehtiä* for men's choir is quoted in *Angels and Visitations*, in the finale of the opera *The House of the Sun*, and as the second movement of *Autumn Gardens*, when *Notturno* for violin and piano turn into the third movement of *Angel of Light*, or when passages from the opera *Thomas* recur in the third and fourth movements of the Eighth Symphony. Sometimes Rautavaara reorchestrates compositions and gives them a new title or includes them in different compositions: thus the reworked orchestral movements of *Kaivos* become Cantos I and II[21] and the fourth movement of the Second Symphony recurs in *Angels and Visitations*. Reorchestrated compositions might retain their original title, as is the case in the thrice-rescored First Symphony (1956/1988/2003) and in

---

[19] See Abbate, 215.

[20] "My method is to write first the piano score and during that work I already plan what kind of instruments I need to use, but I do not start its score immediately because one of the reasons is that in this large work I cannot know at the beginning what I am going to need later; it is better to leave that for later." Personal communication, Helsinki, 30 April 2008.

[21] More about the reworking of passages from *Kaivos* as Canto I and Canto II can be found in Sivuoja-Gunaratnam, *Narrating with Twelve Tones*, 93-103.

the Second Symphony; or they might receive a new title, as when the First String Quartet (1952) became the *Suite for Strings* (1952). These tendencies reflect the composer's intertextural approach to his musical material, which he recycles several times to "make works live longer and at the same time to emphasize their form in 'the now'."[22] New orchestrations "refresh" the compositions, giving them a greater range of colors and sonorities, and the new titles provide different semantic contexts for interpretation.[23] The best example is the orchestral work *Garden of Spaces* (2003), previously entitled *Regular Sets of Elements in a Semi-regular Situation* (1971).[24] The orchestration of a work seems to bring the material to its "most perfect state," so instrumentation must be an essential element in understanding the composer's music.

Rautavaara's approach to instrumentation evolved through his different stylistic periods. His "breakthrough" work, the Third Symphony, is in Sivuoja-Gunaratnam's opinion the one that started the process of the hierarchization of instrumental texture, in which every group of instruments is entrusted with a different role.[25] During Rautavaara's long career, the principle of "hierarchization of instruments" remains largely unchanged.[26] He has created a kind of "instrumental vocabulary" in which certain instruments possess symbolic meaning. Hence the hierarchization of instruments reflects the hidden symbolism in his music, and in this sense the Greimassian model of mythical actants (realized through the use of the "disturbance" technique), together with the role and significance of mechanical elements, provide the basis on which to understand the symbolic function of instruments in compositions referring to angels. Rautavaara classifies instruments into six groups: woodwinds, metallophones, strings, brass, non-metallophone percussion instruments, and solo instruments, according them different significations.[27]

---

[22] See Tiikkaja, "Einojuhani Rautavaara":49.

[23] See Sivuoja-Gunaratnam, "Narcissus Musicus": 12.

[24] In a reverse scenario, Rautavaara occasionally changes a work's title without any modifications to its musical material, primarily in the interest of widening its appeal to audiences. With regard to the work originally known as *Hommage à Zoltan Kodaly* (1982) but later advertised as *Bird Gardens*, he commented: "The work was commissioned in 1982 by the Kodály Society. Later I understood that the title limited performances of the composition to Hungarian connections." Personal communication, 8 February 2007.

[25] See Sivuoja-Gunaratnam, *Narrating with Twelve Tones*, 58.

[26] Even in the entirely serial Fourth Symphony *Arabescata* there is a division of roles: each instrumental group employs a different form of the row: the percussion uses the prime form, "[...] the plucked and keyed instruments its inversion, the woodwinds the 'fifths' row and the brass the 'fourths' row." Aho, *Einojuhani Rautavaara as Symphonist*, 94.

[27] Some instruments, such as the piano, join the metallophones in some works, but act as soloists in others and therefore belong to a different group.

Woodwinds

Generally, Rautavaara treats the woodwind group as homogeneous, giving it arabesque-like material in the form of short melodic lines based on scales or symmetrical modes that often exhibit mirror writing or engage in *ostinato* figurations. The most typical texture has the instruments playing in rhythmic monotony in a medium or high register. The woodwinds rarely carry the composition's crucial material or even expressive melodic lines like the solo cantilenas they typically get to play in Romantic music. The result is a kind of ornamented backdrop that by means of multiple repetitions of overlapping, arabesques gives the illusion of permanent movement.[28] In this manner, the woodwind group contributes to the *"impassibilité"* technique already mentioned (Ex. 75).

A well-known example of permanent woodwind ornamentation occurs in the arabesques that imitate birdsong in the *Cantus arcticus*. Rautavaara describes this ornamentation as "birdsong," and the symbol of the bird is essential for his aesthetic: "The appearance of birds in my works is unintentional, so I suppose they must have deeper symbolic meaning for me. Birds are mysterious citizens of two worlds. But the swan, like man, is unfortunately bound to an element in which it must suffer, to a being that is dualistic ... that is why the fate of birds is reminiscent of the fate of man."[29] Rautavaara shares Messiaen's belief that flying birds are messengers between Heaven and Earth, and hence the most spiritual animal. Through their singing they are like terrestrial angels, conveying a spiritual message in an unknown language. For Rautavaara, some birds share the "terrifying" aspect of angels: "It happened in Helsinki in a park. I went to a park and sat on the bench near a huge amount of small birds, and they were terribly mechanical, not like birds in the countryside."[30] In *Angels and Visitations* and *Angel of Dusk*, he asks for modern performing techniques such as multiphonics, whistle tones, and flutter-tonguing to create sonoristic passages. It must be stressed, however, that while arabesques suggestive of birdsong appear in all of Rautavaara's instrumental compositions referring to angels, they do not function as markers of this particular extramusical signified but are characteristics of Rautavaara's style in general. Birdsong imputes angelic qualities into all of his works, making them reflect his mystical attitudes.

---

[28] Mikko Heiniö argues that the technique of arabesques is reminiscent of Ravel's style. See Heiniö, "A Portrait of the Artist at a Certain Moment": 9.

[29] Rautavaara quoted in Sivuoja-Gunaratnam, "Vincent – not a Portrait": 11.

[30] Personal communication, Helsinki, 19 June 2007.

EXAMPLE 75: *Angel of Dusk*, mvt. III, mm. 31-33

Metallophones

Although harps are string instruments and marimbas rely on wooden keys, Rautavaara groups both instruments alongside celesta, glockenspiel, and vibraphone, claiming that their sound shares certain qualities with the metallophones.[31] In some works the group is extended through the addition of synthesizer and piano; see, e.g., the opera *Vincent*. As with the other instrumental groups, Rautavaara treats the metallophones as a homogeneous ensemble and frequently uses several or all of them together. Their function is similar to that of the woodwinds: they accompany the main melodic line by creating a background consisting of figurations and arpeggios, employed as their idiosyncratic counterpart to the woodwinds' arabesques.[32] This provides a "bright" instrumental color, which Rautavaara uses in his operas' dreamy passage, particularly at the beginning of *Thomas* and *Vincent*. Thus the most important technique of the metallophones, like the woodwinds, is the *"impassibilité"* technique, and it is in this role that they are used most commonly in Rautavaara's music (Ex. 76).

The symbolization attributed to the metallophones is a crucial component of Rautavaara's mystical attitude. Their timbre is bell-like: an unsurprising observation, since the sound of many metallophones is produced by striking metal surfaces. The bell-like, sustained quality of metallophone sounds creates a specific atmosphere, the timbre evoking religious and spiritual practices. All religions use bells, usually entrusting unique functions to them in accordance with their different sizes. These functions range from signals within the Divine Service in Christian churches[33] through to the noises made to drive away demons. The imitation of church-bells is easily detectable in "The Death of the Mother of God" from the piano suite *Icons*.[34] Bell sounds have fascinated Rautavaara from an early age. On a trip with his parents to the Orthodox monastery in Valamo, he had his first mystical experience, which stuck in his mind and returned in compositions such as *Icons* and *Vigilia*:

---

[31] Particularly when the harpist is instructed to play *glissandos* with a metal tuning key.

[32] The group is never defined by rhythm, only by color. Rautavaara sometimes introduces new hues by requesting uncommon brushes, beaters, or sticks. As a result, the sound of the metallophone can be harsher, and hence better suited for playing rhythmic material more distinctly; in that case they may join with the rest of the percussion, as happens in the first movement of *Angel of Dusk*, where the vibraphone, played at measure 59 with hard beaters, becomes a sheer rhythmic instrument.

[33] Many Catholic churches have an "Angelus" bell, which is rung for the Angelus prayer, in the morning, at midday, and in the evening.

[34] Eila Tarasti, "Icons," 559.

> The summer before the Winter War in 1939 my parents took me on a tour of eastern Finland, to Karelia—a land which was shortly to vanish for ever. On the islands swimming in the middle of the immense Lake Ladoga there was a monastery—Valamo. One went there in a little ship, early in the morning, so that the ten-year-old boy standing at the prow saw around him only dreary grey morning mist. But then, suddenly without warning the mist dispersed and most wonderful islands sprang forth. They seemed to be floating in the air, and in the midst of the trees rising on them appeared a dome, many domes, towers which in the sun shone full of colors! And suddenly they began to ring—bells, large and small, high tinklings and deep festive booms. The whole world was all at once full of sound and color, so that one's breath caught in the throat and one no longer understood where one was and what could happen. A world full of towers, sounds, visions! And then after landing, black-bearded monks, a strange language, white corridors in the monastery, soaring high arches in the church. Covered with painted saints, kings and angels...[35]

Although woodwinds and metallophones both contribute to the *"impassibilité"* technique, they stand for different extramusical symbols. While the woodwinds arabesques evoke birdsong, the metallophones imitate bells. Both sounds have spiritual connotations; for Rautavaara, they function as signs of something beyond human comprehension. In the context of angelic beings, the two instrumental groups create a specific atmosphere that can be called spiritual or sacred—a space for angelic visitations, as it were.

Strings

The strings are treated as yet another homogeneous group that Rautavaara occasionally uses to create a special celestial atmosphere. While the beautiful cantilenas so typical of his style are often given to the violins, the same violins may also be divided into twelve strands to create a rustling effect or support the percussion group with short rhythmic motifs. These moving backgrounds often start and end an orchestral works (see the beginning and the middle section respectively of *Angels and Visitations*). The effect may be intensified by tremolos that make the backdrop pulsate, corresponding with the composer's idea of treating the work as a living, organic form.[36] Furthermore, Rautavaara sometimes thickens the cantilena lines by dividing the violins and doubling their lines at various intervals, placing an *ostinato* harmony in certain parts, and thus treating them as a harmonic background.

---

[35] Rautavaara, "On a Taste for the Infinite": 110.

[36] "I think that it all comes down to an organic approach." Rautavaara, *Orchestral Works*, 4.

"Angelic" Features in Rautavaara's Instrumental Works

EXAMPLE 76: *Angels and Visitations*, m. 49, marimba, celesta, harp, and strings

In his compositions evoking angels, Rautavaara often uses violins and violas in a high register without the support of cellos and basses.[37] This creates a celestial atmosphere: the mild and soft timbre of strings without harmonic support seem to float in the air without touching ground, and thus suggest as space close to heaven, reminiscent of the composer's childhood experience of Valamo Island as it appears from the mist (Ex. 76). The string timbre is an important part of Rautavaara's orchestral sound, for it gives his works a soft and warm color[38] in which the violins carry the main melodic line (sometimes together with the cello in the baritone range). On the symbolic level, one could thus summarize that whereas the woodwinds have a connotation with birds and the metallophones with bells, the strings (together with trumpet and trombones) are cast as the voice of the angelic messengers themselves.

Brass

Brass instruments form the most significant orchestral group in Rautavaara's works in general,[39] but also and more specifically in compositions referring to angels because of their role in the "disturbance" technique. This group thus has two main roles: to "disturb" (i.e., to carry divine messages into the human sphere) and to play chorales (i.e., to carry human praise and prayer back to God). In the first case, the material used in the noisy outbursts that interrupt a melodic process in other instruments is both mechanical and symmetrical; as with the woodwinds, melodic lines are avoided in favor of combinations of short motifs. While the woodwind material is modal, that of the brass is chromatic. In the second case, the brass conveys a religious mood in diatonic formulations and chordal constructions using triadic four-part harmonies. This harmonic language was probably inspired by Bruckner's music, which Rautavaara admired in his youth; it is from this source that the tuba has come to play "[...] a 'glorificational' role" in Rautavaara's music."[40] The material in chorale style evokes men's choirs, a musical institution that bears some significance for the composer, who explicitly refers to the closed

---

[37] For examples, mm. 39-72 in *Angels and Visitations* and mm. 1-18 in movement III of *Angel of Light*.

[38] The one time Rautavaara decided to use avant-garde string techniques was in *Angel of Dusk* in the soloist's cadenza.

[39] The Third Symphony is the first work in which Rautavaara gave the brass ensemble a significant role. Here, they play in many chorale-like passages and appear in magnificent orchestral *tutti*. Brass chorales are an important element of the composer's style and appear in most of his works.

[40] See Sivuoja-Gunaratnam, *Narrating with Twelve Tones*, 58.

"Men's House," another curious phenomenon in Finnish choral culture: this is a chorus of male voices "whose significance as a mythical ritual ground for the bucks of the species can only be guessed at."[41] As remarked at the beginning of this chapter, Rautavaara very often took the material for his instrumental music from his vocal and choral scores. The brass representation of the men's choir is noticeable; hence the "mythical ground" becomes visible not only in the choir but also in the brass. Just as the men's choir in *Vigilia* is a reflection of Rautavaara's childhood memory of the trip to Valamo, the brass ensemble may symbolize both the singing of Orthodox monks and the pagan Finnish ritual "Men's House."

The Rest of the Percussion Group

If the metallophones tinge the works about angels with "bright" colors, the rest of the percussion, particularly the membranophones, serve to "darken" the orchestral palette and to add rhythmic emphasis. Some instruments have only a coloristic function. A first group, including the lion's roar, metal sheet, and flexatone, are employed to produce noisy, dreadful sounds in support of "disturbance" material played in the brass.

Different coloristic effects are linked to tubular bells, tam-tam, cymbals, gong, and whip. Yet other percussion instruments emphasize rhythm, as do the bass drum, tom-toms, woodblocks, and snare drum. The composer widens the palette of sounds by requiring cymbals to be placed on the skin of kettledrums, by treating the xylophone as a means of coloring the orchestra with its dry, short sounds, etc.

Solo Instruments

Rautavaara prefers to operate with two or more instruments and with whole instrumental groups treated as choirs, rather than with single instruments. The one exception is the use of a solo horn, which suggests that this instrument functions as a musical symbol. Rautavaara included solos for horn in each of his orchestral works after the Third Symphony: "I use the horn when I need something singable but also solid, not too soft but commending something very truthful."[42] He always gives the horn long, beautiful cantilenas in open, free rhythms in a manner comparable to Pyotr Tchaikovsky's use of solo horns in his symphonic works. Why does a composer who commonly avoids solos in his symphonic output give such a significant place to solo horn?

---

[41] Rautavaara, "Choirs, Myths and Finnishness": 3.

[42] Personal communication, 29 October 2007.

Though he composed concertos for various instruments—piano, violin, cello, double bass, flute, clarinet, harp, and percussion—Rautavaara never wrote one for horn. It is curious that in *Playgrounds for Angels* there are four trumpets and four trombones, but only one each of horn and tuba. He accords the horn an individualized role, contrasting it with the four trumpets and trombones, and makes *Playgrounds for Angels* a kind of *concertante* work for horn.[43]

In Rautavaara's orchestral music, the horn represents a "romantic" character and thus embodies a symbolic role. Like the double bass in *Angel of Dusk*, the horn in *Playgrounds for Angels* symbolizes an individual who is in a conflict with society. Like the cello, the horn plays in the baritone range, and as the heroes in Rautavaara's operas are often baritones, the horn may represent the baritone voice in instrumental music.[44] If the operatic protagonists are Rautavaara's alter egos, then the horn, too, as a solo instrument may reflect the composer. Surprisingly, the horn as an autobiographical instrument is connected with the unicorn, a mythical animal that is important to the composer. This can be word play (from *uni*—solo and *corno*—horn) or a kind of hidden extramusical allusion. According to the most popular Western legends, the unicorn is a rare, wild, and solitary animal whose single horn has marvelous powers. In the presence of a virgin, its fierceness will turn to gentleness. Inspired by James Broughton's book *True and False Unicorn* (1957), Rautavaara, wrote four compositions featuring the animal in the title: *True and False Unicorn*, an unconventional cantata to Broughton's text; two works for solo guitar called *Serenades of the Unicorn* (1977) and *Monologues of the Unicorn* (1980); and *Interludes of the Unicorn* (2006).[45] Rautavaara often discusses the legend of the unicorn and its similarity to his private life, declaring: "The unicorn is my emblem."[46] Others have also noticed the likelihood of the unicorn functioning as the composer's alter ego,

---

[43] As Charles Rosen explains, the horn did not play a significant role prior to the Romantic era, probably because it was restricted to basic triadic and diatonic passages, since the valve mechanism had not yet been invented. In the late classical era, the situation changed because of technical improvements, and the horn became the most popular instrument in the classic and romantic orchestra. The fanfare topic ("horn fifths") enabled it to become the romantic symbol of nature both in literature (*The Youth's Magic Horn*) and in music (Beethoven's Sixth Symphony, Brahms's Third Symphony, Bruckner's Fourth Symphony, and also Debussy's *La Mer*). In addition, in Schubert's music the horn began to symbolize memory or distance, absence, and regret. Rosen, 116-124.

[44] See Sivuoja-Gunarantam, *Narrating with Twelve Tones*, 191.

[45] This latter work is an arrangement of some instrumental interludes from the cantata *True and False Unicorn* for symphony orchestra.

[46] Quoted from the documentary film about Rautavaara, *The Gift of Dreams*.

"the personification of the artist, at times semi-divine and at others a wretch and villain."[47] Undoubtedly the interpretation of the French horn as a symbol of the unicorn is just one possible interpretation; yet it is most consistent with the composer's inspirations and interests. As the solo horn plays a significant role in Rautavaara's instrumental music, it may well be a representation of individualization. It may also be a sign of security, which the composer describes in the following words: "I have always loved all kinds of enclosed places.... As a child I was especially fond of traveling in the night train, in a sleeper car with everything in it, where you can wash and sleep and where you would be as in the womb. All kinds of safe, enclosed places were like *Isle of Bliss* or the Squirrel's nest to me ... [expressing] the same feeling."[48]

Dark versus Light

Two of the subtitles alluding to angels refer to degrees of brightness: *Angel of Dusk* and *Angel of Light*. "Dusk," the time of day when the sun has just set beneath the horizon, suggests darkness or at least, murkiness, in contrast to "light." In the *Angel Trilogy*, the Double Bass Concerto *Angel of Dusk* is followed by the Seventh Symphony; thus the composer clearly planned to juxtapose the two oppositional qualities. In the context of this study, the question is how the two qualities of brightness manifest themselves in the musical material of these works. Is it possible to consider these qualities as thesis and antithesis, as is so typical in Rautavaara's symphonies? Although the composer limits an explicit indication of categories of brightness to these two works, the following discussion will demonstrate that the two categories equally inform the internal structure of the other instrumental compositions referring to angels.

The argument is buttressed by two theories: the first by the French novelist and literary theorist Michel Butor,[49] the second by Eero Tarasti, who draws on classifications by Helmut Lachenmann.[50] Butor distinguishes four categories of color: physiological, modal, tonal and local. The first three categories in particular are intertwined.

---

[47] Aho, "Einojuhani Rautavaara": 4.

[48] From *The Gift of Dreams*.

[49] As explained by Eila Tarasti, "Music: The Art of Light and Shadow; or, How Clarity Appears in Tones," Eero Tarasti. ed., *Music and the Arts. Proceedings from ICMS 7* (Helsinki: International Semiotics Institute, 2006), 266-280.

[50] Eero Tarasti, "A Theory of Light in Music": 681-690.

Physiological color in music in based on the fact that the human ear perceives high registers as bright and low registers as dark, a notion that has a source in the theory of aliquots, since high pitches have many more aliquots than low pitches. If a composer transposes a melodic line into different registers, a listener will perceive it as a melody with different colors. Rautavaara's works about angels include salient examples of this coloring. In "Archangel Michael Fighting the Antichrist," the composer transposes one melodic line to different registers. On its first appearance it sounds in the register between C3 and B4, the second time one octave higher; the third time two octaves higher; finally it returns to its starting position in the third and fourth octave. *Angels and Visitations* features a transposition of the main chorale theme from the brass ensemble to the strings with a similar effect.

EXAMPLE 77: *Angels and Visitations*, mm. 81-82, strings

In addition to this change of register and instrumental color, Rautavaara thickens the melodic line with added seconds, thus enriching the color spectrum. The composer describes this process in the following way: "In my orchestral output violin notes can be very dissonant; in that way there are added notes which give it more splendor. This is something that conductors cannot always understand."[51] The effect is reminiscent of a painting technique in which small spots of white paint are placed in people's eyes to make them seem brighter.[52]

Like the last composition from the piano suite *Icons*, the passage from *Angels and Visitations* demonstrates the process of passing from dark to brighter registers. The next passage in *Angels and Visitations* is the autocitation from *Lehdet lehtiä*, which appears three times with different instrumentation and in different registers: it is first given to the strings in their middle register, then repeated one octave higher; subsequently passing through the middle registers of the woodwind and harp to the high register of metallophones and harp. In *Angel of Dusk* the soloist's cantilena in the middle register is juxtaposed with rapid motifs in celesta and harp in a higher register: this juxtaposition makes the double bass part appear even "darker." Although the soloist's material ascends gradually from a low to a higher register, it never reaches the higher registers of its bright accompaniment. A similar process can be observed in the concerto's third movement, in which the soloist's line wanders from a low to a high register, although in the coda the higher pitches of the soloist are unified with the orchestra. (The case of *Angel of Light* receives a separate explanation later in this subchapter, since that work is full of effects that represent wandering from dark to light.)

Next to physiological colors, modal colors are most easily perceptible in Rautavaara's instrumental compositions. The young Rautavaara learned from Persichetti how to use modulations from one mode to another in order to create an effect of brightness. In this context the last composition from *Icons*, based on such effects, stands as an iconic representation of the fight between the archangel Michael and the antichrist. The Archangel, as a positive character and symbol of light, is symbolized by bright modes, and the antichrist, a dark character and representative of evil forces, by darker modes. The contrast between them and the passing from one mode to another create musical oppositions supported by constant shifts in register. The modulation between symmetrical modes in *Angel of Dusk*, with its progression from Messiaen's mode 2 through to mode 3 in the coda of the composition, is another example of how Rautavaara uses modal brightness (see Fig. 16).

---

[51] Personal communication, Helsinki, 30 April 2008.
[52] Pointillists, such as Georges-Pierre Seurat and Paul Signac, took this effect to an extreme in their pictures built exclusively from small dots of paint.

Modal colors lead over to tonal color, which is a kind of supplementation and extension of the former. Following a long musical tradition, Rautavaara introduces the dark D minor at the beginning of his *Angel of Light*, thereby creating a background over which bright material is superimposed with the introduction of the "Bloomington" theme in the metallophones. In this way, tonal color is intertwined with physiological color (Exx. 78 and 79).[53]

EXAMPLE 78: *Angel of Light*, mvt. I, mm. 1-5, metallophones, harp, and strings

---

[53] Similar instances occur in the second movement, mm. 133-150

"Angelic" Features in Rautavaara's Instrumental Works

EXAMPLE 79: *Angel of Light*, mvt. II, mm. 133-135

The conclusion of the symphony stands in opposition to the beginning, with its dense network of arabesque lines in various instruments, harp glissando, and stable E-major and B-flat-major chords. It provides a kind of illumination effect that can be interpreted as a symbol of light, since in the nineteenth century in particular, the E-major chord had that connotation.

A similar effect is described by Eero Tarasti, with reference to the symphony's third movement. Here, the composer "[...] lets the dark and somber motif ascend against a thick texture of strings in the upper register, so that the motif rises as if from the depths of the orchestra."[54]

Angel of Light is full of dark and light effects, not only in the juxtaposition of motifs as physiological color and the use of tonal colors such as D minor and E major, but also in the employment of ascending motifs that give an illusion of brightening. The composer employs two familiar effects in the strings as part of a closure formula. In the first movement, the effect is achieved by an ascending G-minor chord, played by strings and harp; in the last movement, gradually slowing tremolo clusters produce a similar effect (Ex. 80). Both instances are also typical examples of the dark-light opposition, since the basses and cello do not participate as such; rather, they sustain single low notes to provide harmonic support. The two layers, one high and the other low, are separated by a musical "gulf," which emphasizes the strong contrast between these extremes.

The broad spectrum of dark-light effects in *Angel of Light* proves that there is an integral correspondence between the title and the musical material of the work. The music starts in the first movement with a dark D minor (associated with death), leading to E major and finally closing in B-flat major in the fourth movement. The Symphony thus continues the classical tendency initiated by Haydn's overture to *The Creation* and Beethoven's Ninth Symphony, in that it demonstrates the process of passing from dark to light. In the Christian faith this passage represents the transition from death to life, from sin to redemption. The oppositional terms darkness and lightness are another binary opposition, and hence another mythical structure. As in Crumb's *Star-Child*,[55] Rautavaara uses orchestration that reflects the dichotomy of contrasting shades: the dark timbres of the double basses, cellos, violas with bassoons, lower brass and aggressive percussion contrast with the light effect of strings, metallophones, flutes, clarinets, oboes, and harp. Rautavaara's use of instrumental color extends to his using new avant-garde methods of sound production that emphasize the role of sonoristic qualities and coloristic attitudes.[56] In all of the work concerning angels, such avant-garde methods create "noisy sounds" for dark effects, whereas traditional performance techniques belong to the category of light effects.

---

[54] Eero Tarasti, "A Theory of Light in Music": 685.

[55] Crumb describes this composition as "finding the light in a world of darkness ... progression from darkness to light." See Adamenko, 43.

[56] See Eero Tarasti, "A Theory of Light in Music": 687-688.

"Angelic" Features in Rautavaara's Instrumental Works 211

EXAMPLE 80: *Angel of Light*, mvt. IV, mm. 118-119

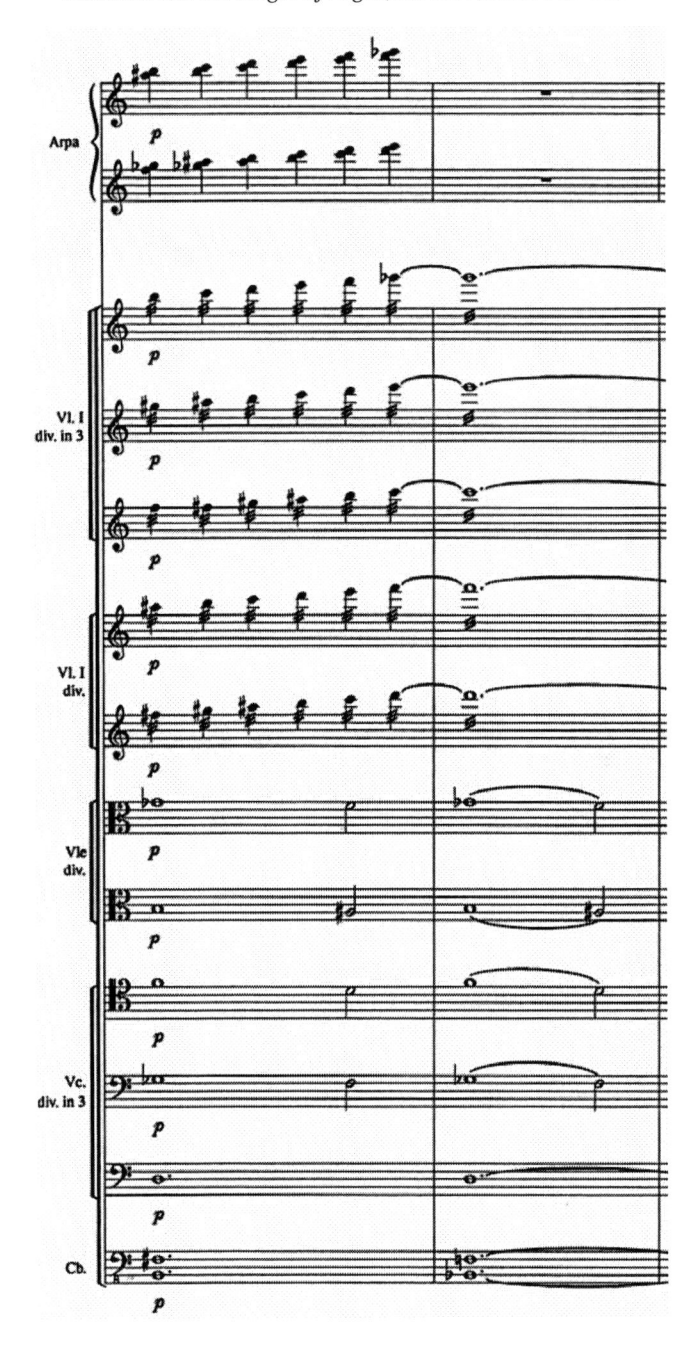

The dark-light dichotomy in Rautavaara's compositions about angels may also be examined as local color. In Finland, the opposition between dark and light days is most noticeable in the comparison of the seasons. Winter days are very short, while summer days are extraordinarily long; in Lapland spends winters in perpetual night and summer in what seems like a single long day. These circumstances have great impact on the Finnish people, their behavior, their architecture, and their way of living. As a result, not only are dark effects typical of Finnish music, but also the contrast between darkness and light.

In *Angels and Visitations*, groups of instruments further contrast with each other or with solo instruments through different types of articulation. This may explain the duality in the title between angels (light) and visitations (dark). In *Angel of Dusk* and *Playgrounds for Angels*, a duality exists between the soloist (double bass, solo horn) and the aggressive material in the trumpets, trombones and percussion; moreover, the concerto features avant-garde performance techniques in the soloist's cadenza. *Angel of Light* enacts a symphonic progression from dark to light, and new techniques of sound creation are explored in the second movement. This supports a hypothesis that Rautavaara uses more traditional performance techniques in the symphony because he wanted to underline the "light" of the title. (Thus far, the argument is strictly theoretical and does not provide an answer to the fundamental question of how the dark-light dichotomy refers to the figure of the angel in the music. *Angel of Light* will provide an answer of sorts.)

Mandala Form

The use of simultaneous time in Rautavaara's operas can be interpreted as related to the composer's most important spiritual symbol, the mandala. Mandalas are geometrical symbols such as circles, spheres, squares, and pyramids read as models of the Universe. A mandala can be described as a mythologem, which in Lévi-Strauss's words is "[...] a kind of language in which an entire myth can be expressed in a single word."[57] The term mandala derives from the Hindu word for "concentric energy circle." Its symbol can be found in Hinduism and Buddhism, but also to a certain extent in Judaism, Christianity, and Islam. During the 1970s and '80 s, Rautavaara was strongly influenced by Jung's notions of archetypes and synchronicity. Jung wrote extensively about the mandala, which he considered to be "[...] a representation

---

[57] Lévi-Strauss, *Structural Anthropology*, vol. II, Monique Layton, trans. (New York, NY: Basic Books, 1976), 144.

"Angelic" Features in Rautavaara's Instrumental Works

of the unconscious self." Rautavaara responded to this, recognizing that the mandala represents the perfect visual symmetrical form. He had long had a strong interest in symmetry in art, an interest that was developed further in Persichetti's harmony courses.[58] Rautavaara's first important work employing symmetry was *Seven Preludes*, later used as material in his Second Symphony. In his compositions concerning angels, symmetrical formulations are particularly common in the material for brass: as has been shown above, their motifs of "disturbance" employ mirror writing.

While Rautavaara often makes use of symmetrical scales, modes, harmonies, and rhythms, these features are not characteristic of, let alone limited to, his instrumental compositions referring to angels. A very convincing case, however, is *Angel of Light*, in which the composer employs the twelve-tone technique and symmetrical rows. The frequently employed row VI is taken from the choral work *Die erste Elegie*. It consists of four chords—two minor and two major triads—and exhibits a symmetrical and mirror construction: the row's the second half is the retrograde inversion of the first.

FIGURE 33: Row VI from *Angel of Light*

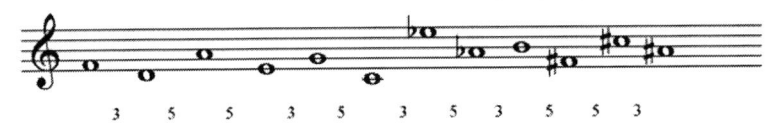

At this point, it is important to mention the Fourth Symphony, particularly the section "Arabescata II" in which Rautavaara tries to portray graphic elements in music, such as letters in the fourth movement (*dedicatio*) and circles in the fifth (*rotatus*).[59] If the symmetrical and mirror structure of row VI is also such a graphic portrayal, then it may be represented as a circle in which the first six pitches are half of the circle, and the next six the remaining half, as a retrograde inversion of the first half.

In Figure 34 the two corresponding pitches of row VI are connected with a straight line, creating the musical representation of a circle. A circle or sphere is the most important geometrical symbol of mandala form. This archaic, mythical and magic form of the row provides another proof for my claim that Rautavaara is a mythical composer.

---

[58] Persichetti explained to his students the notions of symmetrical scales and mirror harmonies, and encouraged them to write short exercises.

[59] See Aho, *Einojuhani Rautavaara as Symphonist*, 95-96; Sivuoja-Gunaratnam, *Narrating with Twelve Tones*, 200.

214 *Chapter 6*

FIGURE 34: Graphic representation of row VI as a circle

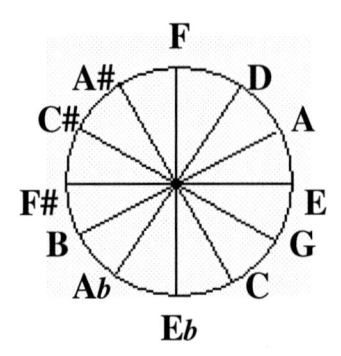

The symphony sets out from the $P_{VI}0$, which is then transposed ($P_{VI}9$, $P_{VI}4$, $P_{VI}11$, $P_{VI}2$, and (after a short passage using the first row) $P_{VI}2$, $P_{VI}11$, $P_{VI}6$, $P_{VI}3$, $P_{VI}10$, $P_{VI}5$ and $P_{VI}0$, thus closing the circular form. When this sequence is repeated, the circular form is broken $P_{VI}9$ by the introduction of $P_{VI}1$ and $P_{VI}7$, followed by a jump to $P_{VI}2$:

FIGURE 35: Graphic representation of the circular form in *Angel of Light*, mvt. I

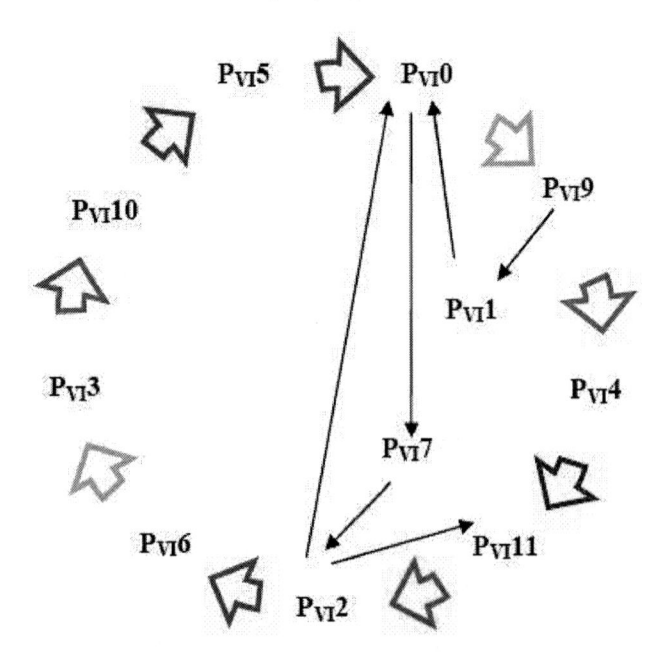

In the second movement, Rautavaara uses row VI less frequently; the third movement, however, is based on another circular series of row transpositions. Beginning with $P_{VI}2$, the series of transpositions passes through $P_{VI}7$ and $P_{VI}10$, before returning to the start; there is then a repetition followed by $P_{VI}3$, $P_{VI}6$, and finally $P_{VI}2$. The circular form here is different from that detected in the first movement, because only five transpositions are employed, but the element of repetition seems even stronger.

FIGURE 36: Graphic representation of the circular form in *Angel of Light*, mvt. III

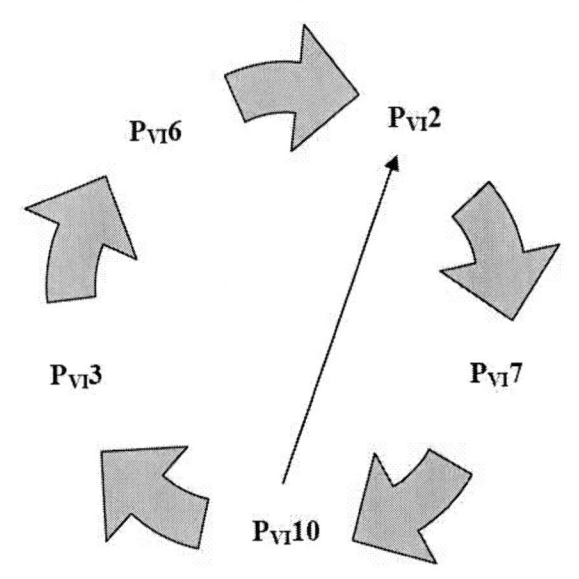

Such circular series of transpositions are not used in the final movement; here, row VI is employed vertically in the form of chords and subsequently abandoned in favor of row V. Although such circular series of transpositions are not to be found throughout the whole symphony, the fact that they appear in the first and third movements is evidence of Rautavaara's admiration of mandala form. With omnipresent symmetries and the mirror-forms of row VI, *Angel of Light* constitutes a kind of spiral symphony, a magic mantra.[60] It is not a journey but a contemplation, an eternal return to the obsessive twelve-tone row and to the obsessive personal myth that may be the figure of the angel itself.

---

[60] Note, though, that its construction is different from the spiral form of the Fifth Symphony. See Aho, *Einojuhani Rautavaara as Symphonist*, 98-102.

216 *Chapter 6*

The circular form of row VI and its circular series of transpositions in the first and third movements are not only reminiscent of the mandala but also of angelic choirs, as described by Pseudo-Dionysius the Areopagite, Hildegard von Bingen, and Thomas Aquinas. If row VI can be called the figure of an angel, then transpositions of this figure create movement. In Pseudo-Dionysius's theory, the nine angelic choirs are like circles, spheres or rings that surround God; Hildegard von Bingen described these choirs as the emanation of God, Divine light, and twinkling. Thomas Aquinas summarized these theories in his philosophical and theological writings, subsequently described by Dante Alighieri in his *Divine Comedy* (Paradiso 28.88-129). At a first glance, Gustave Doré's illustration of this passage is close to the form of a mandala; moreover, the concentric angelic choirs are presented as pure, blinding light (Plate 3).

PLATE 3: Gustav Doré,
"Dante and Beatrice see God as a point of light surrounded by angels"

Both the mandala form and the theory of light are congruent with the idea of angels. In the Judeo-Christian tradition, the adjectives "dark" and "light" correspond to different kinds of angels. Dark symbolizes evil, death, and hell, so the dark angel is the same as the black angel, an evil spirit (a demon or even Satan). Conversely, light is the symbol of God, eternal life, and positive values, therefore referring to good angels and their hierarchies, which emanate God's light. The mandala forms of row VI in two movements of *Angel of Light* may be a perfect example of the notion of light-emanating angels applied to music. Yet while there can be two oppositional categories in one composition – by way of comparison: the tenth movement of Crumb's *Black Angels* contains "God-music" that stands in opposition to the titular Black Angels with their "devil-music" – none of Rautavaara's angelic compositions contain the dichotomy of dark and light angels. While the apparent opposition of the two movement titles in the *Angel Trilogy* may momentarily give this impression, the sequence *Angel of Dusk ... Angel of Light* actually constitutes a process, a transition from dusk to light.

Chapter 7:
Musical Ekphrasis

Angels are symbols by nature because they have no equivalent in reality, only in the sphere of signification. The issue is further complicated by the fact that the reality of symbols arises out of conventions. When considering symbolic representations of angels, it is necessary to refer to cultural codes in which the angels as symbols can be understood. Rautavaara's commentaries provide insights into the understanding of his angelic symbols, situating them in a broader cultural context that includes numerous interrelations to art, poetry, religion, and psychology. These signs join music and the external world, creating a correspondence between music and the other arts.[1] The correspondences between Rautavaara's musically cast angels and their external sources can be regarded as instances of musical ekphrasis. Yet there are also internal sources: Rautavaara regularly links his musical portrayals of angels with his private symbols: his childhood dreams, memories, archetypes, and myths. His numerous commentaries on the angelic series provide a spectrum of interpretative codes by which to understand angels as an extramusical phenomenon in his music.

Although separate program notes exist for each of the instrumental compositions referring to angels, the most important commentaries can be found in three unrelated sources: the program to the choral work *Die erste Elegie*, the documentary film about Rautavaara entitled *The Gift of Dreams*, and an interview he gave to the weekly newspaper *National Catholic Reporter*.[2]

Rautavaara rejects the view of angels as "[...] swan-winged blondes in nightshirts presented by classical kitsch," saying that "the world of fantasy behind the 'Angel Series' has met with misunderstanding."[3] He tries to explain the figure of the angel through other non-musical sources, drawing on literature (Rilke's poetic cycle *Duino Elegies*), psychology (Jungian archetypes common to all civilizations), religion (the biblical Jacob's wrestling

---

[1] Eero Tarasti, *A Theory of Musical Semiotics*, 57.

[2] Rich Heffern, "Conveying the Inexpressible: Interview with Einojuhani Rautavaara," *National Catholic Reporter* December 13 (2002).

[3] Rautavaara, commentary on *Angel of Dusk*, in the booklet accompanying the recording, Finlandia Records 4509-99969-2 (1981).

with the angel), and private obsessions (the terrifying creature that visited him in his childhood dreams). Although Rautavaara readily describes the many associations of his musical angels, he maintains that his music remains absolute, without programs, stories, or fixed imagery.[4]

> My youthful encounter with the poetry of Rainer Maria Rilke turned out to be quite a discovery, not only in literary terms but also for the development of my world view. I still associate it strongly with the mysticism surrounding the ruins of post-war Vienna. It was there that I composed my *Fünf Sonette an Orpheus*, and two years later in Cologne I started writing the song cycle *Die Liebenden* to Rilke's texts. From that time onwards I continued to carry with me—both mentally and in my suitcase—the *Duino Elegies*, Rilke's seminal work. Over the years I would take it out, finding myself particularly drawn to the first elegy, whose angel figure took on the role of a personal *animus*. My orchestral works *Angels and Visitations*, *Angel of Dusk* and *Playgrounds for Angels* are all musical personifications of this figure.[5]

The theory of musical ekphrasis allows to respect the composer's insistence on absolute music, considering the angel works as "mildly programmatic," alluding to but not specifically representing one or several of the aforementioned sources.

The Angel in Rilke's *Duino Elegies*

Rilke began writing his *Duineser Elegien* in 1911 while staying at Duino Castle; they mark his return to writing after a long period of inactivity. The opening lines of the *First Duino Elegy*, "Who, if I cried out, would hear me among the angels' hierarchies?"[6] came to Rilke as he was walking on the cliffs during a strong storm; he assumed that a voice from the sea had shouted these sentences to him. In a letter to his Polish translator Witold Hulewicz, he stressed a crucial distinction regarding the mysterious figure: "The 'angel' of the Elegies has nothing to do with the angel of the Christian heaven (rather with the angel figures of Islam)."[7] Karen J. Campbell examines the connection between the angels in *Duino Elegies* and those of Islam

---

[4] See Rautavaara, "On a Taste for the Infinite": 115.

[5] Rautavaara, commentary in the score of *Die erste Elegie* (Helsinki: Fazer, 1994).

[6] *The Selected Poetry of Rainer Maria Rilke,* trans. Stephen Mitchell (New York, NY: Vintage Books, 1989), 151.

[7] Karen J. Campbell, "Rilke's *Duino Angels* and the Angels of Islam," *Alif: Journal of Comparative Poetics* 23 (2003): 191.

and maintains that when writing the *Elegies*, Rilke was indeed influenced by the Quran: "[...] his primary source of Islamic inspiration was unquestionably Quranic material itself."[8] According to Campbell, Rilke's focus was on the nature of Mohammed's call to prophecy in the Quran, as he "[...] saw the (spectacular) relation of his own Duino angels to his poetic persona prefigured in the relation of the archangel Gabriel to the prophet Mohammed."[9] Moreover, the poet chose Islamic rather than Judeo-Christian[10] inspiration for his angels because he was "[...] more inclined to religions in which the mediator appears to be less essential or almost tuned out." The traditional Muslim proclamation of faith claims that only one messenger exists, Mohammed, and that the Quran was revealed only to Mohammed and without intervention of divine messengers. Both Mohammed and Rilke had subsequent revelations after long periods of waiting—Rilke wrote the next eight *Duino Elegies* in 1922, ten years after his First and Second Elegies,[11] whereas Mohammed had his second angelic revelation twenty years after his first.

In the *Duino Elegies* and in the subsequent cycle, *Sonette an Orpheus* (Sonnets to Orpheus, 1922), Rilke develops the concept of the transcendental function of poetry—"[...] transforming visible things into the invisible object of language, the imagination and the spirit."[12] This concept is already apparent in his *Neue Gedichte* (New Poems, 1907), but receives its most thorough articulation in the later two cycles. In the *Elegies*, Rilke's aim is to create a new image of the universe without the divisions of past and future, physical and spiritual dimensions, or being and non-being. Hans Georg Gadamer, in his essay *Mythopoetic Inversion in Rilke's Duino Elegies*, illustrates the significance of this cycle when he writes:

---

[8] Campbell: 191.

[9] "Mohammed is portrayed as being awakened from a deep sleep by a blinding light; after his eyes adjust to it he perceives an angel standing before him who spans the distance between heaven and earth, and is terrified. The angel lifts him to his feet by his hair—Mohammed feels no pain—and addresses him in a voice that fills him with fear. In the name of their common creator, he hands him a scroll and orders him to read. Mohammed responds that he is unable to read, but the angel admonishes him to do so before he leaves for the first time. According to other accounts, Mohammed later has the sense that the writing has descended into his heart and, after three years of keeping word of his visitations private, he is enjoined by the angel to make his message public." Campbell: 191.

[10] In 1912 Rilke's conception of angels returned to that of the Judeo-Christian tradition in his cycle of poems *Das Marien-Leben* in which the figure of the angel Gabriel is central in relation to the Virgin Mary. See Bruhn, *Rilkes Marien-Leben*, 21-32.

[11] For more on Rilke's process of writing the *Duino Elegies*, see Kathleen L. Komar, *Transcending Angels: Rainer Maria Rilke's Duino Elegies* (Lincoln, NE: University of Nebraska Press, 1987), 18.

[12] Patricia P. Brodsky, *Rainer Maria Rilke* (Boston, MA: Twayne Publishers, 1988), 14.

Like all elegies Rilke's *Duino Elegies* are laments. What is lamented is the unattainability of true happiness for lovers, or rather: the incapacity of lovers, and especially the man in love, to love in such a way that true fulfillment would become possible. Therewith, however, the theme of the elegies is broadened to something more general. The issue is the powerlessness of the human heart, its failure before the task of surrendering itself completely to its feeling.[13]

This is the context in which the Angel appears, who exceeds human beings in terms of absolute and explicit feelings. This creature has nothing in common with its Christian counterpart, for it is not a divine messenger but rather the symbol of spiritual perfection. Gadamer claims:

> Thus it is one of the highest possibilities of the human heart itself which is called upon as angel–a possibility before which it fails, which it cannot manage, because many things condition human beings, making them incapable of unequivocality and unrestricted surrender to their feelings.[14]

Such an angel is neither human nor divine; it stands for the constant feeling that humans will never attain. It terrifies humans, making them aware of their imperfection. Angelic greatness is beyond human reach, angels surpass humans in their smallness and imperfection. Humans find their world to be dark and sinister. In his letter to Hulewicz, Rilke explains his concept of the transformation of the visible earthly world into that of the invisible: "The angel of the Elegies is that being which vouches for our being able to recognize a higher level of reality in the realm of the invisible."[15]

Rilke clarified his conception of the transformation during his stay in Toledo, where he arrived to finish the cycle of his elegies. Although he did not complete them, the Castilian landscape made a strong impression on him, and his angelic figure became ever closer to the angels painted by El Greco. Thus the powerful and distant angel from the *Duino Elegies* is terrifying— "Ein jeder Engel ist schrecklich"— "For beauty is nothing but the beginning of terror, which we are still just able to endure"[16] ("Denn das Schöne ist nichts als des Schrecklichen Anfang").

---

[13] Hans Georg Gadamer, "Mythopoetic Inversion in Rilke's Duino Elegies," in J.M. Connolly et al., eds./trans., *Hermeneutics versus Science? Three German Views* (Notre Dame, IN: University of Notre Dame Press, 1988), 83 (Originally published as: "Mythopoietische Umkehrung in Rilkes *Duineser Elegien*," 1966).

[14] Gadamer, 84.

[15] "Der Engel der Elegien ist dasjenige Wesen, das dafür einsteht, im Unsichtbaren einen höheren Rang der Realität zu erkennen." English translation after Campbell: 191; original from Rainer Maria Rilke, *Briefe* (Wiesbaden: Insel, 1950), 900.

[16] *The Selected Poetry of Rainer Maria Rilke*, 151.

Musical Ekphrasis 223

Rilke follows the tradition of German elegies by juxtaposing the figure of the angel with puppets in order to present the process of the progression of consciousness. In his essay *Über das Marionettentheater* (1810), Heinrich von Kleist distinguishes three levels of consciousness that he assigns to the three characters of puppet, human, and God. "Puppets can be perfectly graceful because they are not reflective; they are not self-conscious."[17] In contrast, the human being is self-conscious and as a result ungraceful. God is all conscious—superconscious—and thus as with the puppet, not self-conscious. Rilke discovered Kleist's works while working on the *Duino Elegies* and probably absorbed this triadic relationship into his own thinking, in which God was replaced by angels. Thus puppets and God possess the same quality of gracefulness, which corresponds to the idea of not being self-consciousness. "The puppet and the god thus exist on a plain in which 'self' and world are unified, whereas self-conscious man is always alienated from the world."[18]

FIGURE 37: Kleist's progression of consciousness (diagram according to Komar)

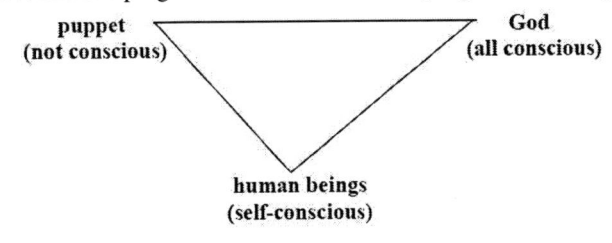

```
puppet                          God
(not conscious)                 (all conscious)
         \                    /
          \                  /
           \                /
            \              /
             \            /
              \          /
               \        /
                \      /
                 \    /
                  \  /
               human beings
              (self-conscious)
```

Rilke's *Duino Elegies* in Rautavaara's Music

In his work commentaries, the composer argues that his conception of angels was strongly influenced by Rilke's *Duino Elegies*, especially the first and second, in which the angel is the dominant actor in the poetic narration. Rautavaara carried a copy of Rilke's Elegies with him everywhere in Vienna (1955), the United States (1955-57), and in Switzerland. He explained that he "[...] had just been waiting for the right time to turn them into music,"[19] and that the influence of these two elegies brought forth all his instrumental works referring to angels.

> Angels were with me very early, which I did not remember when in the 70s I read the "Duino Elegies" by R. M. Rilke, poems which had been with me always. Then I realized that it is so much about angels and I found out that his angels had something very

---

[17] Komar, 9.

[18] Komar, 10.

[19] Paul Cutts, "Angel Voices," *Choir&Organ* 11/12 (1998): 22.

special. He says "Every angel is terrible." It was exactly what Jacob in the Bible does with his angel. He has to wrestle with it, and then I thought probably everybody must wrestle with his angel. This was mine.[20]

It may not matter whether Rautavaara knew that the *Duino Elegies* resulted from Rilke's encounter with Islam, because the fundamental thing is the profound influence the poetic cycle had on his compositions. Certainly the model of puppet relates to Rautavaara's process of composition. Rautavaara argues that he is not the mother of his works but rather a midwife, imagining himself in the role of medium (or even a puppet or other kind of automaton). As he explains: "It occurs to me that I could never have produced anything like that. These works must always have existed, perhaps in some Platonic world of ideas. My skill lies in putting them down, not in forcing them to conform to my idea."[21] Such a compositional process requires from the composer sufficient skills, humility, and acceptance of the internal rules of his pre-musical material. Rautavaara sees the composer's role as that of a messenger who performs in a manner analogous to the poet in Rilke's *Duino Elegies*; somebody between the fully self-conscious and superconscious level in the scheme of progression of consciousness (Fig. 38). Rilke's notion of being a messenger, a kind of medium, is also vividly present in Rautavaara's artistic outlook, so in fact Rilke (a poet) and Rautavaara (a composer) share the same artistic attitude: they both feel that they are like angels who transmit works of art from the ideal to the real world.

FIGURE 38: Rilke's progression of consciousness (diagram according to Komar)

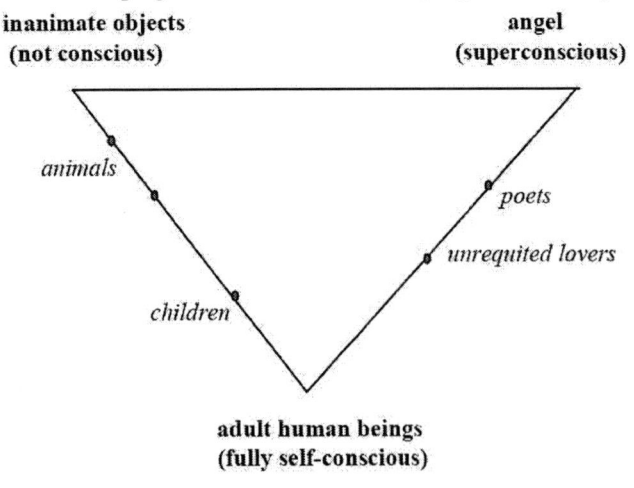

[20] Rautavaara in the documentary film *The Gift of Dreams*.
[21] Cutts: 22, see also Hako, "Music Has a Will of Its Own": 19.

Although Rautavaara rejects the notion of there being a hidden program behind his instrumental works concerning angels, he quotes on a number of occasions the opening lines of Rilke's elegies, which had a great impact on him: "Who, if I cried out, would hear me among the angels' hierarchies? and even if one of them pressed me suddenly against his heart: I would be consumed in that overwhelming existence."[22] Another line he regularly quotes is the most famous line of this *First Duino Elegy*: "Every angel is terrifying."

While these compositions may thus not offer the kind of re-representation required by the strict definition of musical ekphrasis, they may indeed constitute associative transformation. "Association" in the context of ekphrastic poetry or its sisters in other artistic field is used in the same (somewhat vague) sense as in other fields. "A sensory or mental input—an image, a sound, a phrase, a thought—triggers memories or mental links that, if they proceed in several steps, may lead to intriguing domains that may often be rather remote from the stimulus."[23] The three most prominent musical elements identified in the preceding chapters as characteristic of Rautavaara's compositions about angels lead the way here. The "disturbance" technique places two oppositional musical features in confrontation. The conflict between solo instruments and brass ensemble creates a tension that can easily be interpreted as corresponding to the opening lines of the *First Duino Elegy*: a weak human being stands transfixed by a powerful, archetypal angel. On other occasions, Rautavaara portrays angels by allusions to music boxes: mechanical elements typical of soul-less, unfeeling creatures. By this mechanicalness, Rilke's angels in Rautavaara's music seem distant and beyond human comprehension. Conversely, solo instruments like the horn in *Playgrounds for Angels* and the double bass in *Angel of Dusk* represent human existence with free, open melodic lines. The signification of the brass, and in particular of trumpets and trombones, can be regarded by virtue of traditional depictions as the terrifying angels of the *Dies irae*. Mechanical material given to trumpets and trombones emphasizes the terrifying aspect of angels by means of the performance technique of blowing into the instruments without producing a tone.

Another point of similarity between Rilke's *Duino Elegies* and Rautavaara's works about angels is the fact that, just as Rilke started writing his *Elegies* after he "heard" a strange voice from the sea, Rautavaara claims that the titles of his works come to him without his conscious intervention. The majority of Rautavaara's angelic titles contain binary oppositions: "Archangel Michael Fighting the Antichrist," *Angels and Visitations* and the opposition

---

[22] *The Selected Poetry of Rainer Maria Rilke*, 151.

[23] Bruhn, *Musical Ekphrasis*, 67.

of dark and light in *Angel of Dusk* and *Angel of Light*. As demonstrated in the previous chapter, the aspect of light is not only apparent in the titles but also in the modulation of scales, in harmonic oppositions, in instrumentation, and in the musical representations of the mandala. This invites the hypothesis that the contrast between light and dark must exist in Rilke's *Duino Elegies* and that the composer took it upon himself to convey this idea in his music. In the effort of tracing how these categories are presented in the poetic cycle, the popular signification of the word "dusk" in the title of *Angel of Dusk* seems like a good starting-point. Dusk is a very specific time: the day is ending and the night beginning; one may see a beautiful sunset, and then light gives way to darkness. The association of the day with life and the night with death is probably present in every culture: hence dusk is likely to suggest the waning of life force. This raises the question whether dusk and night were significant concepts for Rilke and if so, how he treats them poetically. The *First Duino Elegy* (which Rautavaara claims is the most angelic in the cycle) contains an interesting passage about the night:

> Oh and night: there is night, when a wind full of infinite space gnaws at our faces. Whom would it not remain for--that longed-after, mildly disillusioning presence, which the solitary heart so painfully meets.[24]

Komar interprets "the night" as a so-called final category: at night, the boundaries of the physical world become indistinct, and it "devours boundaries of self-consciousness as well."[25] Rilke writes that "a wind full of infinite space gnaws at our faces," which means that the face, which represents the identity of every human being as an individual, is "torn away to reveal a more essential being beneath it."[26] The night tries to get beyond human self-consciousness to reestablish the unity of all existence on some higher level of consciousness, to transform the visible into the invisible. If, in Rautavaara's music, the solo instrument is the main hero and its part from beginning to end unfolds like a mythical journey, this can be interpreted as a trajectory from the invisible to the visible, from the imperfect human world to the perfect angelic world in the final movement of the composition. Assuming that the soloist embodies the titular Angel of Dusk, it seems that this protagonist is in the process of becoming an angel, moving from day to night, from the visible word into the invisible. Hence there is an association between the symbol of Rilke's night from the *First Duino Elegy* and Rautavaara's title *Angel of Dusk*.

---

[24] *The Selected Poetry of Rainer Maria Rilke*, 152.

[25] Komar, 28.

[26] Komar, 28.

By contrast, *Angel of Light*, as mentioned several times above, is arguably the least characteristic of Rautavaara's series of compositions concerning angels. The challenge of finding an equivalent "angel of light" in Rilke's poetry and linking it with this problematic composition is facilitated by the position the composition occupies as the final work within the *Angel Trilogy*. The hypothesis I wish to pursue here is that the *Angel Trilogy* refers not only to the *First Duino Elegy* but to the whole ten-part cycle. Therefore, if *Angels and Visitations* corresponds to certain passages from the *First Duino Elegy*, then the symphony, as the final work in the Trilogy, may relate to the cycle's final poems.

In the conclusion of her study of Rilke's *Duino Elegies*, Komar groups the ten elegies into a scheme of thesis and antithesis, identifying the fifth poem as the significant center. The *First Duino Elegy* outlines the main concepts, which are developed and resolved in the *Ninth Elegy*, so that the initial poem can be considered an introduction and the penultimate one, a conclusion. In the *Ninth Elegy*, Rilke assumes that humans will never attain the superconscious position held by powerful angels, and begins to refocus his opinion about the weak, tiny, and imperfect human realms introduced in the *First Elegy*. In contrast with the *First Elegy*, in the *Ninth Elegy* Rilke turns to affirm the physical world that is not perceptible by angels. Thus the powerful angelic realms are not yet so frightening, since the poet disposes of them in human language, which also possesses the ability to transform things from visible to invisible: "The poet comes to realize that the one capacity he possesses and the angel does not is that of transforming the world into conscious form."[27] The human being, having become master of the physical world's transformation, is no longer terrified of angels but able to praise them, which Rilke expresses thus: "Praise the world to the angel, not the unsayable." In this context, the concept of darkness (which is associated with death) receives a new dimension as "holy inspiration," because it removes the object from the physical world into consciousness.

In a manner similar to Rilke's affirmative *Ninth Elegy*, Rautavaara's *Angel of Light* follows the dark first movement and "disturbed" second movement with the calm and serene atmosphere of the third movement and concluding solemnity of the fourth. In addition to the *Ninth Elegy*, the *Tenth Elegy* can help with the interpretation of the symphony. This problematic poetic afterthought depicts angels not as subjects (superconscious creatures) but as the objects of the *Ninth Elegy*. The poetic battle with powerful angels has made the poet stronger than he was before, and the angels "[...] have

---

[27] Komar, 163.

disappeared in favor of personified human emotions."[28] The *Angel of Light*, composed fourteen years after the *Angel of Dusk* and sixteen years after *Angels and Visitations*, recalls the fact that Rilke completed his *Ninth* and *Tenth* elegies ten years after the first (1912).

Rilke's Angel as a Jungian Archetype

Rautavaara generally portrays Rilke's angel as a terrifying, alien, and powerful creature, but in his commentary to his choral work *Die erste Elegie* he links such angels also to Jung's concept of the archetypal *animus*. Examining the theory of archetypes in this context is crucial for two reasons. First, the composer often alludes to his interest in Jung's theories. On one such occasion, he said: "I think I have five or six of his [Jung's] books. I was fascinated by his texts and theories and had read most of them in the 1970s and later in the '80s. So, he was very important for my outlook on life."[29] This is precisely the period during which Rautavaara composed most of his works referring to angels. Second, the Jungian term "archetype" appears in his very commentaries.

> I have set several of Rainer Maria Rilke's poems to music. He speaks of angels as terrifying archetypes common to all civilizations. My conviction is that there are other kinds of realities, other kinds of consciousness. They are real but beyond rational approach. If you want to use words you can say "angel," for lack of a better word.[30]

According to Jung, the human psyche is the sum of consciousness (thoughts and actions under the control of the will) and unconsciousness (which is divided into the personal and collective). The personal unconscious is a reservoir of individual memories to which people occasionally gain access through dreams or sudden flashes of recollection. The collective unconscious is a deep level within the psyche which harbors instinctive patterns of thought and behavior common to all civilizations throughout the ages.[31] These patterns can be examined only in symbolic form as images projected by our minds: archetypes (Fig. 39).

---

[28] Komar, 196.

[29] Personal communication, Helsinki, 22 September 2006.

[30] Heffern, "Conveying the Inexpressible."

[31] See Anthony Stevens, *On Jung* (London, UK/New York, NY: Routledge, 1990), 28.

> From the unconscious there emanate determining influences which, independently of tradition, guarantee in every single individual a similarity and even a sameness of experience, and also of the way it is represented imaginatively. One of the main proofs of this is the most universal parallelism between mythological motifs, which, on account of their quality as primordial images, I have called archetypes.[32]

FIGURE 39: Division of psyche into consciousness and unconsciousness in Jung's theory

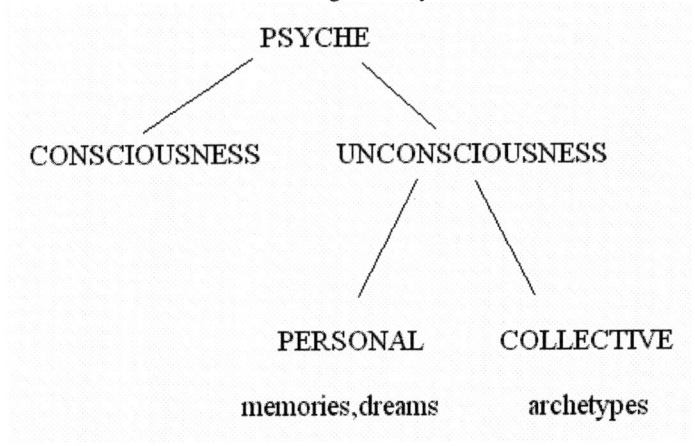

```
                    PSYCHE
                   /      \
         CONSCIOUSNESS   UNCONSCIOUSNESS
                         /        \
                   PERSONAL      COLLECTIVE

                memories, dreams   archetypes
```

Jung distinguishes between a number of archetypes, including the anima, animus, mother, father, trickster and shadow. Rautavaara initially suggested that he regarded the terrifying figure of the angel as his personal animus, which he attempts to render in his music. The archetype of the animus is the collective image of man in the female unconscious, which emerges symbolically as the ideal of manhood, as a hero-prince who fights evil or, in its negative aspect, as a cruel, destructive, aggressive, power-seeking man.[33] It therefore seems a little surprising that a male composer should treat the figure of an angel as his personal animus. Rather then an archetype of man in the female psyche, Rautavaara evidently considers the animus a representation of the negative aspects of his own personality (evil, aggression). This observation triggers a logical problem for the further investigation of archetypes in his music. Confronted with this apparent

---

[32] Carl Gustav Jung, *The Archetypes and the Collective Unconscious* [*The Collected Works of C.G.Jung*, IX/1, R.F.C.Hull, trans.] (New York, NY: Pantheon Books for Bollingen Foundation, 1959), 58.

[33] See Fontana, 14.

discrepancy in a private communication, the composer admitted that he had made a mistake: he had meant to identify the angel with the archetype of the shadow rather than that of the animus.

The term "shadow" refers to the interior nature of this archetype. Every human being has his or her own personal shadow, the dark and evil side of any personality. The shadow embodies a disruptive energy, an inner terror or a set of antisocial desires of which we are ashamed and which we attempt to bury in the unconscious.[34] The shadow is a moral problem for every human nature, a "[...] potentially terrifying experience so much so that we usually protect ourselves from such disturbing awareness by making use of ego-defense mechanisms: we deny the existence of our shadow and project it onto others."[35] Rautavaara expresses this concept with reference to the Old Testament scene of Jacob wrestling with the angel:

> I realized that it is so much about angels and I found out that his [Rilke's] angels had something very special. He says "Every angel is terrible." It was exactly what Jacob in the Bible does with his angel. He has to wrestle with it, and then I thought probably everybody must wrestle with his angel.[36]

In this context, the angel as a shadow archetype is "[...] one of mankind's oldest traditions and perennial companions [...] It must follow us and we must follow it, even today, if we wish to control our lives and understand the world."[37]

In fact, the Jungian shadow coincides with Rilke's terrifying angel in what can be regarded as an ekphrastic transposition of the poetic figure into a psychological concept. Generally, the role of the archetype is to help analyze dreams through visible images that emerge into consciousness in order to discover the hidden invisible world, the unconscious.[38] The symbol of the shadow can represent the process of gaining self-knowledge, of unifying the unconscious with the conscious. It is therefore compatible with Rilke's conception of the transformation through poetry of visible earthly things into invisible ones. This process has a similar function to that of the angel, which joins Heaven and Earth; as Gadamer writes about Rilke's angel:

---

[34] See Fontana, 16-17.

[35] Stevens, 44.

[36] Rautavaara's commentary in the documentary film *The Gift of Dreams*.

[37] Rautavaara, note about *Angel of Light,* in the booklet accompanying the recording, Ondine 869-2 (1996).

[38] See Fontana, 8-13.

> Again and again it is the power and powerlessness of human feeling which gives occasion for thinking of the angel as one whose feeling is not limited by the feeling of something else, but instead so fills him that his emotion is completely identical with him. An emotion which does not evaporate but which rather stands in itself is what Rilke calls "angel," because such feeling surpasses human beings.[39]

As the thoughts expounded above demonstrate, the symbol of the angel in Rautavaara's instrumental compositions can be understood not only as an ekphrastic representation of Rilke's "Every angel is terrifying," but also with respect to the idea of Jung's shadow archetype. Both concepts provide similar codes to aid the interpretation of Rautavaara's angels with reference to the composer's titles and commentaries. Moreover, in addition to these concepts Rautavaara also discusses other, related terrifying angels: the fight between Jacob and the angel from the Old Testament, Ezekiel's vision of angels, and powerful images of huge, masculine angels from Blake's paintings.[40] All of these offer opportunities to seek out ekphrastic links. But above all, they emphasize the same aspect of Rautavaara's angels: angels are terrifying beings whom he seeks to represent in music through the use of oppositional categories of expression, instrumentation, timbre, melodic and harmonic structures, and contrasts between dark and light qualities.

Rilke's Terrifying Angels in Rautavaara's Instrumental Music

Rautavaara's instrumental music depicts the terrifying aspect of angels not only through the use of trumpets and trombones as symbols of the apocalyptic trumpets, but also, more broadly, through special musical ideas given to the brass instruments. The first of these is the use of modern performance techniques for brass, including blowing or breathing into the instruments without tone, in order to create special "noisy" effects such as rustling, flutter-tonguing, and tremolo. Although the composer integrated some of these techniques on several occasions before and after his compositions about angels (as in his opera *Vincent* and the related Sixth Symphony *Vincentiana*), they occur with greatest frequency in relation to angels.

The technique of blowing into the instruments without tone, in particular, appears so frequently that it merits special attention.[41] The resulting sound is marked by the absence of traditional sound qualities. It thus

---

[39] Gadamer, 85.

[40] See Rautavaara, "On a Taste for the Infinite": 113-114.

[41] Cf. *Angels and Visitations*, mm. 37-38, 325-327, 330, 332; *Angel of Dusk*, third movement, mm. 2, 4, 9-10, 22-23, 26, 28, 230-32; *Playgrounds for Angels*, mm. 182-83, 185-86, 190-91.

232 *Chapter 7*

constitutes a kind of "non-sound," which creates a strong opposition with other pitches.

EXAMPLE 81: Blowing into the instruments without tone, *Angel of Dusk*, mvt. III, mm. 1-2

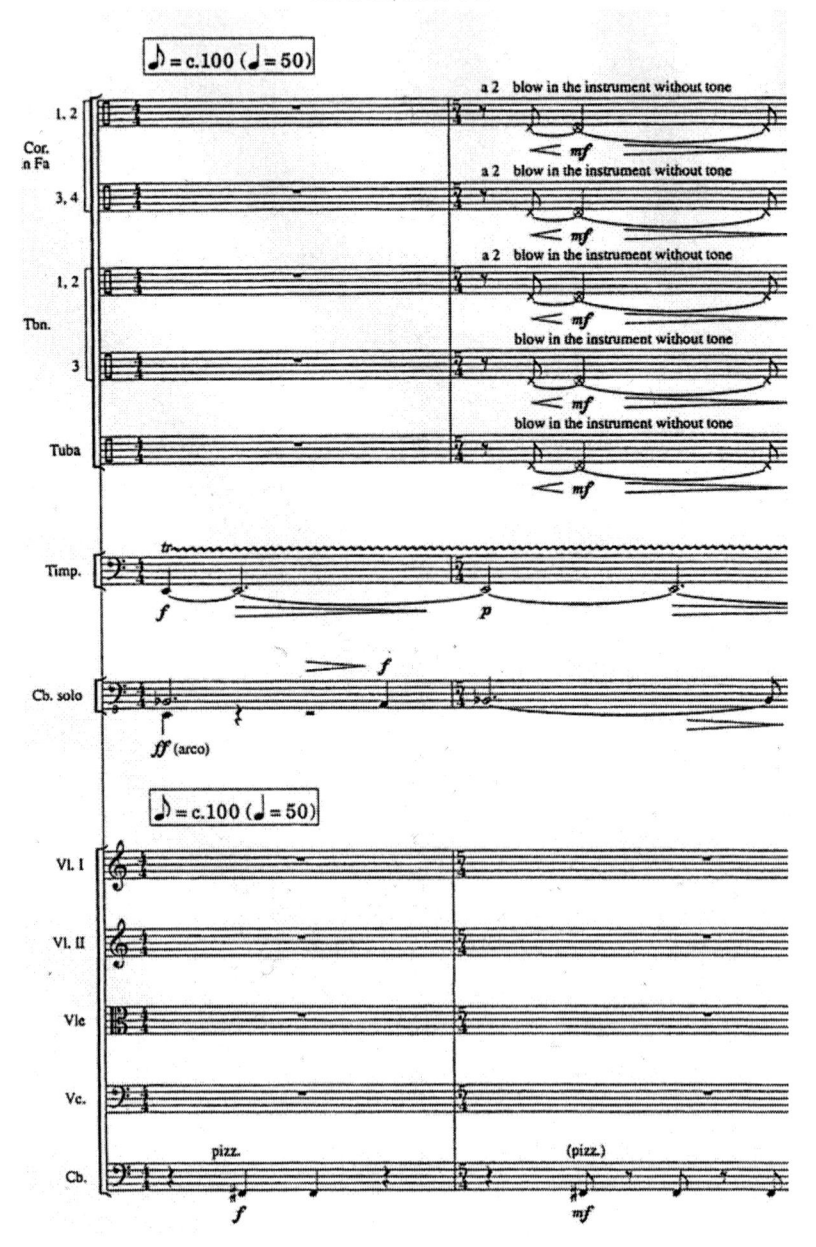

Both the Old and New Testaments mention angelic trumpets but say nothing about the manner of playing being the same as human playing, as was assumed in later years. According to the Bible, the sound of angelic trumpets is neither gentle nor soft, but rather like destructive thunder that brings death and extermination to the unfaithful; angelic singing is not like human singing but reminiscent of a roar or loud speech. Voices of angels are always loud and terrifying; some Biblical scholars have claimed that it can be compared to the sounds of trumpets at the destruction of Jericho (Book of Joshua 6: 16-21) and the trumpets of the Apocalypse. In this context the strange sound of blowing without tone can be a sign of the angels' blowing trumpets at the Last Judgment or angelic voices that are comparable to loud roars. In *Angels and Visitations*, Rautavaara specifically requests that this terrifying aspect be emphasized through the use of two Lion's Roars (mm. 126, 246). Another possible source for the composer's choice of this technique is the biblical account of the Creation, according to which "[...] the Lord God formed man from the dust of the ground and breathed into his nostrils the breath of life, and man became a living being" (Genesis 2: 7). Thus, breathing into an instrument without tone can be a musical icon of God's breathing. Several scholars have suggested that this effect may also be understood as muteness and symbolize death or the Angel of Death;[42] similarly, literary scholars have interpreted the angels from Rilke's *Duino Elegies* as symbols of death.[43]

Other representations of terrifying angels in Rautavaara's instrumental compositions include passages in which the brass instruments (particularly the trumpets and trombones) play material associated with the "disturbance" technique. In such cases they begin with a thin texture of two or three instruments, *piano*; gradually, other instruments are added in increasingly rapid tempo, creating a strong dynamic and textural crescendo.[44] As an extra-musical sign this can function as an index of fear or a terrifying experience; it is often used in horror movies and thrillers. This procedure therefore refers to interpretations of the angel as an object of fear and dread, as can be found in the Old Testament, the Apocalypse, Rilke's *Duino Elegies* and the composer's obsessive dream.

If musical features point toward the terrifying aspect of the angel, then it is a short step to psychoanalytic readings of the music, for the "terrifying" is one element in Freud's theory of the uncanny. Furthermore, those elements

---

[42] See Naomi Cumming, "Horrors of Identification: Reich's 'Different Trains'," *Perspective of New Music* 35 (1997): 129-149, also Välimäki, 281.

[43] See Eva-Maria Simms, "Uncanny Dolls: Images of Death in Rilke and Freud," *New Literary History* 27 (1996): 663-677.

[44] Refer back to Exx. 27, 72, 73, and 74.

of the compositions that distinguish them as angelic (the "disturbance" technique, *musica automata*, the prominent role of trumpets and trombones) are all categories within the musical uncanny.

Aspects of the Uncanny in Rilke's and Rautavaara's Angels

The "disturbance" technique, in which two oppositional instruments or groups are in permanent conflict as mythical actants that push back the subject, is a perfect example of the repression of the musical subject, as with the orchestral outbursts of Tchaikovsky's Sixth Symphony.[45] The "disturbance" technique can also be understood as an unexpected appearance of the uncanny at the levels of actorialization and inner temporality: a breaking of time and an opposition of the mechanical and the free. Automatism of the material given to brass instruments (the trumpets in particular) underlines the aspect of repression and does not require further comment. The mechanical motifs and chorales in the trumpets and trombones have military connotations, but can also be symbols of death, resurrection, or mystical appearances, and of the Apocalypse or the attributes of its angels.[46] Conversely, the peaceful chorales, which frequently appear in the instrumental compositions concerning angels as monolithic chords, can be read as representations of the male choir in instrumental terms, such a choir having mythical and ritual signification in Rautavaara's music.[47] Indexes of fear in the material given to trumpets and trombones emphasize the frightening aspect of angelic visitations both in religious thought and in their presentation in other arts.

All categories of the uncanny in Rautavaara's instrumental compositions are bound up with the brass ensemble in which trumpets play the role of opponent in the "disturbance" technique and so have no individual subjectivity, hence representing dolls or puppets as in Tchaikovsky's Sixth Symphony, "[...] a kind of gothic horror symphony, in the form of a demonized requiem, playing with the theme of non-subjectivity."[48] The "non-subject" stands in opposition to the subject; if at the symbolic level the subject is human, then the opponent is non-human or inhuman. Rautavaara's terrifying angel thus did not originate in Rilke's poetry but rather in the composer's obsessive childhood nightmare. According to Freud, uncanny feelings stem from childhood experiences or fairy tales in which such feelings are accepted

---

[45] See Välimäki, 283.

[46] See Välimäki, 276-294.

[47] See Rautavaara, "Choirs, Myths and Finnishness": 3.

[48] See Välimäki, 287-289, 294, 300.

Musical Ekphrasis

rather than rejected. Rautavaara made an interesting observation about this in his autobiography, when he noted that "Perhaps the tendency towards angelography had its origins in the grammar lessons of my school days, where one spoke about this mysterious 'inside being'."[49]

Richard Cohn suggests that a sense of the uncanny is created by a particular division of a hexatonic scale into "hexatonic poles": two chords (one major, one minor) that are derived from the scale but that share no common tones (C-minor and E-major chords may serve as an example).[50] The hexatonic pole is a significant feature in Rautavaara's instrumental compositions referring to angels, giving rise to both a hexatonic scale and (through the addition of three notes) to Messiaen's mode 3.

FIGURE 40: Hexatonic poles (1), the hexatonic scale (2), Messiaen's mode 3^2 (3)

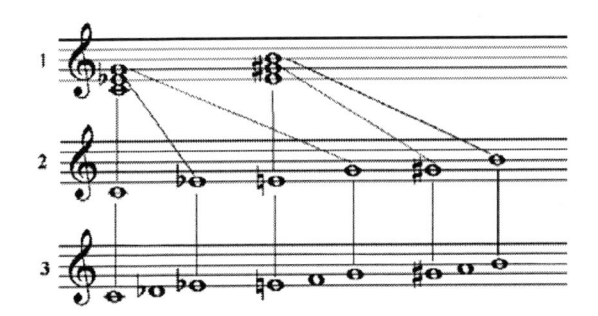

The hexatonic scale appears twice in *Angels and Visitations* as the basis of the expressive second theme; mode 3 is the harmonic basis for the finale of *Angel of Dusk*.[51] Both elements add new qualities to the respective compositions, their surprising effect suggesting the uncanny. There are no tensions within these scales; instead, their usage in the music of these two compositions results in a kind of immobility, a sense of the unreal and transcendent. Furthermore, the two passages are accompanied by metallophones which imitate bells. These bells have strong connotations for the composer, reminding him of the trip he took with his parents to Valamo, which made an imprint in his mind and stayed with him for his whole life as a source of inspiration. The association of bells with death and spirits is common in many religions. Their primary role is to disperse bad spirits and

---

[49] Rautavaara, *Omakuva*, 327.

[50] See Cohn: 305.

[51] Cf *Angels and Visitations*, mm. 29-72, 296-310, shown in Exx. 20 and 74; *Angel of Dusk*, mm. 200-233.

demons and underline God's holiness in the liturgy.[52] In the works concerning angels there are many such passages that employ celesta, vibraphones, glockenspiel, and bells, thus conjuring up symbolic associations with his childhood memories.

The atmosphere of fantasy is underlined also by the use of "naive" themes. In their timbres as well as in their simplicity of construction and their mechanical nature, such themes are reminiscent of children's musical automata such as music boxes. *Angels and Visitations* contains such a music-box passage, as does the third movement of *Angel of Light*. Both are monotonous and repetitive, aspects that are obscured by changing time signatures and hence "secret." Secrecy is also a quality of the uncanny as well as being a category of the magical.[53] As an example of the uncanny, the third movement of the symphony displays extreme nostalgia with its expression *Come un sogno* (Like a dream), underlined by the use of the soft string timbre and thematic attenuation.[54] All of these qualities are reminiscent also of the pastoral topic and a lost Arcadia; extreme nostalgia represents the composer's longing for an ideal world and the lost paradise. Lovejoy has argued that this slow movement is the best example of Rautavaara's depiction of safety, enclosed places, and glimpses of eternity.[55]

Beyond Rilke: Rautavaara's Musical (Self-)Ekphrasis

> When I was a small boy, with no personal contact with music as yet, I painted "music" on paper with watercolors and put these paintings on display in my bedroom as "compositions."[56]

Some twentieth-century composers were amateur painters: the most famous among them are Schoenberg[57] and George Gershwin, though neither painted anything deriving from their musical compositions. Probably the most famous artist who was professional both as a composer and as a painter is Mikalojus Konstantinas Čiurlionis. His compositions have pictorial titles and structures, such as the symphonic poems *Jūra* (The Sea) and *Miške* (In

---

[52] See Välimäki, 281.

[53] See Susan Youens, *Retracing a Winter's Journey* (Ithaca, NY: Cornell University Press, 1991): 161; also Välimäki, 255, Eero Tarasti, *Myth and Music*, 97-103.

[54] See Välimäki, 297.

[55] See Lovejoy, 13.

[56] Rautavaara, *Orchestral Works*, 3.

[57] He painted self-portraits, nature scenes, and visions, and had several exhibitions of his paintings.

the Forest); whereas his paintings have musical titles and structures, including his cycle of *Sonatas* (1907-1908) and the diptych *Prelude and Fugue* (1908). Although he linked the two activities of music and painting, he never created a composition and painting with the same title. Schoenberg and Gershwin were amateurs who treated painting as a hobby, so they did not feel the necessity to express their musical ideas in a different art form.[58] Schoenberg stated that "I used to paint [...] but that was years ago. I did not do much with it. Maybe I shall take it up again. But painting and my music have nothing in common. My music is the result of purely musical theory and must be judged from purely musical results."[59]

When studying in the United States in the 1950s, Rautavaara was interested in the work of a crippled painter whom he met during one of his journeys. He noticed that the process of painting was very similar to that of composition: one must choose the material and subsequently shape it expressively and structurally. The meeting with the painter not only showed Rautavaara similarities between the arts but also encouraged him to paint; as a result he finished his first painting entitled *Angel of Dusk* (Plate 4).[60] In subsequent years painting became his hobby, and he painted several pictures containing the symbol of the mandala.[61] In 1980 he used *Angel of Dusk* as a title for his Double Bass Concerto; four years later, the early painting with the same title was used by Finlandia Records as a cover for their LP recording of the concerto.[62] Why would a composer who claims that there are no interrelations between a composition and a painting allow his painting to be on the cover of a work with the same title?

The pursuit of this question led to even more unexpected discoveries. A digital photo of the LP cover reveals the words "MONOLOGUE WITH ANGELS" in the right-hand corner of the painting. This inscription points to a composition Rautavaara wrote about three decades later, his Fifth Symphony, which was originally entitled *Monologue with Angels*. The question of changing titles therefore seems to be essential for the examination of correspondences between Rautavaara's paintings and his compositions. In his autobiography,

---

[58] "I must answer that as a painter I was absolutely an amateur; I had no theoretical training and only a little aesthetic training, and this only from general education, but not from an education which pertained to painting. In music it was different." Halsey Stevens, "A Conversation with Schoenberg about Painting," *Journal of the Arnold Schoenberg Institute* 3 (1978): 178.

[59] Interview with Arnold Schoenberg in Berlin (12 October 1913), published on the occasion of a performance of Five Pieces for Orchestra, op. 16, in Chicago.

[60] Reproduced in Hako, *Unien lahja*, 49-50.

[61] Some of Rautavaara's paintings can be seen in the biographical film *The Gift of Dreams*.

[62] Finlandia Records FA 339.

Rautavaara noted that "The composition project was never, in any case, taken up";[63] he planned a work with this title,[64] but during the process of composing he abandoned it and began to develop different musical ideas, which resulted in the Fifth Symphony. It is therefore impossible to compare the unwritten composition *Monologue with Angels* with the painting, but it is possible to compare the painting *Angel of Dusk* with the Double Bass Concerto. If there are some interrelationships between these two different works of art, an analysis of the painting may open a space for correspondences.

The painting can be divided horizontally.[65] The upper portion represents a person in red clothes sitting in a kind of levitating ancient stone temple backed by an intensely blue cloudless sky. The lower portion is dominated by the color gray, with geometric figures of cubes and spheres hovering and traveling to the snowy mountain tops. The stony temple and the person inside it dressed in ancient clothes are reminiscent of a monk in an isolated cell. This might be a symbol of meditation or of an alienation from the

---

[63] Rautavaara, *Omakuva*, 327.

[64] All of the composer's manuscripts can be found in the National Library of Finland in Helsinki. Among the sketches for *Angel of Light* I found sketches (National Library coll. no. 586.5) of a completely unrelated and unfinished orchestral score totaling 27 pages. Its compositional techniques are completely different from those of the symphony, reminiscent of those which Rautavaara used during the 1970s and '80s, although the symphony was written in 1994. It is obvious that this composition had nothing in common with the Seventh Symphony; this can be proved by comparing the instrumentation with those of the Fifth and Seventh Symphonies. An English Horn is missing both in the untitled composition and the Seventh Symphony, and the presence of the harp may suggest that the sketches are from an early draft of the Symphony. However, both the untitled sketch and the Fifth Symphony employ one bass clarinet and one contrabassoon; these instruments are not used in the Seventh Symphony. Similarly, the percussion scoring is closer to the dry sounds of the tom-toms, found in the Fifth Symphony, than to the metallophone-dominated Seventh Symphony. The use of four trumpets in C rather than the three trumpets in B-flat of the Seventh Symphony convinces me that this is an early sketch for the Fifth Symphony. Also, Rautavaara set out to compose the Seventh Symphony knowing that the composition would be performed by the Bloomington Symphony Orchestra which commissioned it; he probably had no choice about which instruments to use. On closer inspection, however, the unfinished score could also represent the first 85 measures of an orchestral sketch for Rautavaara's opera *Thomas*, despite the absence of vocal parts. Was the unfinished score a sketch for the opera, or was it initially the orchestral work *Monologue with Angels* which the composer subsequently used at the beginning of *Thomas*? These are questions much like those that arise from the hypothesis that *Angel of Dusk* was derived from the musical material of the withdrawn opera *En dramatisk scen.*

[65] I am indebted to Laura Gutman-Hanvihaara from the Ateneum Museum in Helsinki who not only helped me in the interpretation of this painting but also advised me of correspondences between it and other twentieth-century paintings.

Musical Ekphrasis

PLATE 4: Rautavaara's painting *Angel of Dusk* (or *Monologues with Angels*)

material world. The spiritual aspect is emphasized by the levitation, a state that is said to be attained by certain mystics and spiritual masters in every culture. The person, neither man nor woman, is in another, spiritual world; it is also a world of itself, safely enclosed in a glass box hovering in the sky. The lower plane of the painting reinforces this idea of a safe, enclosed place, a world of spiritual beings, with the succession of geometrical figures ascending to the mountain. There are two shapes, the cube (which can symbolize the masculine side of the personality) and the sphere (the feminine side, which at first is bigger and gradually becomes smaller). The progression of spheres to the mountain seems to flow, with a meta-rhythm that links the foreground of the temple, the person, and the first two geometric shapes with the background of the mountains.[66] The levitating shapes in connection with the mountains may be interpreted as symbols of a spiritual development reminiscent of Rilke's idea of the progression of consciousness. The meta-rhythm of ascending cubes and spheres show not only two planes through their flow, but also movement, which can be interpreted as a transposition of musical ideas of time and rhythm.

As in Čiurlionis's works, Rautavaara's picture can be read as a kind of musical score from left to right, from introduction to final climax. Indeed, the titles of the painting (initially *Monologue with Angels*, later *Angel of Dusk*) correspond with the person enclosed in the box-temple and the idea of the progression of consciousness that is represented by the geometrical figures. The painting's overriding colors, blue and gray, create an atmosphere of coldness and loneliness: only the clothes on the person are red. As static colors, blue and gray provide the meditative character of the picture, whereas the person in red presents human life, imperfect like the surroundings but in the process of becoming perfect. Both titles can provide material for interpretation: With the first, the idea of loneliness encapsulated in a "monologue with angels" is presented as the flow of cubes and spheres. In the case of the second title, the "angel" can be the person inside the stony temple, with "dusk" emphasized by the gray and blue color scheme.

So what is the link between the painting *Angel of Dusk* and the composition bearing the same title? In the one case, the "angel of dusk" refers possibly to the person in the stony temple, in the other case, to the double bass concerto's soloist. The work's three movements, alluding to the double bassist's first appearance, monologue, and last appearance, encapsulate a musical progression from the "disturbance" technique of the first movement through to the spiritual mountain tops symbolized by a coda based on the hexatonic scale. Significantly, in the commentary on his Fifth Symphony Rautavaara stated that for the first time he did not feel he was *making* music but rather *being* in music—"I was not making an art-work but the life in which I was residing—or rather that I was wandering through perpetually new vistas and landscapes."[67] Hence the composer himself can be said to be

---

[66] Geometrical shapes in paintings have historically symbolized spiritual ideas and linked mathematics and the visual arts. In the twentieth century, painters such as Paul Serusier, Alberto Giacometti, and Francis Bacon used shapes levitating in space to present mystical ideas. In addition, in every culture mountains have a spiritual association as places that connect heaven and earth, God and people, and are symbols of spiritual progression.

[67] Rautavaara quoted in Aho, *Einojuhani Rautavaara as Symphonist*, 102.

represented by the person in red in the box-temple which floats through the landscape. In his autobiography, the composer compared this journey to flying on a red carpet and the symphony to a musical journey through different landscapes.[68] Analysis and interpretation of the painting provide the following important set of ideas: the progression of consciousness as in Rilke's *Duino Elegies*, the topic of journey, the question of monologue, the color of dusk, and the angelic title. Although an amateur work of art, the painting offers an important key to the understanding of Rautavaara's musical world and its language. Rautavaara presents similar ideas through different art forms; he has said that "Perhaps what makes art individual is the method and procedure through which a work of art is created. Everyone has to find his own process for himself. After that, it does not really matter what one works with: words, colors, shapes, or music. They are all materials to choose from."[69] In light of these words, the painting *Monologue with Angels* may be interpreted as the source of an unusual instance of self-ekphrasis; it either anticipates by visual means what the composer otherwise expresses through music, or serves as an inspiration of Rautavaara's much later musical representation of the same imagined subject matter. In a wider sense, the painting thus constitutes an additional, very early "composition" in Rautavaara's series of artistic representations of angels, albeit one created in a medium different from the one preferred in most of his works.

---

[68] See Rautavaara, *Omakuva*, 327.

[69] Rautavaara quoted in Hako, *Unien lahja*, 50.

Conclusion

Rautavaara as an erudite composer has a strong tendency to treat music as a sign of the spiritual world beyond human existence. This approach merges his diverse artistic activities as a composer, writer, poet, amateur painter, and philosopher. Rautavaara seems to attempt the creation of his idiosyncratic version of a "total work of art" by re-using parts of one composition in other works. In this way he offers a rich network of mutual interrelations and this intertextuality.[70] Moreover, Rautavaara's operas have similar plots in which the main theme is that of a conflict between an individual and his or her environment, between past and present, life and death, the real world and dreams, and similar opposites. Such binary oppositions correspond to the mythical elements in music revealed by the structural anthropology of Lévi-Strauss and to Greimas's model of mythical actants. Ancient rituals and pagan mythology play important roles in several of Rautavaara's operas, including *The Myth of Sampo*, *Marjatta, The Lowly Maiden*, and *Thomas*; they can also be found in his choral works, particularly in those for male choir. These works in turn have exerted a strong influence on his instrumental compositions, as can be seen in his frequent auto-citations. Although the operatic passages quoted in instrumental works necessarily come without the text originally associated with the music, the imports do not entirely lose their semantic level or their signification. For Rautavaara as for Mozart, opera is the most important site for experiments: he rarely works in the opposite direction, citing material first composed for an instrumental composition in his operas. Moreover, most of his works have titles or subtitles that point to extramusical references, which he claims were sources of inspiration or starting points for his music. Finally, commentaries and program notes in staggering number offer often very detailed explanations of how certain musical figures relate to painting, literature, and psychology.

The aim of the present study has been to provide a hermeneutic analysis of a certain group within the body of Rautavaara's instrumental works. His music invites such approach since it is full of profound correspondences with

---

[70] Rautavaara's striving for a *Gesamtkunstwerk* may be compared to Wagner's use of leitmotifs in his operatic tetralogy *The Ring of the Nibelung* or to the seven novels collectively entitled *À la recherche du temps perdu* (1909-1922) by Marcel Proust.

extramusical ideas. The composer frequently emphasizes such correspondences with autobiographical details. The method of inquiry employed here could be applied not only to instrumental music concerning angels, but to almost all of his other music, particularly to his instrumental works. Rautavaara uses symbolic representation in all musical parameters. Some of it is easily recognizable owing to its references to traditional concepts. For the most part, however, he invents his own symbolic means to represent extra-musical ideas. Through auto-citations and the characteristic usage of instruments, he alludes to and comments on topics that are also featured in his operas. Prominent among these are all those that correspond to his belief in a different reality existing above this world, the signs of which include birds, powerful angels, mystical appearances, saints, and the Virgin Mary. According to Paul Ricoeur, each authentic symbol unites three dimensions: the cosmic, indicating the symbols of the sacred; the oneiric, indicating the archaic symbols of the unconscious and of dreams; and the poetic, indicating the embodiment of the sacred and the oneiric in language.[71] For Rautavaara, the symbol of the angel has precisely these three dimensions: in its cosmic aspect, it refers to the terryfing angel with whom Jacob wrestles in the Old Testament; in its oneiric aspect, it is one of Jung's archetypes; and in its poetic aspect, it is incarnated in the angel of Rilke's *Duino Elegies*.

For Rautavaara, "a glimpse of eternity" is the only true justification for all art. Rautavaara aims for a spiritual art that is able to lift humans from their normal existence into a timeless infinity. He is therefore frequently described as a mystic, although he does not intend for his music to convey mystical visions. Rautavaara, together with twentieth-century composers like Messiaen, Crumb, and Stockhausen, desires to rescue the spiritual significance of music and to point out the spiritual experience of every human being. His autocitations are like spiritual mantras that remind people of the lost paradise for which Western art should search. To paraphrase the composer's own words, any art without this glimpse of eternity has no foundation for its existence.

---

[71] See Paul Ricoeur, *The Symbolism of Evil*, Emerson Buchanan, trans. (New York, NY: Harper & Row, 1967), 10-14.

Appendix:

Rautavaara's short version of the text of
Die erste Elegie / The First Elegy by Rainer Maria Rilke,
matched with Stephen Mitchell's English translation of the excerpts

Wer, wenn ich schriee, hörte mich denn aus der Engel Ordnungen? und gesetzt selbst, es nähme einer mich plötzlich ans Herz: ich verginge von seinem stärkeren Dasein. Denn das Schöne ist nichts als des Schrecklichen Anfang, den wir noch grade ertragen, und wir bewundern es so, weil es gelassen verschmäht, uns zu zerstören. Ein jeder Engel ist schrecklich.

Ach, wen vermögen wir denn zu brauchen? Engel nicht, Menschen nicht, und die findigen Tiere merken es schon, daß wir nicht sehr verläßlich zu Haus sind in der gedeuteten Welt. Es bleibt uns vielleicht irgend ein Baum an dem Abhang, daß wir ihn täglich wiedersähen; es bleibt uns die Straße von gestern.

O und die Nacht, die Nacht, wenn der Wind voller Weltraum uns am Angesicht zehrt -, wem bliebe sie nicht, die ersehnte, sanft enttäuschende, welche dem einzelnen Herzen mühsam bevorsteht.

Ja, die Frühlinge brauchten dich wohl. Es muteten manche Sterne dir zu, daß du sie spürtest. Es hob sich eine Woge heran im Vergangenen, oder da du vorüberkamst am geöffneten Fenster, gab eine Geige sich hin.

Who, if I cried out, would hear me among the angels' hierarchies? and even if one of them pressed me suddenly against his heart: I would be consumed in that overwhelming existence. For beauty is nothing but the beginning of terror, which we are still just able to endure, and we are so awed because it serenely disdains to annihilate us. Every angel is terrifying.

Ah, whom can we ever turn to in our need? Not angels, not humans, and already the knowing animals are aware that we are not really at home in our interpreted world. Perhaps there remains for us some tree on a hillside, which every day we can take into our vision; there remains for us yesterday's street.

Oh and night: there is night, when a wind full of infinite space gnaws at our faces. Whom would it not remain for-- that longed-after, mildly disillusioning presence, which the solitary heart so painfully meets.

Yes – the springtimes needed you. Often a star was waiting for you to notice it. A wave rolled toward you out of the distant past, or as you walked under an open window, a violin yielded itself to your hearing.

Stimmen, Stimmen. Höre, mein Herz, wie sonst nur Heilige hörten: daß sie der riesige Ruf aufhob vom Boden; Es rauscht jetzt von jenen jungen Toten zu dir.

Freilich ist es seltsam, die Erde nicht mehr zu bewohnen, kaum erlernte Gebräuche nicht mehr zu üben, Rosen, und andern eigens versprechenden Dingen nicht die Bedeutung menschlicher Zukunft zu geben, und selbst den eigenen Namen wegzulassen wie ein zerbrochenes Spielzeug. Alles, so lose im Raume flattern zu sehen.

– Aber Lebendige machen alle den Fehler, daß sie zu stark unterscheiden. Engel (sagt man) wüßten oft nicht, ob sie unter Lebenden gehn oder Toten. Die ewige Strömung reißt durch beide Bereiche alle Alter immer mit sich und übertönt sie in beiden.

Ist die Sage umsonst, daß einst in der Klage um Linos wagende erste Musik dürre Erstarrung durchdrang; daß erst im erschrockenen Raum, dem ein beinah göttlicher Jüngling plötzlich für immer enttrat, das Leere in jene Schwingung geriet, die uns jetzt hinreißt und tröstet und hilft.

Rainer Maria Rilke, from
Duineser Elegien,
completed in Duino on 21 January 1912.

Voices. Voices. Listen, my heart, as only saints have listened: until the gigantic call lifted them off the ground. It is murmuring toward you now from those who died young.

Of course, it is strange to inhabit the earth no longer, to give up customs one barely had time to learn, not to see roses and other promising Things in terms of a human future; to leave even one's own first name behind, forgetting it as easily as a child abandons a broken toy. Strange to see meanings that clung together once, floating away in every direction.

Though the living are wrong to believe in the too-sharp distinctions which they themselves have created. Angels (they say) don't know whether it is the living they are moving among, or the dead. The eternal torrent whirls all ages along in it, through both realms forever, and their voices are drowned out in its thunderous roar.

Is the legend meaningless that tells how, in the lament for Linus,the daring first notes of song pierced through the barren numbness; and then in the startled space which a youth as lovely as a god has suddenly left forever, the Void felt for the first time that harmony which now enraptures and comforts and helps us.

Stephen Mitchell, trans., from
The Selected Poetry of Rainer Maria Rilke,
(New York, NY: Vintage Books, 1989), 151-55.

BIBLIOGRAPHY

General music research

Abbate, Carolyn, *In Search of Opera*, Princeton, NJ: Princeton University Press, 2001.

Adamenko, Victoria, *Neo-Mythologism in Music. From Scriabin and Schoenberg to Schnittke and Crumb*, Hillsdale, NY: Pendragon Press, 2007.

Agawu, Kofi, *Playing with Signs. A Semiotic Interpretation of Classic Music*, Princeton, NJ: Princeton University Press, 1991.

Bruhn, Siglind, *Messiaen's Contemplations of Covenant and Incarnation. Musical Symbol of Faith in the Two Great Piano Cycles of the 1940s*, Hillsdale, NY: Pendragon Press, 2007.

——, *Musical Ekphrasis. Composers Responding to Poetry and Painting*, Hillsdale, NY: Pendragon Press, 2000.

——, *Musical Ekphrasis in Rilke's Marien-Leben*, Amsterdam/Atlanta, GA: Rodopi, 2000.

——, *Saints in the Limelight: Representations of the Religious Quest on the Post-1945 Operatic Stage*, Hillsdale, NY: Pendragon Press, 2003.

——, *The Temptation of Paul Hindemith: Mathis der Maler as a Spiritual Testimony*, Stuyvesant, NY: Pendragon Press, 1998.

——, "Wordless Songs of Love, Glory, and Resurrection: Musical Emblems of the Holy in Hindemith's Saints," in S. Bruhn, ed., *Voicing the Ineffable. Musical Representations of Religious Experience*, Hillsdale, NY: Pendragon Press, 2002, 157-188.

Cohen, F.L., "Shofar," I. Singer, ed., *The Jewish Encyclopedia* 11, New York/London: Funk and Wagnalis, 1905, 301-306.

Cohn, Richard L., "Uncanny Resemblances: Tonal Signification in the Freudian Age," *Journal of the American Musicological Society* 57/2 (2004): 285-323.

Cone, Edward, *The Composer's Voice*, Berkeley/Los Angeles, CA: University of California Press, 1974.

Crumb, George, commentary on the String Quartet *Black Angels*, in the booklet accompanying the recording Elektra-Nonesuch 7559-79242-2 (1990).

Cumming, Naomi, "Horrors of Identification: Reich's 'Different Trains'," *Perspective of New Music* 35 (1997): 129-149.

——, *The Sonic Self. Musical Subjectivity and Signification*, Bloomington, IN: Indiana University Press, 2000

Drabkin, William, "Tritone," *The New Grove Dictionary of Music and Musicians* 19, London, UK: Macmillan, 1980, 154-155.

Einstein, Alfred, *Die Romantik in der Musik*, Vienna: Berglandverlag, 1950.

Grabócz, Márta, "Affect and Narrative Transformation in 18th Century Sonata Forms: The First Movement of Mozart's Symphony in C major K.338," Eero Tarasti, ed., *Musical Semiotics Revisited*, Helsinki: International Semiotics Institute, 2003, 40-59.

Hako, Pekka, *Finnish Opera*, Helsinki: FIMIC, 2002.

Hamel, Peter Michael, *Durch Musik zum Selbst*, Berg/Munich/Vienna, Scherz Verlag, 1976.

Hanslick, Eduard, *Vom Musikalisch Schönen. Ein Beitrag zur Revision der Aesthetik der Tonkunst*, Leipzig: Rudolph Weigel, 1854.

Harnoncourt, Nikolaus, *Baroque Music Today: Music as Speech: Ways to a New Understanding of Music*, M. O'Neill, trans., Portland, OR: Amadeus Press, 1988. (Originally published as: *Musik als Klangrede: Wege zu einem Neuen Musikverständnis: Essays und Vorträge*, 1982.)

Harwood, Ian, "Angel Lute," Stanley Sadie, ed., *The New Grove Dictionary of Musical Instruments* 1, London/New York: Macmillan Press, 1984, 60.

Jarociński, Stefan, *Debussy: Impressionism and Symbolism*, London, UK: Eulenberg, 1976. (Originally published as: *Debussy a impresjonizm i symbolizm*, 1966.)

Kaczyński, Tadeusz, *Conversations with Witold Lutosławski,* Yolanta May, trans., London, UK: Chester, 1984. (Originally published as: *Rozmowy z Witoldem Lutosławskim*, 1972.)

Kessner, Dolly,"Structural Coherence in Late Twentieth-Century Music: The Linear Extrapolation Paradigm Applied in Four American Piano Compositions of Diverse Musical Styles (Martinů, Rzewski, Crumb, and Adams)," dissertation, University of Southern California, 1992.

King, Alec H., "Musical glasses," *The New Grove Dictionary of Musical Instruments* 1, London/New York: Macmillan Press, 1984, 59.

Korhonen, Kimmo, *Finnish Concertos*, Jyväskylä: Finnish Music Information Centre, 1995.

——, *Finnish Orchestral Music 2*, Jyväskylä: Finnish Music Information Centre, 1995.

——, *Finnish Orchestral Music and Concertos 1995-2005*, Jyväskylä: Finnish Music Information Centre, 2006.

Kramer, Lawrence, *Classical Music and Postmodern Knowledge*, Berkeley, CA: University of California Press, 1995.

——, *Music as Cultural Practice, 1800-1900*, Berkeley, CA: University of California Press, 1990.

Landon, H.C. Robbins, *Haydn: The Years of "The Creation," 1796-1800*, London, UK: Thames and Hudson, 1977.

Leland, Kurt, *Music and the Soul: A Listener's Guide to Achieving Transcendent Musical Experiences*, Charlottesville, VA: Hampton Roads, 2005.

Messiaen, Olivier, commentary about *Regard des Anges*, in the booklet accompanying the recording of *Vingt Regards*. Erato 4509-91705-2 (1973).

Meyer, Leonard B., *Emotion and Meaning in Music*, Chicago, IL: University of Chicago Press, 1956.

Mianowski, Jarosław, *Semantyka tonacji w niemieckich dziełach operowych XVIII-XIX wieku* [The semantics of keys in German operas from the 18th to the 19th century], Toruń: Adama Marszałek, 2000.

Monelle, Raymond, *Musical Topics: Hunt, Military and Pastoral*, Bloomington, IN: Indiana University Press, 2006.

Nowak, Anna, *Współczesny koncert polski: przemiany gatunku* [The contemporary Polish concerto: transformation of genre], Bydgoszcz: Akademia Muzyczna im. F. Nowowiejskiego, 1997.

Ogden, Dunbar H., *The Staging of Drama in the Medieval Church*, Newark, NJ: University of Delaware Press, 2002.

Orton, Richard, "Ondes Martenot," *The New Grove Dictionary of Musical Instruments* 2, London/New York: Macmillan Press, 1984, 816-818.

Palisca, Claude, "Stile Rappresentativo," *The New Grove Dictionary of Music and Musicians* 18, London, UK: Macmillan, 1980: 145.

Persichetti, Vincent, *Twentieth-Century Harmony*, London: Faber and Faber, 1962.

Pesic, Peter, "Schubert's Dream," *Nineteenth Century Music* 23/2 (1999): 136-144.

Poizat, Michael, *The Angel's Cry: Beyond the Pleasure Principle in Opera*, A. Denner, trans., Ithaca, NY & London: Cornell University Press, 1992. (Originally published as: *L'Opera, ou Le Cri de l'ange: Essai sur la jouissance de l'amateur d'opera*, 1986.)

Pople, Anthony, *Berg: Violin Concerto*, Cambridge, UK: Cambridge University Press, 1996.

Rae, Charles B., *The Music of Lutosławski*, London, UK: Faber&Faber, 1994.

Ratner, Leonard G., *Classic Music: Expression, Form, and Style*, New York, NY: Schirmer Books, 1980.

Reese, Gustave, *Music in the Middle Ages: With an Introduction on the Music of Ancient Times*, London, UK: Dent, 1940.

Rosen, Charles, *The Romantic Generation*, Cambridge, MA: Harvard University Press, 1995.

Rowlands, Walter, *Among the Great Masters of Music*, London, UK: E. Grant Richards, 1906.

Schoenberg, Arnold, Interview published on the occasion of a performance of Five Pieces for Orchestra, op. 16, in Chicago, 12 October 1913.

Schweitzer, Albert, *J.S.Bach* II, E. Newman, trans., Neptune: Paganiniana Press, 1961.

Smith, Joseph, "Some Aspects of the Tritone and the Semitritone in the Speculum Musicae: The Non-emergence of the Diabolus in Music," *Journal of Musicological Research* 3 (1979): 63-74.

Steblin, Rita, *A History of Key Characteristics in the Eighteenth and Early Nineteenth Centuries*, Rochester, NY: University of Rochester Press, 2002.

Stevens, Halsey, "A Conversation with Schoenberg about Painting," *Journal of the Arnold Schoenberg Institute* 3 (1978): 178.

Stuckenschmidt, Hans H., *Arnold Schönberg*, E. T. Roberts and H. Searle, trans., London, UK: Calder, 1959. (Originally published as: *Arnold Schönberg*, 1957.)

Tagg, Philip, *Kojak-50 Seconds of Television Music: Toward the Analysis of Affect in Popular Music*, Göteborg: Göteborgs University, 1979.

Tarasti, Eero, "A Theory of Light in Music," M.Janicka-Słysz, T. Malecka, K.Szwajgier, eds., *Muzyka w kontekście kultury* [Music in the context of culture], Cracow: PWM, 2000: 681-691.

——, *A Theory of Musical Semiotics*, Bloomington, IN: Indiana University Press, 1994.

——, "Music Models through Ages: A Semiotic Interpretation," *International Review of the Aesthetics and Sociology of Music* 17/1 (1986): 22-32.

——, *Myth and Music. A Semiotic Approach to the Aesthetics of Myth in Music, especially that of Wagner, Sibelius and Stravinsky*, Helsinki: Acta Musicologica Fennica, 1978.

——, *Signs of Music. A Guide to Musical Semiotics*, Berlin/New York: Mouton de Gruyter, 2002.

Tarasti, Eila, "Music: The Art of Light and Shadow; or, How Clarity Appears in Tones," Eero Tarasti. ed., *Music and the Arts. Proceedings from ICMS 7*, Helsinki: International Semiotics Institute, 2006, 266-280.

Tatlow, Ruth, *Bach and the Riddle of the Number Alphabet*, Cambridge, UK: Cambridge University Press, 1991.

Välimäki, Susanna, *Subject Strategies in Music. A Psychoanalytic Approach to Musical Signification*, Imatra/Helsinki: International Semiotic Institute, 2005.

Walton, Kendall, "Listening with Imagination: Is Music Representational?," *Journal of Aesthetics and Art Criticism* 52/1 (1994): 47-61.

Youens, Susan, *Retracing a Winter's Journey*, Ithaca, NY: Cornell University Press, 1991.

Young, Percy M., *The Oratorios of Handel*, London, UK: Dennis Dobson, 1949.

Einojuhani Rautavaara, publications

"Choirs, Myths and Finnishness," *Finnish Music Quarterly* 1 (1997): 3-6.

Documentary movie *The Gift of Dreams*, Leipzig: Arthaus Musik, 1997.

Omakuva [Autobiography], Juva: WSO, 1989.

"On a Taste for the Infinite," *Contemporary Music Review* 12/2 (1995): 109-115.

Preface to *Orchestral Works*, Helsinki: Warner/Chappell, 1999, 3-5.

"Seven Questions for Einojuhani Rautavaara," *Highlights* 22 (2007): 7.

"Some Reflections on a Symmetrical Year," *Highlights* 12 (2002).

"Thomas—Analysis of the Tone Material (An Experiment in Synthesis)," *Finnish Music Quarterly* 1-2 (1985): 47-53.

— with Sini Rautavaara, *Säveltäjä ja Muusa* [Composer and muse], Juva: Werner Söderström Osakeyhtiö, 2001.

Einojuhani Rautavaara, program notes

on *Angels and Visitations,* in the booklet accompanying the recording Ondine 881-2 (1997).

on *Die erste Elegie,* in the score, Helsinki: Fazer, 1994.

on Double Bass Concerto *Angel of Dusk*, in the score, Helsinki: Warner/Chappell Music Finland Oy, 1980.

on Double Bass Concerto *Angel of Dusk*, in the booklet accompanying the recording Finlandia Records 4509-99969-2 (1981).

on *Icons,* in the score, Helsinki: Fazer, 1963.

on *Isle of Bliss*, in the booklet accompanying the recording Ondine 881-2 (1997).

on *Playgrounds for Angels,* in the booklet accompanying the recording Ondine 957-2 (2000).

on songs, in the booklet accompanying the recording BIS-CD-1141 (2003).

on the opera *Aleksis Kivi*, in the booklet accompanying the recording Ondine 1000-2CD (2002).

on the Seventh Symphony *Angel of Light,* in the booklet accompanying the recording Ondine 869-2 (1996).

on the Seventh Symphony *Angel of Light,* in the booklet accompanying the recording Naxos 8.555814 (2003).

Studies on Rautavaara

Aho, Kalevi, *Einojuhani Rautavaara as Symphonist*, Helsinki: Sibelius-Akatemia/Edition PAN, 1988.

——, "Einojuhani Rautavaara – Avant-Gardist, Mystic and Upholder of Values," *Highlights* 5 (1998): 2-5.

Anderson, Martin, "Einojuhani Rautavaara, Symphonist. The Finnish Composer Talks to Martin Anderson," *Fanfare* 7/8 (1996): 63-71.

Creutlein, Tarja von, *Einojuhani Rautavaaran 'Vigilia Pyhän Johannes Kastajan muistolle" ortodoksisen kirkkomusiikin kontekstissa,'* Joensuu: Joensuun yliopisto, 2006.

Cutts, Paul, "Angel Voices," *Choir&Organ* 11/12 (1998): 20-22.

Finch, Hilary, "Guided by Angels," *Gramophone* 6 (1996): 24.

Hako, Pekka, "Music Has a Will of Its Own," *Nordic Sounds* 3 (1998): 18-21.

——, *Unien lahja. Einojuhani Rautavaaran maailma* [The gift of dreams. The world of Einojuhani Rautavaara], Helsinki: Ajatus, 2000.

Heffern, Rich, "Conveying the Inexpressible: Interview with Einojuhani Rautavaara," *National Catholic Reporter* December 13 (2002).

Heiniö, Mikko, "A Portrait of the Artist at a Certain Moment – Focus on the Composer Einojuhani Rautavaara," *Finnish Musical Quarterly* 2 (1988): 3-14.

Levine, Robert, "Taste for Eternity," *Classical Pulse* 4 (1996): 9-11.

Lokken, Fredrick, "The Music for Unaccompanied Mixed Chorus of Einojuhani Rautavaara," dissertation, University of Wisconsin, 1999.

Lovejoy, Donald Gregory, "Annunciations: The Wind Music of Einojuhani Rautavaara," dissertation, University of Washington, 2000.

Luut, Klavier, "Einojuhani Rautavaaren vaskipuhallinmusiikin tausta ja analyysi," M.A. thesis, University of Helsinki, 2008.

Moody, Ivan, "'The Bird Sang in the Darkness': Rautavaara and the Voice," *Tempo* 181 (1992): 19-23.

Nikula, Kaisu, *Zur Umsetzung deutscher Lyrik in finnische Musik am Beispiel Rainer Maria Rilke und Einojuhani Rautavaara*, Jyväskylä: Jyväskylän Yliopisto, 2005.

Sivuoja-Gunaratnam, Anne, "Einojuhani Rautavaara as Opera Composer," *Finnish Music Quarterly* 3 (1993): 40-45.

——, "'Narcissus Musicus' or an Intertextual Perspective on the Œuvre of Einojuhani Rautavaara," Tomi Mäkelä, ed., *Topics, Texts, Tensions. Essays in Music Theory*, Magdeburg: Otto-von-Guericke Universität, 1999, 7-25.

——, *Narrating with Twelve Tones: Einojuhani Rautavaara's First Serial Period (ca. 1957-1965)*, Helsinki: The Finnish Academy of Science and Letters, 1997.

——, "Vincent – not a Portrait," *Finnish Music Quarterly* 2 (1990): 4-13.

Tarasti, Eila, "Icons in Einojuhani Rautavaara's *Icons,* Suite for Piano," *Musical Semiotics Revisited*, Imatra/Helsinki: International Semiotics Institute, 2003, 549-562.

Tiikkaja, Samuli, "Einojuhani Rautavaara – Postmodern Intertextualist or Supermodern Intratextualist? On Auto-Quotations in Rautavaara's Oeuvre," *Musiikki* 2 (2004): 39-60.

——, "Einojuhani Rautavaaran seitsemäs sinfonia Angel of light: materiaali-ja muotoanalyysi," M.A. thesis, University of Helsinki, 2000.

——, "The Harmonic Circle as a Tool for Analyzing the music of Einojuhani Rautavaara," unpublished materials from 11th International Doctoral and Postdoctoral Seminar in Musical Semiotics, Helsinki 2005.

Non-musicological literature

Bialas, A.A., "Angelology," *The New Catholic Encyclopedia*, Detroit, MI: Gale, 2003, 414-415.

Brodsky, Patricia P., *Rainer Maria Rilke*, Boston, MA: Twayne Publishers, 1988.

Campbell, Karen J., "Rilke's *Duino Angels* and the Angels of Islam," *Alif: Journal of Comparative Poetics* 23 (2003): 191.

Cross, Frank L., ed., *The Oxford Dictionary of the Christian Church*, Oxford: Oxford University Press, 1997.

Doniger, Wendy, ed., *Merriam-Webster's Encyclopedia of World Religions*, Springfield, MA: Merriam-Webster, 1999.

Fallon, T.L., "Angels in the Bible," *The New Catholic Encyclopedia*, Detroit, MI: Gale, 2003, 415-418.

Fontana, David, *The Secret Language of Symbols-A Visual Key to Symbols and Their Meanings*, San Francisco, CA: Chronicle Books, 1994.

Freud, Sigmund, "The Uncanny," *The Standard Edition of the Complete Psychological Works of Sigmund Freud*, J. Strachey, trans., 17, London, UK: Hogarth Press, 1981.

Gadamer, Hans Georg, "Mythopoetic Inversion in Rilke's Duino Elegies," in J.M. Connolly et al., eds./trans., *Hermeneutics versus Science? Three German Views*, Notre Dame, IN: University of Notre Dame Press, 1988 (Originally published as: "Mythopoietische Umkehrung in Rilkes *Duineser Elegien*," 1966.)

Gaudefroy-Demombynes, Maurice, *Mahomet*, Paris: Albin Michel, 1957.

Greene, Dana, "Adhering to God: The Message of Evelyn Underhill for Our Times," *Spirituality Today* 39 (1987): 22-38.

James, Jamie, *The Music of the Spheres: Music, Science, and the Natural Order of the Universe*, London: Abacus, 1995.

Jung, Carl Gustav, *The Archetypes and the Collective Unconscious* [*The Collected Works of C.G.Jung*, IX/1, R.F.C.Hull, trans.], New York: Pantheon Books for Bollingen Foundation, 1959.

Komar, Kathleen L., *Transcending Angels: Rainer Maria Rilke's Duino Elegies*, Lincoln, NE: University of Nebraska Press, 1987.

Langer, Susanne K., *Philosophy in a New Key. A Study in the Symbolic of Reason, Rite and Art*, Cambridge, MA: Harvard University Press, 1957.

Lévi-Strauss, Claude, *Structural Anthropology*, vol. II, Monique Layton, trans., New York, NY: Basic Books, 1976. (Originally published as: *Anthropologie structurale*, 1958.)

——, *The Savage Mind*, G.Weidenfeld, trans., Chicago: University of Chicago Press, 1966. (Originally published as: *La Pensée sauvage*, 1962.)

Macdonald, D.B., "Malâ'ika," P. J. Bearman, ed., *The Encyclopedia of Islam*, Leiden: Brill, 1990, 216-219.

Matusiak, Błażej, *Hildegarda z Bingen – teologia muzyki* [Hildegard von Bingen – The theology of music], Kraków: Homini, 2002.

Mauron, Charles, *Introduction to the Psychoanalysis of Mallarmé*, Berkeley, CA: University of California Press, 1963. (Originally published as: *L'Introduction à la psychanalyse de Mallarmé*, 1950.)

Michl, J., "Angels. Theology," *The New Catholic Encyclopedia*, Detroit, MI: Gale, 2003, 418-423.

Nadel, I.B.,Freedeman, W.E., eds., *Victorian Novelists after 1885* [*The Dictionary of Literary Biography* XVIII], Detroit, MI: Gale Research Company, 1983.

Oleschko, Herbert, ed., *Księga o Aniołach* [A book about angels], Kraków: Wydawnictwo WAM, 2003.

Ricoeur, Paul, *The Symbolism of Evil*, Emerson Buchanan, trans., New York, NY: Harper & Row, 1967. (Originally published as: *La symbolique du mal*, 1960.)

Rilke, Rainer Maria, *Briefe*, Wiesbaden: Insel, 1950.

——, *The Selected Poetry of Rainer Maria Rilke*, Stephen Mitchell, trans., New York, NY: Vintage Books, 1989.

Royle, Nicholas, *The Uncanny*, Manchester, UK: Manchester University Press, 2003.

Rzepińska, Maria, *Historia koloru w dziejach malarstwa europejskiego* [The history of color in European painting], Warsaw: Wydawnictwo Arkady, 1989.

Schimmel, Annemarie, *The Mystery of Numbers*, Oxford: Oxford University Press, 1994.

Simms, Eva-Maria, "Uncanny Dolls: Images of Death in Rilke and Freud," *New Literary History* 27 (1996): 663-677.

Steiner, Rudolf, *Anthroposophical Leading Thoughts*, G. and M. Adams, trans., London: Rudolf Steiner Press, 1973. (Originally published as: *Anthroposophische Leitsätze, Der Erkenntnisweg der Anthroposophie – Das Michael Mysterium*, 1924/25.)

Stevens, Anthony, *On Jung*, London, UK/New York, NY: Routledge, 1990.

Stevenson, Robert Louis, *The Strange Case of Fables. Other Stories and Fragments*, London, UK: William Heinemann, 1931.

Underhill, Evelyn, *Mysticism: A Study in Nature and Development of Spiritual Consciousness*, Grand Rapids, MI: Christian Classics Ethereal Library, 2005 [1923].

Webb, Gisela, "Angel," J.D. McAuliffe, ed., *Encyclopedia of the Qur'ân* 1, Leiden: Brill, 2001, 84-92.

Wigoder, Geoffrey, ed., *The New Encyclopedia of Judaism*, New York, NY: New York University Press, 2002.

List of Ilustrations

Music examples

1	Three beginnings of the Sanctus from Masses VIII, IX, and XI	37
2	Monteverdi, long melisma on the word "Sanctus"	37
3	Bach, *St. John Passion*, no. 2, recitativo	42
4	Weber, *Der Freischütz*, Act II, no. 10	43
5	Mozart, *Idomeneo*, Act III, scene X, no. 28c	51
6	Bach, *Christmas Oratorio*, Sinfonia, flutes and violins	52
7	Bach, Cantata no. 40, bass aria "Höllische Schlange..."	52
8	Tartini, Sonata *Il Trillo del Diavolo*, mvt. III, solo violin	56
9	Messiaen, "Les Anges"	61
10	Messiaen, "Regard des Anges," angelic sparkling	62
11	Messiaen, "Danse de la fureur, pour les sept trompettes"	63
12	The three rows from the opera *Vincent* as three basic colors	87
13a	Modulation of brightness in "Archangel Michael Fighting the Antichrist"	98
13b	Modulation of brightness (cont.)	99
14	Mirror writing in "Archangel Michael Fighting the Antichrist"	100
15	Imitation of brass theme in "Archangel Michael Fighting the Antichrist"	102
16	First chorale theme, *Angels and Visitations*, 4 horns and 4 tubas	107
17	Chorale construction of the fifth theme, *Angels and Visitations*	108
18	Seventh theme, *Angels and Visitations*, 4 horns and 4 tubas	109
19	"The Unicorn," *True and False Unicorn* no. 4	109
20	Excerpt of second theme, *Angels and Visitations*, violins	110
21	The polyphonic third theme, *Angels and Visitations*, divided violins	112
22	Fourth theme, Angels and Visitations, four trumpets	113
23	Third Symphony, mvt. IV	116
24	*Angels and Visitations*, brass ensemble	117
25	Opening chorale theme in brass, *Angel of Dusk*, mvt. I	121
26	*Angel of Dusk*, mvt. I, solo part	123
27	The "disturbance motif," *Angel of Dusk*	124
28a	Extended double bass techniques in *Angel of Dusk*	125
28b	Extended double bass techniques in *Angel of Dusk* (cont.)	126
29	Soloist's theme, *Angel of Dusk*, mvt. II, section E	128
30	Part of [c], *Angel of Dusk*, mvt. III	130
31	Part of [c1], *Angel of Dusk*, mvt. III	131
32	*Angel of Dusk*, mvt. III, soloist's line	131
33	*Angel of Dusk*, mvt. III, metallophones, harp, soloist, strings	133
34	"Bloomington" theme, *Angel of Light*, mvt. I	144
35	*Angel of Light*, mvt. I	145
36	*Angel of Light*, mvt. I, harp, and strings	146

List of Illustrations

37	Using different transpositions of row II (II^3), *Angel of Light*, mvt. II	148
38	Analogous motifs and motivic transformations, *Angel of Light*, mvt. II	149
39	Variant of the "Bloomington" theme, *Angel of Light*, mvt. II, oboes	150
40	Similarities between "disturbance" motif and main motif...	150
41	The chorale construction of the cantilena, *Angel of Light*, mvt. III	151
42	Arpeggiated "nocturne" motifs, *Angel of Light*, mvt. I	152
43	Tremolo passages, *Angel of Light*, mvt. II	153
44	Chorale texture, *Angel of Light*, mvt. III	153
45	Horn melody based on the "Bloomington" theme, *Angel of Light*, mvt. III	154
46	Canto IV	156
47	Motif [a], *Playgrounds for Angels*	159
48	Motifs [a] + [a'], *Playgrounds for Angels*	159
49	Motifs [a1']+[a1], *Playgrounds for Angels*	160
50	Motif [b], *Playgrounds for Angels*	160
51	Motif [b1], *Playgrounds for Angels*	160
52	Motif [b2], *Playgrounds for Angels*	160
53	Motifs [a] and [b], *Playgrounds for Angels*	160
54	Combination and singing tones, *Playgrounds for Angels*, trombones	162
55	Passages up and down, *Playgrounds for Angels*, trombones	162
56	Mirror harmony, *Playgrounds for Angels*, trumpets and trombones	163
57	Glissando *con sordino*, *Playgrounds for Angels*, trombones	164
58	Motifs with seconds and thirds, *Playgrounds for Angels*, trombones	164
59	Horn cantilena, *Playgrounds for Angels*	166
60	*Playgrounds for Angels*, horn and tuba	166
61	Fast chromatic motifs, *Playgrounds for Angels*, trumpets	168
62	*Fiddlers*, "Jacob Könni"	180
63	*Lehdet lehtiä*	182
64	*Angels and Visitations*, glockenspiel, celesta, harp	183
65	Second Symphony, final mvt.	184
66	*Angels and Visitations*, percussion and strings	185
67	*Angels and Visitations*, strings	187
68	*Angel of Dusk*, strings	188
69	*Angel of Dusk*, mvt. I	189
70	Musical dialogues between trumpets, *Playgrounds for Angels*	190
71	*Angel of Light*, mvt. III	192
72	*Angels and Visitations*, brass	193
73	*Angel of Dusk*, mvt. I	194
74	*Playgrounds for Angels*	194
75	*Angel of Dusk*, mvt. III	198
76	*Angels and Visitations*, marimba, celesta, harp, and strings	201
77	*Angels and Visitations*, strings	206
78	*Angel of Light*, mvt. I, metallophones, harp, and strings	208
79	*Angel of Light*, mvt. II	209
80	*Angel of Light*, mvt. IV	211
81	Blowing into the instruments without tone, *Angel of Dusk*, mvt. III	232

List of Illustrations

Figures

1	Progression of realms in Messiaen's opera *François d'Assise*	65
2	The triple role of Einojuhani Rautavaara	82
3	Einojuhani Rautavaara's handmade signature and its graphical version	88
4	Persichetti's characterization of modes, ranging from dark to bright	99
5	Intervallic structure of Messiaen's mode 2^1	106
6	Intervallic structure of mode 6^4	106
7	The hexatonic scale	110
8	Harmonic structure of the introductory section [a]	120
9	Two harmonic structures in [b] and [b']	122
10	Correspondences of motivic material and articulation techniques	127
11	Incomplete row from the double bass melody, *Angel of Dusk*, mvt. III	129
12	Messiaen's mode 2^1 without its third and seventh steps	130
13	Juxtaposition of irregular and regular meters in section C	130
14	A palindrome of metric groups in section C	130
15	Intervallic structure of mode 3^2	132
16	Messiaen's modes in Rautavaara's *Angel of Dusk*	134
17	Row I in *Angel of Light*	139
18	Row II	139
19	Row III	139
20	Row IV	139
21	Row V	139
22	Row I	140
23	The chromatic scale combined with the circle of fifths ...	140
24	Row VI	140
25	The row from *Die erste Elegie* as used in *Angel of Light*	140
26	The "Bloomington" theme and its motivic correspondence to row II	141
27	*Angel of Light*, harmonic and melodic foundation of mvt. I	143
28	Descending chords derived from $P_{VI}9$, *Angel of Light*, mvt. II	147
29	*Angel of Light*, the harmonic structure of mvt. III	152
30	Comparison of row V (above) with an inversion of row VI (below)	155
31	Row V presented horizontally and vertically	156
32	Greimas's mythical actants in *Angel of Dusk*	176
33	Row VI from *Angel of Light*	213
34	Graphic representation of row VI as a circle	214
35	Graphic representation of the circular form in *Angel of Light*, mvt. I	214
36	Graphic representation of the circular form in *Angel of Light*, mvt. III	215
37	Kleist's progression of consciousness	223
38	Rilke's progression of consciousness	224
39	Division of psyche ... in Jung's theory	229
40	Hexatonic poles, the hexatonic scale, Messiaen's mode 3^2	235

Plates

1	Einojuhani Rautavaara on the balcony of his home in Helsinki	vi
2	Hildegard von Bingen, the hierarchical order of angels, from *Scivias*	28
3	Gustave Doré, "Dante and Beatrice... "	216
4	Rautavaara's painting *Angel of Dusk* (or *Monologues with Angels*)	239

Tables

1	"Archangel Michael Fighting the Antichrist"	97
2	Disposition of brass instruments in "Archangel Michael ..."	101
3	Formal scheme of *Angels and Visitations*	105
4	Musical oppositions in *Angels and Visitations*	118
5	Formal and harmonic structure of movement I of *Angel of Dusk*	120
6	Formal scheme, *Angel of Dusk*, mvt. III	128
7	Structural overview in the three-movement *Angel of Dusk*	135
8	Formal scheme of *Angel of Light*	142
9	Sections ... in the trumpet parts, *Playgrounds for Angels*	159
10	Trombone sections and their musical material, *Playgrounds for Angels*	161
11	Horn and tuba sections, *Playgrounds for Angels*	165
12	Rautavaara's compositions referring to angels as a cycle	169
13	Chronological order of Rautavaara's compositions referring to angels	169
14	Lévi-Strauss's mythical structure and the sections in *Angel of Dusk*	178
15	Juxtaposition of mythical actants with instruments and *musica automata*	195

Index of Names

Abbate, Carolyn: 13, 15, 179
Adamenko, Victoria: xviii, 9, 12, 14, 173
Aho, Kalevi: xiv, xv, xvii, 115, 136, 177
d'Alembert, Jean-Baptiste le Rond: 4
Aristotle: 35, 38
Augustine (St.): xviii, 25, 26
Bach, Johann Sebastian: xviii, 34, 42, 43, 47, 51, 52, 57, 128
Bacon, Francis: 240
Bartók, Béla: 127
Bartolozzi, Bruno : 108, 111
Baudelaire, Charles: 83, 89
Beethoven, Ludwig van: 6, 34, 39, 41, 204, 210
Berg, Alban: xviii, xix, 43, 56, 57, 60, 128, 135, 138
Berio, Luciano: 108
Berlioz, Hector: 11, 12, 34, 50, 53, 54, 57
Blake, William: 31, 104, 136, 231
Blavatsky, Helena: 31
Bliss, Arthur: 33
Boethius: 38
Boito, Arrigo: 15, 53
Botticelli, Sandro: 88
Brahms, Johannes: 5, 33, 40, 56, 204
Broughton, James: 204
Bruckner, Anton: 33, 71, 167, 202, 204
Bruhn, Siglind: xvii, xviii, xx, 9, 17, 18, 50, 58, 65
Burnham, Scott: 5
Butor, Michel: 205
Cabanel, Alexandre: 88
Caccini, Giulio: 7, 33
Campbell, Karen: 220, 221

Carter, Elliot: 12
Cavalieri, Emilio de: 7
Charpentier, Marc-Antoine: 39
Chavannes, Puvis de: 88
Chopin, Fryderyk: 180
Čiurlionis, Mikalojus Konstantinas: 236
Clement of Alexandria: 35
Cohn, Richard: 15, 235
Cone, Edward: 9, 11, 12, 57, 175
Contractus, Hermannus: 38
Copland, Aaron: 119
Cotton, Johannes: 38
Creutlein, Tarja von: xvii
Crumb, George: xviii, 12, 14, 44, 45, 55, 56, 59, 60, 66, 210, 217, 244
Dali, Salvador: 73, 86
Dante, Alighieri: 216
Dargomyzhsky, Alexander: 15
Debussy, Claude: 18, 88, 204
Delvaux, Paul: 73, 86
Delville, Jean: 31
Desprez, Josquin: 33
Doré, Gustave: 216
Dvořák, Antonín: 34, 53, 54
Eggebrecht, Hans Heinrich: 5
Einstein, Alfred: 4
El Greco (Doménikos Theotokópoulos): 222
Eliot, Thomas Stearns: 83
Ertel, Paul: 40
Fauré, Gabriel: 34
Floros, Constantin: 6
Forqueray, Antoine: 48
Françaix, Jean: 34
Franck, César: 54
Freud, Sigmund: xxi, 9, 12, 14, 15, 77, 233, 234

Gadamer, Hans Georg: 221, 222, 230
Galilei, Vincenzo: 4, 11
Gaudefroy-Demombynes, Maurice: 30
Gautier, Théophile: 17
Gershwin, George: 236, 237
Giacometti, Alberto: 240
Globokar, Vinco: 108
Goethe, Johann Wolfgang von: 53, 54
Gogh, Vincent van: 72, 80, 87, 93
Gounod, Charles: 33, 53
Górecki, Henryk Mikołaj: xv, 33
Grabócz, Márta: 11
Greene, Dana: 70
Greimas, Algirdas Julius: xx, 9, 11-13, 174, 176, 193, 243
Grétry, André: 39
Grieg, Edvard: 53, 154, 169, 180
Grimm, Jacob and Wilhelm: 53
Gropius, Manon: 56
Gropius, Walter: 56
Grünewald, Matthias: 57, 58
Guido d'Arezzo: 38, 42
Gutman-Hanvihaara, Laura: 238
Hako, Pekka: xvi, xvii
Hamel, Peter Michael: 67
Handel, George Frideric: 34, 47, 48, 50-52
Hanslick, Eduard: 3, 5
Harnoncourt, Nikolaus: 9, 10
Haydn, Joseph: 33, 39, 47, 53, 210
Heinichen, David: 106
Heiniö, Mikko: 197
Heinse, Johann Jakob: 39
Henry, Olivier: 78
Hepoluta, Pekka: 137
Hildegard von Bingen (St.): xviii, 26-28, 38, 48, 62, 216
Hindemith, Paul: xviii, xix, 50, 56-60
Hoffmann, Ernst Theodor: 195
Holliger, Heinz: 108
Hulewicz, Witold: 220, 222
Humperdinck, Engelbert: 40, 53
Jackendoff, Ray: 5
James, Jamie: xviii, 3

James, William: 81
Jarociński, Stefan: 6
Joyce, James: 83
Jung, Carl Gustav: xxi, 12, 15, 19, 77, 80, 212, 228, 229, 231, 244
Kellner, David: 106
Kessner, Dolly: 59
Kiilunen, Reijo: 47
Kircher, Athanasius: 38
Kivi, Aleksis: 79, 80, 83
Kleist, Heinrich von: 223
Kneif, Tibor: 5
Khnopff, Ferdinand: 22
Komar, Kathleen: 223, 224, 226, 227
Kosonen, Olli: 119, 124
Koussevitzky, Olga: 84, 119, 135, 177
Koussevitzky, Serge: 135, 177
Kramer, Lawrence: 6- 8
Kretzschmar, Hermann: 5
Kundera, Milan: 76, 83, 104
Lalande, Jérôme de: 55
Lachenmann, Helmut: 205
Landi, Stefano: 34, 46
Langer, Susanne: 12
Lassila, Sampo: 119
Lehrdahl, Fred: 5
Leland, Kurt: 67
Lennox, Annie: 68
Lévi-Strauss, Claude: xvi, 9, 12- 14, 73, 176-178, 212, 243
Liadov, Anatoly: 54
Liszt, Franz: 48, 50, 54
Lokken, Fredrick: xvii
Lorca, Federico García: 78, 83
Lorenz, Alfred: 40
Lortzing, Gustav Albert: 53
Lotman, Yuri: 12
Lovejoy, Donald Gregory: xvi, 236
Lutosławski, Witold: 174
Luut, Klavier: xvi
Mâche, François-Bernard: 12
Magritte, René: 73, 86
Mahler, Gustav: 40, 57
Mahler Werfel, Alma: 56, 57

Index of Names

Mallarmé, Stéphane: 18, 89
Mann, Thomas: 75
Marais, Marin: 48
Marschner, Heinrich: 40, 53
Mattheson, Johann: 10, 39
Mauron, Charles: xvi, 89
Mei, Girolamo: 4
Mendel, Auguste: 48
Mendelssohn-Bartholdy, Felix: 33, 47, 53, 54
Menotti, Gian-Carlo: 34
Messiaen, Olivier: xviii, 34, 44, 45, 49, 51, 56, 60- 66, 87, 106, 113-115, 120, 129, 130, 132, 134, 135, 141, 142, 197, 207, 235, 244
Meyer, Leonard B.: 8
Meyerbeer, Giacomo: 15, 53
Mianowski, Jarosław: 41
Michelangelo Buonarroti: 49
Milhaud, Darius: 33
Milton, John: 26, 33
Monelle, Raymond: 6, 16
Monet, Claude: 86
Monteverdi, Claudio: 7, 37, 46, 50
Moreau, Gustave: 22
Mozart, Wolfgang Amadeus: 15, 16, 34, 47, 50, 51, 175, 243
Munch, Edvard: 22
Mussorgsky, Modest: 54, 102, 103
Müller, Wilhelm Christian: 41
Narmour, Eugene: 5
Nikula, Kaisu: xvii
Nowak, Anna: 174, 176
Ockeghem, Johannes: 43
Ogden, Dunbar H.: 47
Origen: 25
Paganini, Niccolò: 48, 60
Palisca, Claude: 7
Palestrina, Giovanni Pierluigi: 33
Pauer, Ernst: 40
Pärt, Arvo: xv
Peirce, Charles Sanders: 7, 9
Penderecki, Krzysztof: 33
Peri, Jacopo: 46,

Persichetti, Vincent: 13, 94, 96, 97, 99, 101, 118, 207, 213,
Peter Lombard: 26
Peter (St.): 26
Picasso, Pablo: 169
Pickett, David: 137
Plato: 3, 4, 23, 35, 38
Pockrich, Richard: 48
Poe, Edgar Allan: 78, 84
Poizat, Michael: xvii
Prokofiev, Sergei: 180
Propp, Vladimir: 11, 13
Proust, Marcel: 243
Pseudo-Dionysius the Areopagite: 26, 27, 36, 53, 62, 216
Pythagoras: 43
Quantz, Johann Joachim: 10
Rameau, Jean-Philippe: 39
Rasputin, Grigori: 79, 80
Ratner, Leonard: 16
Rautavaara, Mariaheidi: 93
Rautavaara, Sini: 93
Rautawaara, Aulikki: 83
Ravel, Maurice: 15, 102, 180, 197
Reich, Steve: 12
Respighi, Ottorino: 17
Ricoeur, Paul: 244
Riemann, Hugo: 106
Rilke, Rainer Maria: xvii, xix, xxi, 19, 58, 64, 83, 89, 94, 103, 104, 219-228, 230,231, 233, 234, 240, 241, 244
Rimsky-Korsakov, Nikolai: 53, 54
Rostropovich, Mstislav: 174
Rousseau, Jean-Jacques: 4, 7, 39
Rubinstein, Anton: 15, 33, 53
Schafer, Murray: 34
Schenker, Heinrich: 5
Schering, Arnold: 5, 6, 40
Schnittke, Alfred: 12
Schoenberg, Arnold: xviii, 14, 18, 44, 138, 236, 237
Schopenhauer, Arthur: 5
Schubart, Christian Friedrich Daniel: 39, 4 39, 40

Schubert, Franz: 40, 78
Schumann, Robert: 56
Schütz, Heinrich: 34
Schweinitz, Wolfgang von: 34
Schweitzer, Albert: 51, 52
Scriabin, Alexander: 12, 31, 54
Segerstam, Leif: 95, 119
Serusier, Paul: 240
Sessions, Roger: 119
Seurat, Georges-Pierre: 207
Shakespeare, William: 54, 83
Shostakovich, Dmitri: 147
Sibelius, Jean: 12, 54, 111, 118, 136, 137, 158
Signac, Paul: 207
Sikorski, Filip: 158
Sivuoja-Gunaratnam, Anne: xv, xvi, 14, 72, 73, 85, 87, 93, 129, 174, 180, 196
Socrates: 3
Steiner, Rudolf: 31
Stevenson, Robert Louis: 80
Stockhausen, Karlheinz: 12, 14, 42-45, 50, 56, 66, 67, 244

Strauss, Richard: 40,71
Stravinsky, Igor: 12, 60, 147, 180
Tame, David: 67
Tarasti, Eero: 6, 12, 157, 174, 178, 205, 210
Tarasti, Eila: xvii, 94, 101
Tartini, Giuseppe: 55, 56, 60
Tavener, John: xv, 33, 34
Tchaikovsky, Pyotr Ilyich: 203, 234
Thomas Aquinas (St.): xviii, 26, 27, 36, 38, 53, 62, 216
Tiikkaja, Samuli: xv-xvii, 106, 138, 141, 147, 155,
Underhill, Evelyn: 70, 75
Välimäki, Susanne: 6, 15, 16
Verdi, Giuseppe: 34, 50
Vogel, Vladimir: 140
Vogler, Georg Joseph: 39
Wagner, Richard: 12, 40, 41, 53, 243
Weber, Carl Maria von: 15, 39, 41, 42, 43, 53
Weber, Gottfried: 106
Wipo of Burgundy: 34
Zarlino, Gioseffo: 38, 39

About the Author

Wojciech Stępień, born in Chorzów, Upper Silesia, Poland, is a musicologist, music theorist, and composer. He completed his M.A. degree in music theory *summa cum laude* at the Karol Szymanowski Academy of Music in Katowice, and his PhD in musicology at the University of Helsinki, under the direction of Prof Eero Tarasti. His M.A. thesis about the Polish contemporary composer Eugeniusz Knapik won the Grand Prix at the XIVth National Competition of Master's Thesis in Warsaw. The original version of his doctoral dissertation, entitled *Signifying Angels. Analyses and Interpretations of Rautavaara's Instrumental Compositions*, was published in the series Studia musicologica Universitatis Helsingiensis in 2010.

Dr. Stępień is an active member of the International Music Signification Project and of the Polish Composer's Union. Since 2011 he has been working as assistant professor at the Karol Szymanowski Academy of Music in Katowice. His post-doctoral research builds on his earlier studies by focusing on different aspects in the relationship between music, religion, and psychology.